Facebook® Marketing

6th Edition

by Stephanie Diamond and John Haydon

for dummies®

A Wiley Brand

Facebook® Marketing For Dummies®, 6th Edition

Published by: **John Wiley & Sons, Inc.**, 111 River Street, Hoboken, NJ 07030-5774, www.wiley.com

Copyright © 2018 by John Wiley & Sons, Inc., Hoboken, New Jersey

Published simultaneously in Canada

No part of this publication may be reproduced, stored in a retrieval system or transmitted in any form or by any means, electronic, mechanical, photocopying, recording, scanning or otherwise, except as permitted under Sections 107 or 108 of the 1976 United States Copyright Act, without the prior written permission of the Publisher. Requests to the Publisher for permission should be addressed to the Permissions Department, John Wiley & Sons, Inc., 111 River Street, Hoboken, NJ 07030, (201) 748-6011, fax (201) 748-6008, or online at http://www.wiley.com/go/permissions.

Trademarks: Wiley, For Dummies, the Dummies Man logo, Dummies.com, Making Everything Easier, and related trade dress are trademarks or registered trademarks of John Wiley & Sons, Inc. and may not be used without written permission. Facebook is a registered trademark of Facebook, Inc. All other trademarks are the property of their respective owners. John Wiley & Sons, Inc. is not associated with any product or vendor mentioned in this book.

For general information on our other products and services, please contact our Customer Care Department within the U.S. at 877-762-2974, outside the U.S. at 317-572-3993, or fax 317-572-4002. For technical support, please visit https://hub.wiley.com/community/support/dummies.

Wiley publishes in a variety of print and electronic formats and by print-on-demand. Some material included with standard print versions of this book may not be included in e-books or in print-on-demand. If this book refers to media such as a CD or DVD that is not included in the version you purchased, you may download this material at http://booksupport.wiley.com. For more information about Wiley products, visit www.wiley.com.

Library of Congress Control Number: 2018937407

ISBN 978-1-119-47621-4

ISBN 978-1-119-47620-7 (ebk); ISBN 978-1-119-47637-5 (ebk)

Manufactured in the United States of America

10 9 8 7 6 5 4 3 2 1

Contents at a Glance

Table of Contents

Introduction

With more than 2 billion active users — including more than 1 billion who log in every day — Facebook has become a virtual world unto itself. Harvard dropout Mark Zuckerberg started Facebook as a dorm-room exercise to extend the popular printed college directory of incoming freshmen online, but he has since developed it into an international organization employing more than 7,000 programmers, graphic artists, and marketing and business development executives, with offices across the United States as well as in Dublin, London, Milan, Paris, Stockholm, Sydney, and Toronto.

For many people, Facebook is a social experience, a place to reconnect with an old college chum or poke a new friend. But in April 2007, Zuckerberg did something so revolutionary that its aftershocks are still being felt throughout the business web. He opened his virtual oasis to allow anyone with a little programming knowledge to build applications that take advantage of the platform's *social graph* (network architecture). In that open software act, Facebook redefined the rules for marketers looking to gain access to social networks, and it will never be business as usual again.

About This Book

Facebook Marketing For Dummies, 6th Edition, provides you, the marketer, with an in-depth analysis of the strategies, tactics, and techniques available to you so that you can leverage the Facebook community and achieve your business objectives. By breaking down the web service into its basic features — including creating a Facebook Page for your business, adding applications for your Page, hosting an event, creating a Facebook Group, advertising, and extending the Facebook platform to your website through social plug-ins — we lay out a user-friendly blueprint for marketing and promoting your organization via Facebook.

To help you absorb the concepts, this book uses the following conventions:

>> Text that you're meant to type just as it appears in the book is in **bold.** The exception is when you're working through a step list: Because each step is bold, the text to type is not bold.

>> Words for you to type in that are also in *italics* are meant as placeholders; you need to replace them with something that works for you. For example, if you see "Type ***Your Name*** and press Enter," you need to replace *Your Name* with your actual name.

>> We also use *italics* for terms I define. This means that you don't have to rely on other sources to provide the definitions you need.

>> Web addresses and programming code appear in monofont. If you're reading a digital version of this book on a device connected to the Internet, you can click the live link to visit a website, like this: http://www.dummies.com.

>> When you need to click command sequences, you see them separated by a special arrow, like this: File ⇨ New File, which tells you to click File and then New File.

Foolish Assumptions

We make a few assumptions about you, the marketer and aspiring Facebook marketing professional:

>> You're 13 years of age or older, which is a Facebook requirement for creating your own profile.

>> You're familiar with basic computer concepts and terms.

>> You have a computer with high-speed Internet access.

>> You have a basic understanding of the Internet.

>> You have your company's permission to perform any of the techniques we discuss.

>> You have permission to use any photos, music, or video of your company to promote on Facebook.

Icons Used in This Book

Icons in the margins of this book indicate material of special interest. These icons include the following:

TECHNICAL STUFF

This icon points out technical information that's interesting but not vital to your understanding of the topic being discussed.

REMEMBER

This icon points out information that's worth committing to memory.

WARNING

This icon points out information that could have a negative effect on your Facebook presence or reputation, so please read the info next to it!

TIP

This icon points out advice that can help highlight or clarify an important point.

Beyond the Book

Extra content that you won't find in this book is available at www.dummies.com. To find the Cheat Sheet for this book, go to www.dummies.com and search *Facebook Marketing For Dummies Cheat Sheet*. Updates to this book, if any, are also available at www.dummies.com.

Where to Go from Here

If you're new to Facebook and an aspiring Facebook marketer, you may want to start at the beginning and work your way through to the end. A wealth of information sprinkled with practical advice awaits you. Simply turn the page, and you're on your way.

If you're already familiar with Facebook and online marketing tactics, you're in for a real treat. We provide you the best thinking on how to market your business on Facebook — based in part on our own trials and tribulations. You may want to start with Part 2 of the book, but it wouldn't hurt to take in some of the basics in Part 1, such as Chapter 3, which speaks directly to creating a marketing plan and finding ways to generate more engagement from your followers. Also, a reminder: Read about some of the new menus and software features. You're sure to pick up something you didn't know.

If you're already familiar with Facebook and online marketing tactics but short on time (and what marketing professional isn't short on time?), you might want to turn to a particular topic that interests you and dive right in. We wrote the book in modular format, so you don't need to read it from front to back, although you're certain to gain valuable information from a complete read.

Regardless of how you decide to approach *Facebook Marketing For Dummies*, 6th Edition, we're sure you'll enjoy the journey. Here's to your success on Facebook!

1

Getting Started with Facebook Marketing

Chapter 1

Marketing in the Age of Facebook

F acebook is a social media juggernaut! As of the publication date of this book, Facebook has more than 2 billion people worldwide. In fact, if it were a country, it would be the most populated country in the world, ahead of India and China!

In addition to being the largest social network on the planet, it's the most active. In fact, as of December 2017, 1.4 billion people use Facebook every day! Also, according to a report by eMarketer in 2017, more than half of the population of the U.S. used Facebook in 2016.

TIP

Think about this: Most smartphones and tablets are preloaded with a Facebook app or at least have features that allow for Facebook sharing.

Facebook grew at a staggering rate because it fit the needs of both consumers and businesses. However, early in 2018, Facebook changed its algorithm (an algorithm determines the order in which you see items in your Timeline) in response to a major controversy involving the use of automated bots that didn't represent content from actual users.

All Facebook users have a Facebook *profile*, which includes a main image, or *avatar*; a Timeline listing their latest activities and comments from friends; and a sidebar that includes links for photos, personal information, and other apps.

Facebook's goal in changing the algorithm was to encourage more social interaction among friends and family. Consumers use Facebook to connect with friends and share their lives in the form of updates and activity.

Businesses use Facebook Pages to engage customers and prospects; they also run highly targeted ad campaigns for the Facebook community. However, this algorithm change impacts how businesses need to market their products and services. (See details for dealing with these changes in Chapter 3.)

Businesses need to adjust their strategies and tactics to engage users by creating more value. Posting quality content is more important than producing a steady stream of articles and photos. If used correctly, Facebook is still an attractive platform for virtually all industries to achieve concrete business goals such as:

>> **Increasing brand awareness:** Companies of all sizes are reaching Facebook's massive community with Facebook Social Plugins (for websites), Facebook Ads, and Facebook Pages.

>> **Launching products:** Brands are using Facebook to announce new products with Facebook Ad campaigns and custom apps as part of their overall product launch strategy.

>> **Providing customer service:** Brands also realize that consumers expect to be able to get their issues resolved by contacting the company via its Facebook Page by using Facebook Messenger.

>> **Selling products and services:** Businesses like DODO case (https://www.facebook.com/DODOcase) and Calm the Ham (https://www.facebook.com/CalmTheHam/) sell their products on Facebook through the use of e-commerce applications that can be added to a Facebook Page.

This book shows you how you can achieve some of these business goals.

In this chapter, we give you an overview of why Facebook has grown so big and how marketers are taking advantage of its potential. We also explain why you need to create a Facebook Page for your business.

What Is Facebook, and Why Is It So Popular?

The social networking site Facebook was launched in 2004 by a kid at Harvard University named Mark Zuckerberg. It started with the name Thefacebook (shown in Figure 1-1) and was available only to Harvard students or anyone else who had a `harvard.edu` email address. The social network spread quickly throughout Harvard because it was exclusive.

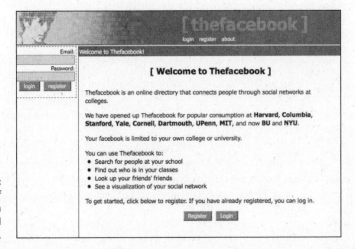

FIGURE 1-1: Screen shot of Thefacebook.com as it appeared in 2004.

Although it was launched as a network for Harvard students, Facebook was eventually made available to students at other universities and finally to anyone with access to a computer. Now, just a few years later, it has become the largest social networking site in history. As of the publication date of this book, Facebook has more than 2 billion users worldwide.

But it's not just the biggest social networking site in history; it's also the most active. According to Facebook (`http://newsroom.fb.com/company-info`), the company has

>> 1.4 billion daily active users on average for December 2017

>> 2.13 billion monthly active users as of December 31, 2017

According to Zephoria Digital Marketing (`https://zephoria.com/top-15-valuable-facebook-statistics/`)

>> 1.15 billion mobile daily active users for December 2016

>> 1.74 billion mobile monthly active users as of December 2016

FACEBOOK FACILITATES CONNECTION

Karen Graham and Tim Garman are a brother and sister who were reunited after 40 years because of Facebook. Separated at birth and adopted by two separate families, they were reunited only when their younger sister, Danielle, began searching for them on Facebook.

After three months and more than a few dead ends, Danielle found the Facebook profile of Karen Graham's daughter. She sent her the message "I think your mom is my mom's daughter," which eventually led to the reunion.

Today, Karen and Tim are very close, attending family gatherings around holidays and reunions. The two had a desire to meet each other, but they lacked the means to find each other until Facebook provided the opportunity for connection.

Similarly, in 2011, I (John) was able to meet an old friend I hadn't seen since high school. In middle school and high school, I was a very unpopular, shy nerd who was bullied by the "cool kids." Needless to say, I wasn't very excited to get friend requests from many of these classmates.

But with Clark, I said, "Now that's someone that I'd be very interested in reuniting with!" I remembered Clark as being extremely smart and creative. (The figure shows Clark [left] with me in Chicago.) We initially connected through a Facebook Group someone created for our high school, and then we arranged to connect in Chicago when I was there on business.

But now we want to talk about you. If you're like most people, your mom is on Facebook. Most of your friends are on Facebook. Maybe you reconnected with a long-lost high school friend by using Facebook. Maybe you even met your spouse there.

You may be wondering why Facebook — and not formerly popular Myspace or FriendFeed — got to where Facebook is today. Although an entire book can be written on this topic, it's worth exploring at least briefly here.

Here are a few reasons why Facebook has blown past all other social networks:

>> **Facebook has used existing social connections to promote the platform.** From Day One, the sign-on process has included inviting anyone you've emailed! Its assumption is that if you've exchanged an email with someone, there's a good chance that you have some kind of relationship with that person and may be inclined to invite him or her to join you on Facebook.

>> **Facebook is heavily covered by mainstream media.** Whether it's a newspaper article about a teacher getting fired for making thoughtless comments about a student or a TV interview with two siblings who were separated at birth but reunited on Facebook, not a day goes by without some kind of mention of Facebook in the news.

>> **Facebook keeps us connected.** Young people famously use Facebook to stay connected, but they're not alone. One of the fastest-growing segments on Facebook continues to be people over 55. Many of them use Facebook to keep up with their children and sometimes grandchildren.

Understanding the Marketing Potential of Facebook

In the 1950s, this gadget called television exploded throughout American culture. At first, there were black-and-white TVs, and then, toward the end of the decade, there were color TVs in every middle-class living room. As more consumers started watching TV instead of listening to the radio, marketers had to adopt their strategies to the new medium. Successful ad executives and writers took the time to understand how TV fit within American culture. They researched how and why TV became a focal point for families at the end of each day (remember TV dinners?). They researched the ways men watched TV differently from women and which television shows kids preferred on Saturday morning.

Only after this research were they able to create successful TV advertisements. They learned to condense their messages to 30 seconds. They created ads with jingles that imitated popular TV themes and effectively placed their products within popular shows.

In the same way, today's successful brands must understand how to best use Facebook to market their brands.

If you're reading this book, there's a good chance that you've heard about how brands like Harley-Davidson and Nutella, as well as thousands of small businesses and nonprofits, are using Facebook to market their products and services.

Through a variety of strategies and tactics, these businesses are tapping into Facebook to achieve a variety of objectives:

>> They're increasing awareness of their brands through highly targeted Facebook Ads.

>> They're getting to know what their customers really want by having daily conversations with them.

>> They're launching new products and services with Facebook Pages and custom Facebook applications.

>> They're increasing new and repeat sales with coupons, group deals, and loyalty programs.

>> They're enhancing the native experience by using such innovations as Facebook Live and the extensive use of video.

Part of the reason why these businesses are successful is that they understand Facebook isn't just a static website; it's a way for people to connect and be heard.

Leveraging the power of word-of-mouth marketing

Word of mouth is the most powerful way to market any business. In fact, many studies have shown that consumers are more likely to make purchase decisions based on recommendations from people they know than from a brand's marketing materials. Each time a user likes, comments on, or shares content on Facebook, that action spreads to his network of friends. This is how "word of mouth" happens on Facebook (see Figure 1-2).

According to a Nielsen report in 2015, 83 percent of online users in 60 countries trust brand recommendations from friends and family. And this makes perfect sense.

Think about the last time you made a major purchase decision (a car, a TV, or even a contractor). Which influenced you more in that decision: an ad about that product or service, or the experience of a friend who purchased that product or service?

The most powerful aspect of Facebook is the deep ties among users. Large portions of friend networks are based on work relationships, family relationships, or other real-life relationships. Some marketers refer to these connections as *strong ties*, meaning that they go beyond the boundaries of Facebook. Such connections are in contrast to *weak ties* — online connections that lack stated common interests or goals.

Think about it this way: Would you be more influenced by the Facebook friend with whom you went to college or the Facebook friend who sent a friend request simply because she met you at a concert this past weekend?

When a Facebook user likes, comments on, or shares a piece of content you publish on your Facebook Page, many of that user's friends can also see that content. And those friends essentially view those actions as digital word-of-mouth recommendations.

Using marketing tools for all kinds of businesses

Facebook offers marketers several unique ways to interact with customers and prospects, including the following:

>> **Facebook Pages, Groups, and Events:** These tools are free for any business and have the very same social features (including News Feeds; comments; and the capability to share links, photos, videos, and updates) that more than 2 billion people use to connect with their friends on Facebook. In other words, Facebook allows businesses to connect with customers in the same way that these customers connect with their friends. This business-is-personal paradigm has helped Facebook transform the way companies market themselves.

>> **Facebook Social Plugins for websites:** Facebook offers several free plug-ins for websites that allow your website visitors to share your content with their Facebook friends. The Comments plug-in, for example, lets people comment on content on your site by using their Facebook profiles. When they do so, a story is generated in their friends' News Feeds, exposing their friends to your website content.

>> **Facebook Ads:** Facebook Ads, which can be purchased on a cost-per-click (CPC) or cost-per-impression (CPM) basis, are increasingly popular because they enable marketers to reach as narrow or as wide an audience as desired, often at a fraction of the cost of other online media outlets, such as Google Ads. And because Facebook members voluntarily provide information about their personal interests and relationships, Facebook has a wealth of information about its members that advertisers can easily tap. Additionally, Facebook partners with a few third-party consumer data companies such as Acxiom and DLX to provide information about purchasing behavior and income. (See Figure 1-3.)

FIGURE 1-3:
Facebook Ads like these are an extremely cost-effective way to target your exact customer based on a variety of factors.

The new Facebook marketing paradigm is rewriting all the rules. As marketers scramble to understand how best to leverage this powerful new communications channel, those who don't jump on board risk being left behind at the station.

Understanding Why Your Business Needs a Facebook Page

The best (and easiest) way for you to establish a presence for your organization on Facebook is to create a Facebook Page.

A Page serves as a home for your business, as well as a place to notify people about upcoming events; post offers; provide your hours of operation and contact information; display news; and even display photos, videos, text, and other types of content.

Pages also allow you to carry on conversations with your customers and prospects, providing a new means of finding out more about what they want from your business.

Facebook Pages are visible to everyone who's online, regardless of whether that person is a Facebook member. This allows search engines, such as Google and Microsoft's Bing, to find and index your Page. This can improve your company's positioning in search results on those sites.

Here are a few essential components that make Facebook Pages the core marketing tool for all kinds of businesses:

- » **The Publisher:** The Publisher serves as the central component of a Page and allows you, the Page administrator (admin), to post status updates and links, and to upload content such as photos, videos, and links. These actions generate updates and display as stories on your fans' News Feeds.

- » **Like button:** When someone clicks your Facebook Page's Like button, she's expressing her approval of your Page. That action creates a story in her News Feed, which is distributed to her friends, who are then more likely to like your Page because they trust her recommendations.

- » **Cover image:** The cover image is the large image at the top of every Facebook Page. It's the thousand words that express what your business is about!

>> **Views and applications:** Facebook Pages include various views (sometimes called *tabs*), including Photos, Events, and Videos. When Facebook users click the view icons on your Page, they can see all the content for that view (see Figure 1-4). You can also add a variety of apps to customize your Page, such as contest and promotion apps, or apps that display Twitter and Instagram content.

>> **Message feature:** All Pages include an option to allow Facebook users to send the Page administrator private messages (see Figure 1-4). Facebook members use a similar feature to send private messages to their friends. The message featured on your Page (if you choose to use it) allows you yet another opportunity to connect more personally with your customers and prospects. With the advent of chatbots (automated messages using artificial intelligence), you can engage users who can immediately get answers they need.

FIGURE 1-4: Facebook Pages include various views and apps that users can explore when they visit your Page.

TIP

For more details on Facebook Page components, see Chapter 4.

Attracting new fans who are friends of customers

Marketers can post updates — also called *stories* — to engage fans in relevant discussions. When these updates appear in their fans' News Feeds, they can like, comment on, and share that story, which in turn is seen by their friends.

When nonfans see those stories in their News Feeds, they can also comment on or like your Page story and even visit your Page directly to engage with other stories and/or become a fan or a connection of your Page. Additionally, when they mouse over the name of your Page in their News Feeds, a small pop-up window called a *hovercard* appears. In this card, they can also like your Page and see more detailed information about your business (see Figure 1-5).

FIGURE 1-5:
Facebook users can like your Page from your hovercard by hovering their mouse pointers over the name of your Page in their News Feeds.

Changing first-time customers into repeat customers

In marketing, getting people's attention and keeping it is paramount for success, and things are no different on Facebook. This principle applies to your current customers in addition to your prospects.

After customers have liked your Facebook Page, it's your job to nurture and grow your relationships with them by providing added value. In other words, you must use your Facebook Page to enhance the benefit that your customers get from doing business with you. You do this by continually posting exciting and relevant content on the Page, which we discuss in Chapter 7. A car dealership, for example, can post auto-maintenance or travel tips — in addition to live training, discounts on oil changes and other services — on its Facebook Page to turn a first-time customer into a lifetime customer.

Chapter **2**

Researching and Understanding Your Target Audience

S mart marketers, regardless of their medium, know that defining target audiences helps save time, money, and other resources. Small-business owners know that paying for a full-page ad in a national magazine or buying a 30-minute regional television spot isn't a cost-effective way to reach specific audiences. The smart marketer knows who has bought from him in the past. He knows his customer's age, where she lives, what her lifestyle is, and more; by knowing these things, he can target similar people through whatever marketing medium he chooses.

In this chapter, we talk about how to define your target audience, how this understanding relates to changes to the Facebook News Feed, and how to exploit strong and weak ties within that target audience.

Defining Your Target Audience

Your *target audience* is the specific group of consumers to which your business has decided to aim its marketing efforts. If you think about your target audience in the context of everyone on the planet, you can see that defining your target audience prevents you from wasting money by targeting people who will never buy.

Understanding the marketing funnel

A useful model to help you understand and define your target audience is the *marketing funnel*. The marketing funnel shows the categories your customers fall into and describes how those categories are related to one another. So-called *evangelists* or *advocates* are a subset of your loyal repeat customers, for example, and your repeat customers are a subset of more casual customers. The five marketing-funnel categories group customers according to how much they trust you, do business with you, and recommend your products or services (see Figure 2-1).

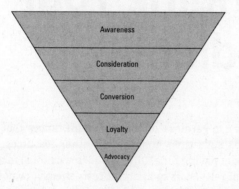

FIGURE 2-1:
Diagram of the marketing funnel.

The purpose of the marketing funnel is to help marketers develop specific marketing strategies for potential customers, new customers, repeat customers, and raving fans. Car dealers, for example, could run different campaigns for different customer categories. New customers, such as new parents who are in the market for a minivan, could receive messages that include TV ads, newspaper ads, and content from a dealership's Facebook Page. Existing customers, on the other hand, would receive emails or direct-mail pieces offering discounts on oil changes and other specials.

In the marketing funnel, the marketplace is broken down into five behavior stages, or phases, as follows:

>> **Awareness:** The people in this stage are aware of your product or service but have yet to consider purchasing it. Awareness is created on Facebook using targeted ads, engagement with your Facebook Page posts, and content shared from your website using Facebook Social Plugins.

>> **Consideration:** The people in this stage are considering your product or service but have yet to purchase it. This is the stage at which the potential customer needs proof, testimonials, guarantees, and anything else that will instill confidence to proceed to the next stage.

>> **Conversion:** The people in this stage have made the leap to purchase your product or service. At this stage, they're at the highest risk of experiencing buyer's remorse. In addition to your normal customer service channels (including email and phone), you want to actively monitor your Page Timeline for customer questions and feedback.

>> **Loyalty:** The people in this stage have decided to purchase your product or service repeatedly. They have done so because your product/service is of high quality and because they trust you.

>> **Advocacy:** The people in this stage actively recommend your product or service to others. Smart Facebook marketers treat these people like gold, giving them special offers, additional discounts, praise, and recognition.

Understanding the ladder of engagement

Facebook is about friendships. It's about reconnecting with old friends and keeping up with close friends. It's about collaborating with small private groups and sharing with the world. This is even more true now that the focus of Facebook is "helping you have more meaningful social interactions."

Facebook isn't about buying things or getting the lowest price. There are already websites for that, such as Amazon and eBay.

In other words, Facebook is *relational*; it's not *transactional*.

In their book *Measuring the Networked Nonprofit* (John Wiley & Sons, Inc.), Beth Kanter and Katie Delahaye Paine use the term *ladder of engagement* to describe the way nonprofit organizations move people in stages from awareness to action. Although they're focusing on nonprofits, the concept of the ladder of engagement applies equally well to any business that deals with people (that is, pretty much every business).

The ladder of engagement shown in Figure 2-2 is one way to express how customers relate to brands they interact with on Facebook.

The diagram in Figure 2-2 (which, by the way, is just one way to represent Facebook's ladder of engagement) contains two important data points:

>> **Trust and affinity:** As people become aware of your business and interact with you at different levels of commitment, trust and affinity increase (or decrease if you're not trustworthy or likable).

>> **Audience size:** Similar to the popular "sales funnel" model, which shows the different audience sizes during the buying process, the steps in this diagram represent smaller but more engaged audience at each stage in this ladder.

In this diagram, each step represents an action someone can take on Facebook that expresses her relationship with your organization.

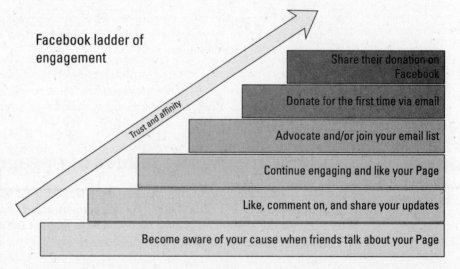

FIGURE 2-2: Customers interact with brands on Facebook based on trust and affinity.

This model is useful for understanding which actions people are comfortable taking on Facebook based on their relationship with your business. As you use Facebook strategically to promote your business, more and more people will naturally move up the ladder and come to like and trust you.

Defining who your best customers are

One of the first steps in developing a target audience strategy is analyzing your current customer base.

Of all your customers, think about the ones who keep coming back — the ones who consistently tell others about your business. Wouldn't it be great to attract more of these types of customers?

Of course it would be!

These people have already demonstrated that they're willing to pull out the credit card or give you cash for your products and services, and you already know that there's a huge difference between someone liking what you sell and buying what you sell.

From this perspective, you can begin to define your target audience as "the ideal person you want to get your product or service in front of." It has essentially the same characteristics as your best customers. Imagine a Vespa scooter dealership in a college town. Through simple research, the dealership discovers that its best customers are parents of students going to universities located around that dealership.

Rather than targeting everyone located within 50 miles of the dealership, then, it would be smarter to target only students (and their parents) who attend local universities. The dealership's marketing resources would be best used for ads in university publications, local newspapers, and targeted Facebook Ads.

Selecting demographic criteria for your target audience

Following are several factors that you should consider when creating a target audience:

>> **Age:** The importance of age depends on the type of product or service that you're selling. If you sell driving lessons — that is, if you own a driving school — obviously you're going to target parents of children who are a specific age. On the other hand, if you're selling pizza, age may not be that important.

One more important thing to think about with respect to age is that sometimes it's best to target a range of ages instead of a specific one. Marketers of clothing for pregnant women, for example, would target a range of ages; marketers of retirement funds, however, might pick a specific age.

>> **Gender:** Is your product or service better suited to one gender than another? Men's Wearhouse, for example, primarily sells clothing for men.

If you must target a specific gender, be careful to consider who the buyers actually are (because this might not be readily apparent), such as wives who buy men's clothing as gifts for their husbands.

>> **Location:** Is the location of your customer an important factor? Again, a pizza shop primarily sells pizza to people who live in the neighborhood, but Amazon.com doesn't care where any of its customers live.

>> **Interests:** Understanding your target audience's interests is very important because it allows you to sell additional related products or services. A store that sells golf accessories could also sell golf lessons or getaways, for example.

REMEMBER

Demographic targeting should consider both the user of your product or service and the buyer of your product or service. The user and buyer may not be the same person.

Using personas to give your target audience personality

When you have a good understanding of the demographics of your target audience, you should look at your customers' behaviors, beliefs, and the stages of life that they're in. This information helps you better understand what motivates your prospects to buy your product or service. New parents, for example, tend to exhibit a specific set of beliefs and behaviors, including being thrifty, creating a secure home, being protective about the family, and choosing healthier eating habits.

Just as playing with imaginary friends helps kids learn to interact with real people, personas that help you learn about your audience as real people, not just as a set of demographic statistics. In practical terms, personas help you come up with creative marketing campaigns and messages that resonate with your prospects.

You can develop personas by following these basic steps:

1. **Figure out who your customers are.**

   Define their needs, demographics, income, occupation, education, and gender. Ask yourself whether they volunteer, how much they donate to charity, and so on.

2. **Create groups of customers who share a lot of characteristics.**

   Include groups for new customers and repeat customers to help you understand why people buy from you in the first place and why they come back to buy again.

3. **Rank these groups in order of importance.**

   Home Depot, for example, might rank professional builders higher than first-time do-it-yourselfers.

4. **Invent fictional characters who represent each group.**

   Add details such as age, occupation, marital status, kids, hobbies, interests, online activity, and more. Anyone who directly connects with your customers on a daily basis should be brought into this discussion (salespeople, tech-support people, and so on).

5. **Give these characters life by using stock photos of actual people and naming them.**

   This step also makes it easier to create products and messaging that speak to these people. It may be tempting to skip this step, but don't. The more real you can make your personas, the more compelling your marketing will be.

6. **Create a short back story for each persona.**

   A food pantry might have the following story for "Beth," one of its volunteer personas:

   "Beth is a 55-year-old empty-nester with two kids in college. She's a busy customer service manager at a local software company but strongly believes in living a balanced and meaningful life. She also values contributing to her local community. When her kids moved to California to go to college, Beth began working at the local food pantry. This gives her a tremendous sense of happiness — not only because she believes in giving back, but also because she has new friends who she has over for dinner parties. For Beth, the food pantry is not at all about food; it's about living a meaningful life."

Researching Target Audiences with Facebook's Ads Manager

Facebook's Ad tools are intended primarily to be used by advertisers to create, launch, and manage advertising campaigns (see Figure 2-3). You can use the Ads Manager for your mobile and desktop ads, or use the Power Editor if you have multichannel ads (Facebook, Instagram, and others). In Chapter 11, we go into great detail about creating Facebook Ads. In this chapter, however, we discuss how to use the Ads Manager to research your target audience segments.

Using the Facebook Ad tool as a research tool allows you to answer questions such as these:

>> How many Facebook users near my business's location are married and between the ages of 35 and 39?

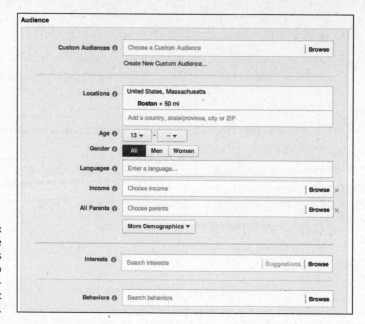

FIGURE 2-3:
You can use
Facebook's Ads
Manager tool to
better under-
stand your target
audience.

>> How many fans of my Facebook Page are also fans of my competitor's Facebook Page?

>> How many of my target customers are already fans of my competitor's Facebook Page?

The following list describes several target segment criteria you can research with the Facebook Ads Manager:

>> **Locations:** You can research a target audience based on where they live (refer to Figure 2-3). You can target broadly with countries or get as specific as cities. Note that if a city has no Facebook users living there, that city may not be available as a selection. (This situation is rare, however.)

>> **Age:** When a person first signs up on Facebook, she's required to enter her date of birth. This information allows you to see how many users are within a particular age range or are a specific age.

Always begin targeting with broad criteria, such as location, and then add more specific criteria, such as interests. This step allows you to get a sense of the possible reach of people you can target on Facebook. As you add or remove targeting criteria in the Ad tool, Facebook automatically updates the estimated audience number (see Figure 2-4).

TIP

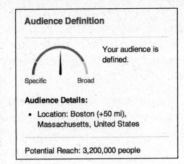

FIGURE 2-4:
Facebook
updates the
estimated
audience as you
select target
criteria.

>> **Gender and languages:** You can research a target audience based on their gender or what language they speak. Note that if you don't make a language selection, the Ad tool automatically defaults to the official language of the country that the user is located in.

>> **Interests:** This selection allows you to research the various interests people have expressed through Pages they liked, group they joined, and other actions they took within and without the Facebook network (see Figure 2-5).

REMEMBER

Researching Facebook interests is very different from researching search-engine keywords. If you sell hiking shoes, for example, you'd use *"hiking boots"* to research search-engine keywords but would use *"backpacking"* or *"National Wildlife Federation"* to research various Facebook audiences.

As you select keywords and phrases to target, Facebook automatically suggests additional likes and interests that other users have selected. As you add these keywords to your criteria, the estimated-reach number updates to reflect the keywords you've added.

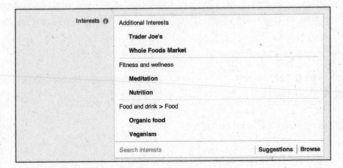

FIGURE 2-5:
Facebook allows
you to target a
wide variety
of interests.

>> **Behaviors:** Facebook has partnered with several third-party data sources for consumer-behavior information such as charitable activity, purchasing behavior, and travel habits (see Figure 2-6). The biggest providers of this third-party data include Acxiom, DLX, and Epsilon.

>> **Connections:** In this section, you can target fans, friends of fans, and so on. Targeting people in this way can help you spread your message by word of mouth (see Figure 2-6).

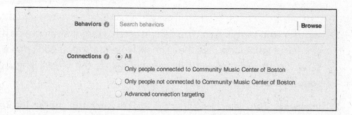

Discovering How Many Customers Use Facebook

More than 2 billion people use Facebook, and there are 1.15 billion mobile daily active users. But although these numbers are impressive, they don't say how many of *your* customers use Facebook. With the Facebook Ads Manager, you can analyze your current customer base by uploading their emails and sifting through Facebook's Graph data.

To use the Facebook Ads Manager to find out how many of your customers use Facebook, you will be taken through the following sequence in the Ads Manager:

>> Add a customer list.

>> Edit data mapping.

>> Perform a hashed upload and creation of an audience.

>> Create a look-alike audience.

Follow these steps to add a customer list:

1. **Export your email lists.**

   Your goal is to find out how many of your customers use Facebook. This process starts with exporting an email list from your current customer database or Customer Relations Management (CRM) tool and uploading it to Facebook's Ad tool.

   You need only a single column (CSV or text) of emails. No other data is required. You can even remove the header row. After you export the data, you should save it to your hard drive.

TIP

   Worried about security? Don't worry about Facebook stealing your emails. When you upload your list, the data is hashed in the browser (you have to use Chrome). This means that Facebook won't have access to any email that's not associated with a Facebook user.

2. **Log in to your Facebook Ads account.**

   Don't worry; you don't have to pay for anything. This exercise uses Facebook Ads only as a research tool.

   When you log in to your account, navigate to www.facebook.com/ads/create and click the Close button at the bottom of the page. From there, you can access the main Ads Manager menu.

3. **Click the Ads Manager menu and then click the Audiences link in the pop-up window, as shown in Figure 2-7.**

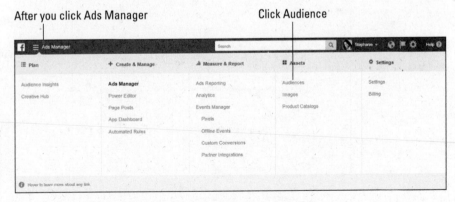

FIGURE 2-7:
Selecting the Audiences link from the Ads Manager Menu.

4. **Select Create a Custom Audience from the Reach the People Who Matter to You screen, as shown in Figure 2-8.**

   Again, you're not buying a Facebook Ad. You're simply preparing to upload your customer file, as shown in Figure 2-9.

Create Custom Audience

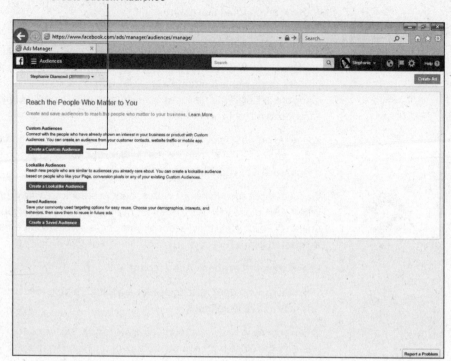

FIGURE 2-8:
Selecting Create a
Custom Audience
in Ads Manager.

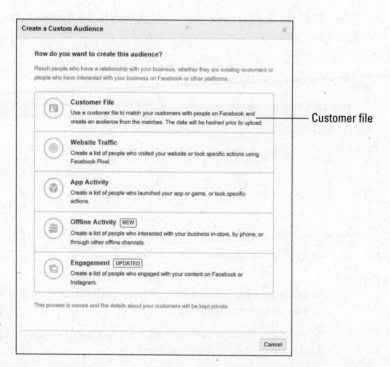

Customer file

FIGURE 2-9:
Preparing to
upload a
Customer File.

5. **Select Customer File and choose Add Customers from Your Own File or copy and paste data, as shown in Figure 2-10.**

   A pop-up menu appears with a place to drag and drop your own file or to copy and paste it, as shown in Figure 2-11.

Add customers

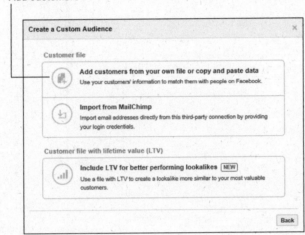

FIGURE 2-10:
Adding customers from your own file.

Drop file here

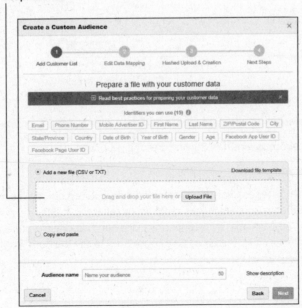

FIGURE 2-11:
Uploading your data file.

6. **Enter the name of your list and a description, select the I Agree to the Facebook Custom Audiences Terms box, and click Next.**

A screen appears that previews your data and allows you to edit data mapping, as shown in Figure 2-12.

FIGURE 2-12: Ads Manager shows you a preview of your file.

Click Upload & Create

7. **Make any changes you want and then click Upload & Create.**

Facebook begins hashing and creating your data.

8. **Get your answer.**

When Facebook finishes hashing the data, you can quickly see how many Facebook users are in your email list by returning to https://www.facebook.com/ads/manager/audiences/manage/ and clicking the name of the custom audience you just created (see Figure 2-13) to see the number of email users on your email list.

Click filename

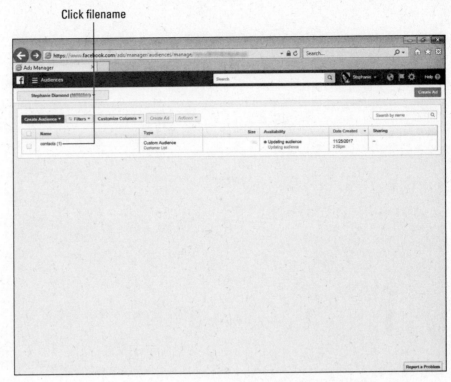

FIGURE 2-13:
Selecting the
name of your new
custom audience.

The number of Facebook users on your email list appears on the right side. The original file had 6,000 emails, 3,800 of whose senders have Facebook accounts, as shown in Figure 2-14.

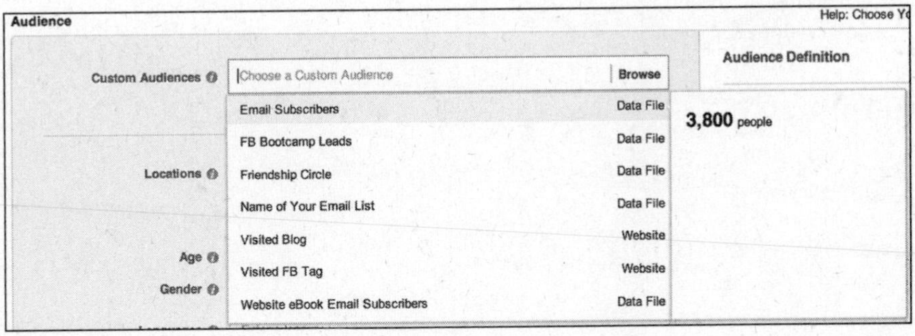

FIGURE 2-14:
Discovering the
number of
customers who
use Facebook.

Now that you know how many of your customers use Facebook, what are you going to do with that information? That's what Chapter 3 covers.

IN THIS CHAPTER

» **Getting to know your audience**

» **Creating engaging content and measuring your results**

» **Integrating your offline and online campaigns**

Chapter **3**

Developing a Facebook Marketing Plan

When George Harrison sang "If you don't know where you're going, any road'll take you there," he could've been thinking about Facebook. Because it's true: If you don't have a plan, you shouldn't expect to achieve exceptional results. In fact, if we had to pick one thing that determines success or failure on Facebook, it would have to be planning.

This point became even truer in January 2018, when Mark Zuckerberg announced that Facebook's highest goal was to generate more social interaction with friends and family and to enhance people's well-being. The change Facebook made to its algorithm (code that determines how something is handled) results in fewer messages from business Pages in user Timelines. So, planning has become even more important now. In a later section of this chapter, we discuss ways that may help you enhance your engagement with users so that your message will be heard.

Planning is a process that forces you to define specific goals and objectives. It's a process that forces you to ask the difficult questions, such as who your audience is and what makes customers engage with and talk about you.

This chapter helps you define Facebook goals, articulate what makes your product or service remarkable, and understand who your target audiences are. You also find out how to develop a content strategy, determine what to measure, and create a more integrated marketing strategy.

Understanding the Power of Word of Mouth on Facebook

Traditional marketing methods like print or TV ads are limited in that they can only shout (so to speak) at your customers to get them to buy something. This approach doesn't work with Facebook because users expect dialogue; they expect that they'll be able to contact and respond to you via your Facebook Page. They also expect that you'll respond in a timely manner. So in contrast to the one-way communication models of TV and print, Facebook is a place where customers and businesses can engage in two-way conversations.

Over time, even marketing approaches on the Internet have undergone a dramatic evolution. Websites once represented a kind of one-way communication, one in which visitors could only view content. Websites were followed by blogs and forums, which allowed visitors to comment on content, and then networks like Myspace and Facebook came along and really gave friends the ability to connect with one another. Finally, tools like Twitter and Foursquare allowed all people (not just friends) to have real-time conversations and even share their real-world locations within those conversations (see Figure 3-1).

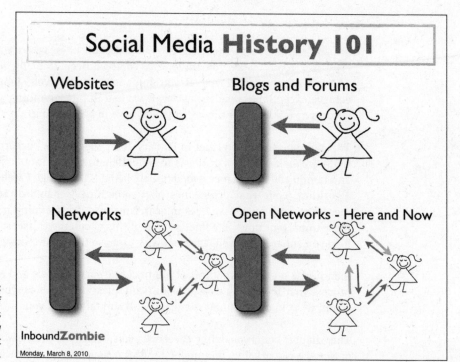

FIGURE 3-1: The advent of social networks influenced how people connect with brands.

Studies have shown that consumers trust what their friends say about a product or service ten times more than they trust what the brand itself says. This phenomenon, known as *word-of-mouth marketing*, has been around for centuries, but it has evolved over time. Friends originally made recommendations in person, then by mail, then by phone, then with email, and now with Facebook. But because of Facebook's viral nature, word-of-mouth marketing can be scaled to a massive degree.

How does this play out on Facebook? Here's an example.

When a Facebook user likes Spotify's Page (www.facebook.com/Spotifyusa) or installs the Spotify application in her profile, these actions are automatically turned into stories that appear in the News Feeds of many of her friends. By performing a simple action such as liking Spotify's Page, the user recommends Spotify to her Facebook friends, expanding word-of-mouth awareness of that brand without any extra effort.

Understanding What to Include in Your Marketing Plan

Before you can take full advantage of the marketing power of Facebook, you need to put together a Facebook *marketing plan*, which is a structured way to align your strategies with your objectives. Here are the general steps for creating your plan:

1. Develop your value proposition.
2. Understand your audience.
3. Define your marketing goals.
4. Develop your content strategy.
5. Encourage audience engagement.
6. Monitor and measure your Page activities.
7. Integrate your online and offline campaigns.

The rest of this chapter explains each of these steps in detail. By putting these steps into practice, you can begin to put your marketing strategy in place by the end of this chapter.

Developing Your Value Proposition

Why should customers buy what you're offering?

When you're developing a marketing plan, the first thing you need to do is define your *value proposition.* How is your product or service different from the competition's? Why should people buy your product instead of the competition's? What value do you add that is unique to your company?

You may have a different value proposition for each audience segment you target or for each product or service you offer. Your marketing plan should detail the ways in which you plan to communicate these values to your target audience.

To understand your value proposition, answer the following questions:

>> **How are you different from your competitors?** By knowing your competition and what separates your offering from theirs, you can begin to develop your *product differential,* a key ingredient that goes into your value proposition. Knowing what makes your product or service different from and better than your competitors' helps you create messaging that gets people's attention. What innovations make your offering stand out in people's minds compared with the competition? Are these differences important to your customers or only to you? How can you articulate these differences in ways that make people tell their friends?

>> **What value do you provide your stakeholders?** *Stakeholders* are your customers, shareholders, employees, partners, and anyone else who is affected by your company. Understanding the value you provide to them is key to developing your messaging and communications strategy. By having a clear picture of what you want to accomplish with your marketing plan, you open a world of opportunities for your business. The key is communicating your plan to your stakeholders. When your employees know and understand your brand messaging, they can pass that information on to your customers in the form of knowledge and better service. When your stakeholders know that you have a clear plan of action, they're more comfortable with the direction in which you're taking the company, which leads to greater support for your future ideas and plans.

>> **What are your big-picture goals?** Some goals are more obvious than others. They could include increasing company sales or driving more traffic to your website, both of which you can do when you clearly define and communicate your value proposition. Other goals aren't as obvious, such as improving your company's reputation or creating a more friendly face for the brand. Whatever your company's goals, make sure that all your Facebook marketing activities align with these goals.

Understanding Your Audience

Whatever your business goals are, always assemble the best information that you can about your audience. The better you understand the culture, desires, motivations, and viewpoints of your audience, the more effectively you can capture their attention and deliver your message. Understanding the lives of your customers and prospects is the key to creating marketing messages that resonate with people so strongly that they take action, such as joining your email list, liking your Facebook Page, or purchasing your product or service. According to Facebook, Insights (the Facebook analytics tool that shows you how your Page is performing; see more in Chapter 10) helps you learn about your three most important groups:

>> People connected to your Page

>> People you've selected to be in your target audience

>> People who are on Facebook

An excellent example of a business that understands its audience really well is the Threadless T-shirt company in Chicago, Illinois. The business was founded on the simple idea of selling T-shirts based on designs submitted by artists and voted on by customers. These designs in turn get published on the company's Facebook Page, where fans can share their favorite designs with their Facebook friends.

The folks at Threadless use Facebook (`www.facebook.com/threadless`) as a way to let fans know about sales; handle customer-support issues; and even engage fans in promotions on other social media sites, such as Instagram (see Figure 3-2).

Facebook gives you some powerful insights into your fans. In fact, identifying and then reaching a specific audience has never been this exact and cost-effective. The Facebook Insights tool helps you find out more about who visits your Facebook Page, including a demographics-and-interests breakdown on your fans, and Facebook's ad-targeting capabilities make it relatively easy to get your message to the right target audience within Facebook.

Gathering this information can be fairly easy if you know where to look and how to go about doing it. Ask your customers to fill out satisfaction surveys or a short questionnaire through your e-newsletter or website, for example. Another option is to search Facebook for companies similar to yours and read the comments posted by *their* fans to see what makes them return to those companies.

FIGURE 3-2:
Threadless displays its latest Instagram feed on its Facebook Page.

Instagram feed

Understanding your fans' psychographic profiles is an important element in knowing who they are. *Psychographic* variables (such as what music they love, politicians they endorse, or causes they support) are any qualities relating to their personality, values, attitudes, interests, or lifestyles. Psychographic variables offer additional insight into *demographics* (such as age and gender) and *behaviors* (such as use rate or loyalty), and can help you better understand your customer segments.

Psychographics is exceptionally relevant in any discussion of social networks because your target audience is more likely to interact with you along the lines of personal interests, values, and lifestyles. Tom's of Maine (https://www.facebook.com/TomsofMaine/), for example, takes advantage of the fact that many people are concerned about making positive changes in their communities and the health of their children. The company's Facebook Page has a #StartFreshSmile tab that allows users to participate in a photo contest (see Figure 3-3).

FIGURE 3-3:
Tom's of Maine
knows that its
customers care
about making
positive changes
in children's
health.

Defining Your Marketing Goals

When you have a better understanding of the makeup of your Facebook audience, you need to define a few goals for your Facebook marketing strategy. You may have other objectives for your business, but these four are the most common:

>> Building your brand's awareness

>> Driving sales

>> Forming a community of people who share your values

>> Listening to feedback about your brand

REMEMBER

We discuss each objective in more depth in the following sections. Keep in mind that these objectives aren't mutually exclusive; they can be combined. You can start with one method and advance your strategy in other areas as you go along.

Building awareness of your brand

The concept of branding traces back to the early Romans, but the practice that has always stuck with me (John) is early livestock farmers branding their cattle with branding irons so that when the animals wandered, everyone would know who owned them. Branding was a way of distinguishing a farmer's animal from other animals that looked very similar.

These days, things aren't that different. A *brand* is how you define your business in a way that differentiates you from your competition; it's a key element in defining your marketing goals. With a Facebook Page, you can build awareness of your brand with all your current and prospective customers.

A Facebook Page (shown in Figure 3-4) serves as the home for your business on Facebook, and it should be created with your company's brand and image in mind. It's a place to notify people of an upcoming event; provide hours of operation and contact information; show recent news; and even display photos, videos, text, and other types of content. A Facebook Page allows for two-way interaction between you and your customers, providing them with a place to post messages. It's also a great feedback loop that helps you find out more about your customers' needs. See more about this in the upcoming section on Facebook Live and Messenger.

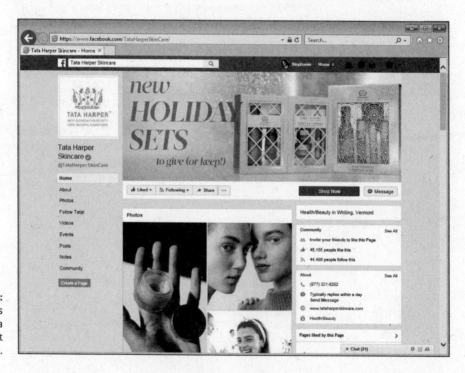

FIGURE 3-4: Facebook allows you to create a Page to market your business.

We discuss building your fan base in more detail in Chapters 7, 8, and 9, but here are three quick tips to get you started on the road to building a thriving presence on Facebook with lots of active engagement:

>> **Reach out to your Facebook friends.** The best place to start promoting your Facebook Page is existing Facebook friends. Use the Invite feature on the right side of any Facebook Page.

>> **Reach out to existing customers, friends, and contacts outside Facebook through your normal marketing channels.** Let these folks know that your business has a Page on Facebook. You can send them an email blast or include the address of your Page in a printed newsletter or flyer. Something as simple as "Join us on Facebook!" does the trick.

>> **Engage with your current fans.** There's no doubt that the people you interact with on Facebook are more likely to do business with you than they would if they'd never heard of you — particularly when you take the time to respond to their wants and needs with useful content and timely responses.

TIP

The Invite feature allows fans to invite their friends to like your Page, as shown in Figure 3-5.

Invite your friends to like Hollywood Express	
■ Beth Kanter	Invite
■ Joe Waters	Invite
■ Kate Rubin	Invite
■ Pamela Grow	Invite

FIGURE 3-5:
Use the Invite link to send a notification about your Page.

REMEMBER

Chapters 7, 8, and 9 discuss many more strategies and tactics for promoting your Facebook Page.

Driving sales

Whether you're a local, a national, or an international business, Facebook can help you drive the sales of your products and services. You can leverage Facebook in several ways to achieve your sales objectives:

>> **Communicate special offerings and discounts, and provide an easy path to purchase with a simple link to your company website.** Some larger retailers bring the entire shopping-cart experience to Facebook. Others simply link their Page to an e-commerce page on their websites. 1-800-Flowers.com offers fan-only discounts within its Facebook Page, shown in Figure 3-6, that links directly to its shopping site.

FIGURE 3-6:
The Facebook Page of 1-800-Flowers.com displays special offers that link to its website.

>> **Target your audience with a Facebook Ad campaign.** In addition to creating a free Facebook Page, many marketers utilize the potential of Facebook as a cost-effective advertising medium. This is likely to increase with the potential decrease in your content reaching your customer's Timeline. You can test and launch targeted ad campaigns that employ traditional direct marketing techniques, such as ads with engaging copy and pictures that capture a reader's attention. The most successful offer is an incentive that appeals to your audience. (We discuss advertising in more detail in Chapter 11.)

>> **Create a Facebook event to generate buzz about a product.** You can hold a new-product launch party or a wine tasting for potential customers, and you can throw a Facebook-only event for fans and allow them to network as well. (See Chapter 13 for a discussion of Facebook Events.)

Forming a community with a Facebook Group

One of the best uses of a social network is to build a *community* — a group of people who have the same interests and passion for a cause. No matter what your marketing goals are, forming a community takes some effort. We generally think that it's arrogant for marketers to feel that they can build a community that people will flock to — the proverbial "build it and they will come" model. With a Facebook Group in addition to a Page for your business, however, that very model is possible.

A *Facebook Group* is about people's shared interests or goals. With a group, you can create a community focused on an existing cause or interest that matches your business goals, and you can give your group members the tools to communicate with one another on Facebook. Another reason to create a group is to share an interest or hobby outside your business. If you own a hardware store and have a passion for building furniture, you can start a group for the purpose of uniting people who share your love of woodworking. (See Chapter 13 for a discussion of Facebook Groups.)

Spirited discussions are prominent in Facebook Groups, so plan for someone in your company — perhaps a product expert or someone on the communications team — to offer additional resources and perhaps lead regular discussion threads on specific topics of interest. The key is to put the needs of group members before the needs of your business.

Listening to feedback

You can listen to feedback from Facebook members in several ways:

>> **Monitor discussions in your group.** As discussed in the preceding section, a Facebook Group lets you create a community and have discussions with your members, but a noteworthy byproduct of forming a Facebook Group is the ability to get feedback. The next time you think about launching a new product or service, consider having the members of your group (in addition to fans of your Page) weigh in on it before it goes to market. Don't worry about a delay in getting the product to market; it takes only a few days to get feedback from members. Of course, you have to build up your member base before you can tap it.

Facebook doesn't publish secret or closed group discussions to Internet search engines, so if getting found via search is part of the strategy of your group, make sure that it's an open group (see Chapter 13).

>> **Search for discussions about your brand.** Facebook is fertile ground for open, honest, peer-to-peer discussions about your business. Just plug any search terms related to your business into the Facebook search box, and see what comes up. You might be surprised to find other fan Pages devoted to your brand.

To search for terms, type your keywords into the main search box at Facebook.com, and filter by pages, posts, or groups.

>> **Review postings on your Page Timeline.** Facebook users can post comments, questions, and even suggestions to your Page. Make sure that you closely monitor those posts and respond appropriately and in a timely manner.

>> **Get feedback directly from the horse's mouth.** Use tools like Facebook Live and Messenger to engage directly with your audience and gather valuable feedback. (For more information, see the upcoming section "Encouraging Audience Engagement.")

Developing Your Content Strategy

Keep in mind that content drives engagement. Content is the foundation of people-centered marketing. As long as social media exists, content will be a primary reason (along with relationship to the referrer) why people share your product or service with their friends. This is why it's so important to keep asking content-related questions such as these:

>> How can you tailor your content to appeal to your fans?

>> How can you provide useful, educational tips and other content?

>> What assets do you already have (such as videos, tips, customer testimonials, and so on) that will enhance your brand while delivering real value to your fans?

When developing your content strategy, look at your different channels of communication — your website, Facebook Page, Twitter presence, e-newsletter, Instagram, and so on — and then decide which content is right for each channel. You may realize that your Twitter followers want a different stream of updates than your Facebook fans do, and that your website visitors would be better served with more product-focused content. Because you want different types of engagement across all your channels, the content you publish needs to address each audience's needs and concerns.

Here are some powerful ways to develop your Facebook content strategy:

>> **Post to engage users.** Although some content you post will be purely informative, such as broadcasting a particular price promotion to your fans, posts that are designed to encourage participation from Facebook will allow you to benefit from Facebook's viral effect. Every time a fan comments on your Facebook Page, a story ends up in many of her *friends'* News Feeds.

These stories provide links back to the original post and often generate additional attention and interaction with that content. In this way, your fans invite others along for the ride.

» **Provide discounts and special offers.** As we touch on earlier in this chapter, Facebook marketers find great success through extending discounts, special offers, and giveaways to attract Facebook fans. Ads that generate the greatest responses on Facebook offer something of perceived value for very little effort on the member's part. Often, these offers are based on a prerequisite, such as completing a form or clicking the Like button.

When developing a promotion, keep in mind that the offer must interest your target audience. Sometimes, the offer doesn't even have to be tangible — merely the chance to have a shot at glory. In Figure 3-7, Klondike appeals to its fans' desires by encouraging them to share funny videos. You don't want your fans to just consume your message, you want them to interact and share their own comments.

FIGURE 3-7: Klondike created a video app for Facebook fans.

» **Deliver content in a format that's accessible to your audience.** When developing your content strategy, you should consider the range of media at your disposal. Facebook allows you to publish content in several formats (including live streaming, photos, and videos), making this content accessible directly through Facebook with a click of the mouse. Why not take advantage of the convenience of having everything in one easy-to-access location?

Likewise, if your fans enter into a dialogue on your Facebook Page's Timeline, continue to use Facebook as your communications channel. Don't reach out to an individual on Twitter, LinkedIn, or some other social network unless requested to do so by the fan (otherwise, you could seem too aggressive). Maintaining a consistent approach to communicating with your Facebook fans keeps them fans for the long term.

REMEMBER

The culture of Facebook is formed by young, digitally fluent adults who understand when they're being talked at versus engaged in a conversation. The key isn't to interrupt them with a continuous stream of messages, but to use content to encourage participation. By creating a steady stream of rich content, you can engage the right audience and get your audience to interact with your brand. For more on fine-tuning and implementing your content strategy, check out Chapter 7.

Encouraging Audience Engagement

As mentioned previously, the change to Facebook's algorithm means that you need to work even harder to engage your audience. As you work on your marketing plan, we recommend that you keep in mind the following tactics to help you achieve your goals. We also mention, where applicable, the specific chapters that go into more depth about these topics.

Creating a rich, customer-centric experience

In addition to incentives, the fierce competition to get your audience's attention requires you to offer an outstanding customer experience. If it's mediocre, you'll lose out to your competition.

Here are some ways you can stand out on Facebook:

>> **Customer support:** Responsive support is the key to developing a loyal customer. Many businesses on Facebook do a mediocre job of helping their customers find information they want and build a relationship. You can set up interactive tools that let you have private one-on-one conversations with users to satisfy their needs. Suggested tools are the following:

- **Facebook Messenger:** Messenger allows you to send/receive private messages directly from Facebook. In addition, you can offer mobile support to show customers that you want to communicate with them in the way they find most convenient.

- **Messenger chatbots:** Setting up chatbots help customers serve themselves to get the answers they are looking for. See Chapter 16 for a detailed look at Messenger and chatbots.

- **Community development:** Setting up a Facebook Group for your community allows you to see what your customers are talking about and how you can serve them better. A tool we suggest is Facebook Groups. Even though Facebook Groups can take some work to maintain, they help you and your members connect with others to build relationships and share information. See Chapter 13 to learn about Facebook Groups.

» **Live streaming:** One of the creative ways to interact with fans on Facebook is to provide live broadcasts that teach, entertain, and let your viewers get to know you better. Ask for their opinions and get them actively engaged. A good tool for this purpose is Facebook Live. You can broadcast directly from your desktop or mobile device to your user, who can watch from either venue (device or computer). Speak directly to your users and show them interviews, events, daily activities, and so on. See Chapter 16 to see how to use Facebook Live

» **Quality content:** You know that if your content is subpar, you won't get users to give you a second look. You need to create great videos, articles, and other content that will cause them to share and respond. A tool we suggest is Instagram Stories, which are easy to set up and use for spontaneous happenings. These stories can get your audience talking with you and each other. See Chapter 14 for more about Instagram and Chapter 7 for information on content marketing.

REMEMBER

Facebook also has a Stories section that is displayed on the upper right of your Facebook profile or Page. As of this writing, this tool hasn't garnered as much interaction as Instagram Stories. Experiment to see whether your audience is interested in finding you on Facebook Stories.

» **Website integration:** Any way that you can help visitors to your website communicate with you is a great step toward increasing their engagement with your brand. If they enjoy using Facebook, you are making it easier for them to talk to you. Consider using Facebook Social Plugins. Plug-ins allow you to integrate your website activity with your Facebook Page. You can also use these tools to track usage data. Chapter 15 tells you much more about how Facebook plug-ins can support your website.

Appreciating your fans and growing your base

Customers want to feel as though they're receiving special treatment on Facebook. They want to know that their support is important to you and that their concerns are heard. They want something in return for their attention and loyalty. Facebook members love free stuff, special discounts, and promotions. But they want to be sincerely appreciated as well, and you might even argue that sincere appreciation is more valuable than free stuff. Offering both is the best approach!

It's not surprising that Facebook members are looking for real value in the form of informative and engaging content from marketers on Facebook. Much as in Google Search, in which users are farther down the intent-to-purchase road by the very nature of their searches, Facebook users aren't necessarily looking for specific products and services to purchase. That's why marketers need to grab their attention through special offers.

People can find special incentive offers throughout Facebook on Facebook Pages. In Figure 3-8, StarKist gives visitors a chance to get discounts and special offers by signing up on its Facebook Page.

FIGURE 3-8:
StarKist gives fans the opportunity to get free merchandise and special offers.

Although discounts and promotions serve as good incentives for some people, savvy marketers want to provide value in different ways that reinforce their proposition value. The Hallmark Channel's *Kitten Bowl* Facebook Page (https://www.facebook.com/KittenBowl/) allows its fans to support an animal shelter with its *Kitten Bowl* events (see Figure 3-9). This sort of promotion creates long-term affinity among fans.

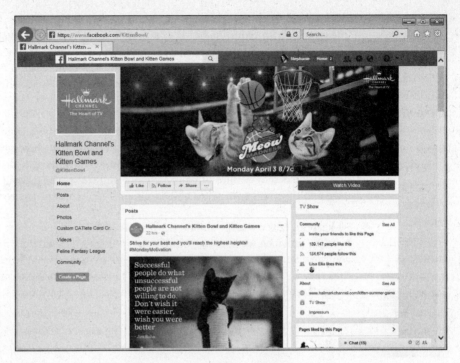

FIGURE 3-9:
The Hallmark
Channel has
Kitten Bowl.

Monitoring and Reporting Page Activity

The last piece of the puzzle for an effective marketing plan is taking the time to monitor and measure your Page activities. Only through careful analysis can you figure out what content resonates with your audience, and because actions within Facebook are measurable, your Page's metrics, or *key performance indicators,* can give you lots of insights into your fans' interactions with your Page.

A marketing campaign is only as good as your ability to measure it. The number of people who like your Page isn't worth anything to your business if you can't peel away the layers to gain greater meaning into those people's actions. You need to translate those analytics into real-world lessons that you can then apply to your content.

Facebook provides some powerful analytic tools to help you discover what's really happening on your Page. The following sections discuss just a few things to keep in mind when taking stock of your Facebook Page's analytics.

Using Insights for Pages

Facebook has an internal analytics system called Facebook Insights, through which you can gain greater understanding of your visitors' behavior when interacting with your Page; it's available for free to all Page admins. By understanding and analyzing trends in your user growth and audience makeup, and by understanding which updates get the most comments, Likes, and shares, you gain valuable insights (pun intended) into what strategies will create the most reach and engagement on Facebook.

Facebook Insights focuses on three areas of data: your fans, your reach, and the ways Facebook users interact with your content, as shown in Figure 3-10. (We explore this topic in greater detail in Chapter 10.) Insights provides information on the demographics of your audience and tracks the growth of fans on your Page and the number of Likes and comments your content has received.

By keeping tabs on some key metrics, such as the increase in the number of fans over the previous week or the number of interactions following a particular post, you can eventually uncover networks and get an idea of what works. If you notice that several fans have opted out of being fans after a particular post, you might draw a correlation between the content you posted and the drop-off rate.

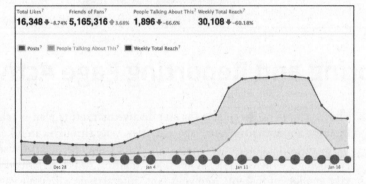

FIGURE 3-10:
Facebook Insights provides metrics on how your fans interact with your Page.

Check out your Insights metrics regularly to stay on top of increases in engagement numbers and activity. Also, keep track of which posts people respond to and which ones they don't. If you don't see any performance changes, it may be time to rethink your content strategy.

TIP

The Insights Dashboard shows you an aggregate of geographic and demographic information about your fans — who you're reaching and who's engaging with your Page — without identifying any individual's location or demographic, as shown in Figure 3-11. This feature is a great way to find out who your audience is.

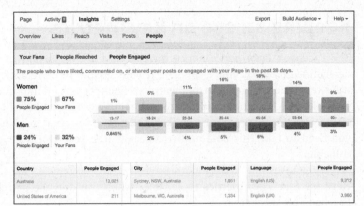

REMEMBER

Flying blindly into your Facebook marketing plan is a fool's journey. The more you know about how and what your fans react to, the easier it is to tailor your content to the audience, giving them more of what they want.

Creating benchmarks and setting goals

As discussed earlier in this chapter, your Facebook efforts are indeed measurable. You need to have an idea of where you stand at the beginning of your efforts to compare it with where you stand at the end of a promotion, ad campaign, event, or other activity. By creating *benchmarks,* the key indicators that define your Page's activity level, you can gauge your progress. Without knowing how many fans your Page had before a promotion, how can you calculate the success of the campaign? Take note of the number of views each specific tab on your Page gets; you can find this information on the Reach tab within Insights. Do certain tabs, such as your Photos tab, get more views than others? Make it a point to update the content on the other tabs to see whether this change increases their views. If views increase, you know that your fans are looking for you to update *all* your tabs more frequently, not just your Timeline.

In addition to setting benchmarks, set goals attached to your various Facebook marketing efforts. Japanese electronics manufacturer JVC set a goal to acquire as many fans as possible over a 60-day period through a daily contest promoted in Facebook Ads. The contest required that members like its company Page before entering the contest. The promotion proved to be so successful that JVC saw an increase in fans from fewer than 1,000 at the outset of the contest to more than 34,000 in 30 days.

Although anticipating the success of a campaign or particular post before going live with it is difficult, by forecasting the outcome, you have to consider the results at the outset of your planning. Therefore, you can better manage your coworkers — and, more important, your boss's — expectations.

Keeping an eye on key metrics

The Facebook Page performance metrics that are important to you are in part determined by what your goals are. If your goal is to drive clicks to an external website, tracking referrals from your Facebook Page is an important indicator for you. Likewise, if your goal is to drive engagement, the number of comments associated with your content is most likely the metric you need to measure. Most of all, you need to take this data and translate it into real-world insights to make it valuable.

Here are seven key metrics to consider when tracking the performance of your Facebook presence:

>> **Views:** A fundamental measurement is the number of views or visitors your content receives, and your Facebook Insights page is the place to go for this information. Understanding where people spend their time on your Facebook Page gives you a good idea of what information they find valuable.

>> **Comments (found under Reach):** The number of comments you receive for a particular post is a great way to track performance. This information also helps you identify which posts resonate with your fans. Typically, the more comments a post receives, the more interested your fans are in that content. Insights provides your Page's comment activity in an easy-to-read graph.

REMEMBER

When measuring the number of comments, don't forget to consider the sentiment of those comments. If all the comments are negative, you could have a backlash if you produce similar posts.

>> **Clicks and downloads:** If you post downloadable content or a link to content on an external website, it should always be trackable. You can use Insights to track them. Several URL shorteners, such as Bitly (http://bit.ly) and Tiny. cc (http://tiny.cc), also provide third-party click-through metrics on any link you shorten through their services. This is an excellent way to track the interest in a particular link or download.

>> **Shares (under Reach):** If your content strikes a chord with your fans, chances are that they'll share the content they find valuable with their own network. By monitoring (with Insights) the number of times content you post is shared, you can get a good sense of what's of interest to people.

>> **Inbound links:** Although linking is more common on external websites, Facebook Pages are linked to by bloggers, media outlets, search engines, and people who are generally interested in your Page. Searching Google by using your Page URL as a search term tells you how many sites link to your Facebook Page. Typically, the more links to your Page, the better.

>> **Brand mentions:** If you're doing a good job marketing your business on Facebook, chances are that it'll have a spillover effect across other social media outlets. Several free social media search sites, such as Social Mention (http://socialmention.com), track brand mentions. Make a point of running a search of your company name on these sites on a regular basis. Monitoring what people say outside Facebook provides numerous insights into your marketing effectiveness.

>> **Conversions:** A *conversion* occurs when a visitor undertakes a desired action, such as completing a transaction on your website, filling out a registration form, subscribing to your e-newsletter, or signing up for an event. Conversions are among the strongest metrics you can measure and track. If you look at it as a ratio of total visitors to those who have converted on a particular action, you see that the higher the percentage of people who undertake that action, the better.

TIP One of the most important metrics not represented in this list is the good old-fashioned practice of listening to your fans. Paying attention to their comments, discussions, and communications helps you better align your content strategy with their interests.

TIP For more on analyzing important metrics, see Chapter 11.

Integrating Your Online and Offline Campaigns

When you start to solidify your Facebook marketing strategy, you may question what support systems and resources you need or wonder how to integrate your social network marketing strategy with your existing marketing plans. In this section, we make some suggestions on how to support the effort without over-loading yourself or your marketing team.

There's no reason why you can't leverage your existing offline campaigns with a social network but be sure that you incorporate the campaigns into Facebook the right way. That is, include all elements of your campaign on Facebook. If you're throwing an Event or starting a campaign, for example, mention it to your Facebook fans. Pretty much anything you currently do can be digitized and used on your Facebook Page.

Here are some ways that you can integrate your offline campaigns with your Facebook marketing activities:

>> **Promote face-to-face Events.** You want people to attend your Event, right? Mention your Event on your Page, and even link to any outside information you've posted, such as on your website. Better yet, create a Facebook Event and get a head start on your head count with those RSVPs that are going to come rolling in via your Page. (See Chapter 13 for more information on setting up Events within your Facebook Page.)

>> **Adapt advertising campaigns to use for Facebook Ads.** Just be sure to make the campaign more social and conversational in tone by creating short, attention-grabbing headlines and using eye-catching pictures.

REMEMBER

You have a limited number of characters to use in a Facebook Ad, so make every character count.

>> **Compare Facebook results with offline efforts.** Have you found that you have a better response rate to your Facebook marketing activities than, say, to sending out a direct mailer? Did you find that you got more visits to your website because of something you posted on your Page than phone calls from prospective customers as a result of your mailers? Take some time to view both your online and offline marketing results to get a clear picture of what's working and what isn't. After you compile this information, you can focus more closely on what gets you the most results.

The following sections explain how to evaluate your media budget and take inventory of your content assets.

Deciding on a media budget

Believe it or not, the cost of the technology used for social network marketing is rather low. A blog costs almost nothing to start, a podcast can cost up to $2,000, a wiki can cost up to $6,500 per year, and a video can cost up to $15,000. Your Facebook Page is free, but a private, branded app on Facebook can cost up to $100,000.

Unlike traditional media (print, TV, and radio) that can cost big money, social networks' upfront costs are very small. A blog or Facebook Page costs nothing to start, but the real (and potentially large) cost is creating a steady stream of rich content to fill these new media channels.

You can also use an online marketing budget calculator like the one at Hubspot `https://www.hubspot.com/ads-calculator?ads-budget=100&cpc=0.8 &conversion-rate=3.00&average-price=400&ltc=10` to help you determine the ROI on ad spending.

TIP

Dedicate up to 25 percent of your traditional media budget to non-traditional media. This amount gives you a healthy budget to experiment with for advertising, apps, and promotions, and for creating content to be successful in social networks like Facebook Pages.

Hiring an online writer

To create a steady stream of rich content that attracts the right audience, plan to have access to some additional, perhaps dedicated, writing resources for all your social content needs.

Social writing is a unique skill because the writing needs to be conversational. Headlines need to be provocative and entice the reader to want to know more. Above all, body copy needs to have a colloquial tone without a trace of sales- or marketing-speak.

TIP

Hire a separate writer for social network marketing content unless you happen to be one. Most people tend to think that they can use the same writing resource for research papers, fact sheets, brochures, website copy, email copy, and social content. This practice is dangerous. Having someone who truly understands the medium can help you tailor existing content, and writing new content helps to ensure that you always put your best foot forward. A great resource for finding web copywriters is `http://jobs.problogger.net`.

2

Building Your Facebook Presence

Chapter **4**

Getting Started with a Facebook Page

F acebook Pages give your business a presence on Facebook where you can promote your products or services. Facebook Pages are the business equivalent of a Facebook member's Timeline.

Facebook users can like your Facebook Page, find out about new products and promotions, post content (photos, videos, and links), send you private messages, and even converse with others in comments on your Page posts. You can also add branded custom tabs with various features to engage customers, capture email addresses, and even sell your products or services, such as the shop tab offered by Dollar Shave Club (see Figure 4-1).

With all these features as well as exposure to thousands of potential customers, the Facebook Page has become a central tool in the marketing toolbox of thousands of brands. In fact, Facebook has added lots of features that turn your static Page into an interactive one. You can now swap out your Page photo for a video (covered in Chapter 7) and communicate with your customers using Facebook Live and Messenger (detailed in Chapter 16.)

In this chapter, you find out what Facebook Pages are all about and what that means for your business. We walk you through creating a Facebook Page and give you tips on how to set up your Page so that you convert more visitors to fans. We also help you understand how to make the most of Facebook marketing resources.

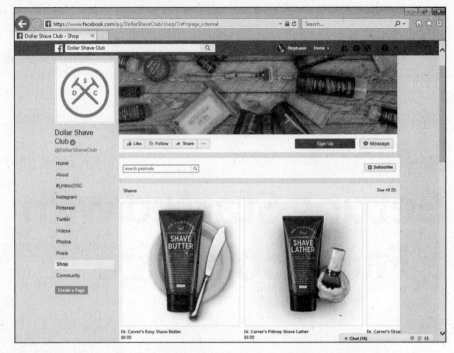

FIGURE 4-1:
Dollar Shave Club enhanced its customer experience on Facebook with an e-commerce app.

Understanding the Differences among Pages, Timelines, and Groups

One of the most common mistakes businesses make when they start using Facebook is using the wrong Facebook tool. Many start by creating a *profile*, which is really intended for people to share personal information on Facebook. Or they start by creating a *group*, which is intended for people to connect with one another on very specific goals and interests.

Each of these Facebook tools serves a very different purpose:

>> **Timelines:** Timelines (otherwise known as Facebook profiles) represent people. They allow Facebook users to connect with friends, upload and share videos and photos, and store their activities over time. If you use Facebook personally, you're using a Timeline.

- » **Pages:** Pages represent businesses, brands, nonprofit organizations, public figures, and celebrities. Pages allow you to create awareness of your product or service within the Facebook community, engage with customers and products, and even sell your products or services.

- » **Groups:** Groups allow people (using Timelines) to organize around shared goals or topics of interest. People can join groups; Pages can't.

Many businesses start with the wrong Facebook tool because they may be comfortable using a Timeline and don't know anything else, or they received no clear direction from Facebook or a marketing expert. Lucky for you that you're reading this book!

Timelines are personal, not business

Timelines limit the number of friends to 5,000. This makes sense, because no human being could actually be friends with an unlimited number of people.

A business, on the other hand, might suffer under such limitations. Your business can post updates to your Page at any time without any concern about a limit on the number of people you can reach.

From one perspective, Facebook users who like your Page are like email subscribers, with Facebook providing the infrastructure for you to reach those subscribers via Page updates, message replies, and the ability to target specific fan segments with updates and ads.

Here are four more key differences between a Facebook Page and a Facebook Timeline:

- » **Timelines don't have any marketing analytics.** Facebook Pages give marketers a powerful tool called Insights that allows you to see how users engage with your Facebook Page updates.

- » **Friending a Timeline is very different from liking a Page.** When Facebook users send friend requests, they're essentially asking that user for access to her photos, her list of friends, her phone number, her relationship status, and other very personal information.

  Facebook Pages offer no such functionality for marketers, which is actually a good thing for both parties. In the real world, a business would never make such personal requests of customers and prospects. Brands that use a Facebook Timeline to market their businesses often unknowingly cross this social boundary. Asking a user to like your Page, on the other hand, doesn't cross any such boundary. Instead, users like Pages (see Figure 4-2).

TIP

Facebook allows Timelines to activate a subscribe feature, allowing Facebook users to subscribe to public updates from that person. This feature is the only marketing feature Timelines have, which is still extremely limited compared with the features offered in a Facebook Page. (Read more about the subscribe feature in Chapter 11.)

FIGURE 4-2:
Facebook Pages require users to like the Page, not request friend-ship, as personal Timelines do.

>> **Using a Facebook Timeline to market your organization is a violation of the Facebook terms and conditions** (www.facebook.com/legal/terms). Facebook terms state: *"You will not use your personal timeline primarily for your own commercial gain, and will use a Facebook Page for such purposes."*

Facebook terms also state: *"If you violate the letter or spirit of this Statement, or otherwise create risk or possible legal exposure for us, we can stop providing all or part of Facebook to you."* This means that even after you spend a lot of resources to build a large number of friends — say, 5,000 — Facebook can simply delete your Timeline.

>> **Facebook Timelines have bad search engine optimization (SEO).** The last key difference between Facebook Pages and Timelines is that Facebook Pages are public by default. This means that anyone can search and find your Page with the Facebook search engine and with Internet search engines (such as Google and Yahoo!), thereby helping your business gain visibility and broadening your audience beyond just Facebook.

If you created a Timeline to market your business and want to switch to a Page, here's the good news: Facebook gives you the opportunity to convert your existing Timeline to a Page. When you do so, your Timeline picture remains, and all your friends become fans of the new Page.

WARNING

When you're converting a Timeline to a Page, though, all other information is removed. So if you opt for this conversion, save any updates, videos, photos, and other types of content to your hard drive so that you can put them on your new Page. You can download your content by clicking the Settings link on your Page.

From the General Settings section at the bottom of the page, click Download Page and follow instructions.

REMEMBER

After you convert your Timeline to a Page, you can't revert back to a Timeline.

To begin converting a Timeline to a Page, go to `https://www.facebook.com/pages/create/migrate` and then follow the steps for creating a Facebook Page outlined later in this chapter (see Figure 4-3).

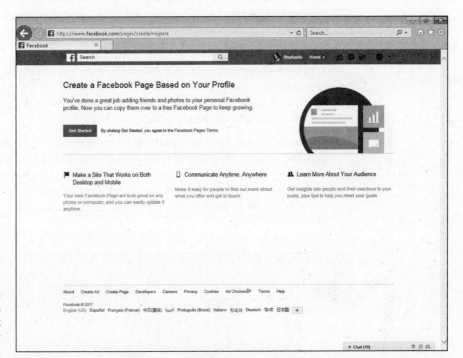

FIGURE 4-3:
Facebook allows users to convert a Timeline to a Page.

Groups are for connection, not promotion

Another very common mistake businesses make is creating a Facebook Group to market their products or services. The problem with this action is that groups are intended for Facebook users to *connect with one another* — not to receive notifications about promotions or new products from businesses.

Most groups are very small and used as tools for people to communicate in real-life social circles. Members of an extended family, for example, can use Facebook Groups to keep in touch with one another, organize family events, and collect and share photos and videos.

Now, this isn't to say that businesses shouldn't use groups. Biggerplate (`http://biggerplate.com`), a mind-mapping company, uses several groups to engage users (see Figure 4-4).

Groups can be valuable for businesses, but here are three reasons that Facebook Groups aren't as good as Facebook Pages for your business:

>> **Groups offer no capability to add custom applications.** One thing that people love about Facebook Pages is that you can add a lot of custom tabs to conduct polls, create photo contests, and collect emails, among other ways to keep prospects and customers connected. You can even add storefront e-commerce applications to a Facebook Page!

>> **Facebook Groups have no viral features.** When users post updates in groups, they're shared only with other members of that group. Pages, on the other hand, automatically generate viral reach each time a person likes, comments on, or shares updates from that Page.

>> **Facebook Groups have no hierarchy.** All members of a Facebook Group are generally seen as being equal players who contribute to a common cause or interest. This situation is different from Facebook Pages in which brands set the agenda for the Page. For this reason, the group members — not a brand — dictate what topics are discussed.

FIGURE 4-4: Biggerplate uses Facebook Groups to engage its community.

In Chapter 13, we go into more depth about Facebook Groups. For now, just know that they're not the best choice for marketing your business.

Understanding the Anatomy of a Facebook Page

Before showing you how to create your own Facebook Page in the following section, we briefly look at its structure. Understanding the structure of a Page makes it easier for you to determine what you want to include on your own business Page. Even though you have probably seen hundreds of Pages, it can be intimidating to decide what to put on your Page if you're not familiar with the layout. Figure 4-5 shows you the main parts that make up a Page as well as how one software company presents its business. You can find this Adobe Page at `https://www.facebook.com/adobe`.

TIP

This is how the Page looked at the time of this writing. Yours may look different, but the structure will be the same.

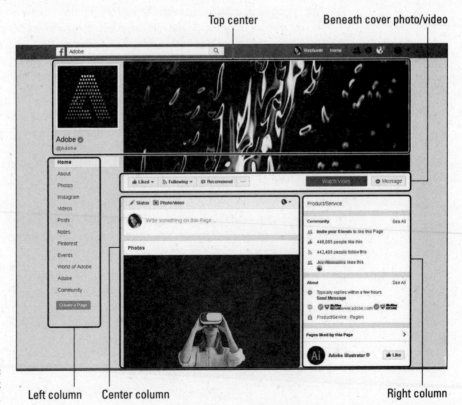

FIGURE 4-5: Adobe Facebook Page.

Top center

Beneath cover photo/video

Left column   Center column

Right column

>> **Top center:** This area includes your profile picture, username, and cover photo or video. These items tell users what your business is about and gives them visual clues about you. Note that Adobe uses a black-and-white picture and cover photo. As a design software company, Adobe wants to set the stage for the colorful content that will populate this page.

Type of content to consider: You need to choose an exciting photo or video that represents your business, as well as choose a profile picture that includes your logo or represents your brand.

>> **Area beneath the cover photo/video:** Right under the cover photo and to the left are the following buttons: Like, Follow, Recommend, and an ellipsis (. . .) button. When you click the . . . button, several other options appear. People who want to become fans can click the Like button, or they can follow you or recommend you to others. To the right is what's known as the call to action (CTA) button (in this case, it's Watch Video). We discuss the CTA button in the "Adding a button (CTA) to your Facebook Page" section, later in this chapter. Adobe uses its Watch Video to show off its latest software innovations. Next to that CTA button is a message button, which is optional. The message button allows users to send you a private message. Adobe uses this button to provide support.

Type of content to consider: For the CTA button, you need to decide what action you want your customer to take and then choose from the options that Facebook provides for that button that aligns with the action you've chosen. You also need to decide whether you'll include a message button. If you offer any kind of customer support, you probably want to consider using this button.

>> **Left column:** Here you find the links that people will use to navigate through your content. The default list will be determined by the Facebook template you choose when you set up your Page. This is also where you add custom tabs and apps. Notice that Adobe takes full advantage of this by adding apps for its Instagram and Pinterest feeds and custom tabs called World of Adobe and Adobe.

Type of content to consider: This is an important section because it will house any apps you decide to include (such as a Pinterest feed) and any custom tabs that will show specific content. You need to decide what content you want to highlight, such as photos or videos, and include them here.

>> **Right column:** In this column, the user sees the designation you use for your business. In this case, Adobe chose Product/Service. Next comes the Community box, which gives users a link to invite friends. It also shows how many people like and follow this page, and it provides the specific name of one of your followers who likes the page. Underneath that box is the company About box, which is where you put important links. Below that is a list called Pages liked by this Page.

Type of content to consider: You can't control the number of likes that display, but you can give careful consideration to the About content that populates this area. Also, you need to determine which Pages you want to like that will show up here.

» **Center column:** This is the timeline area, which is the heart of your Facebook Page. This is where your company posts ongoing updates and where fans can post their content if you choose to allow it. This is also where people comment on your content.

Type of content to consider: Before you publish your Page, make sure that you've thought about how often you'll be posting and what goals you have for that content.

Next, you look at how to set up your own Facebook Page.

Creating a Facebook Page from Scratch

Here are the steps for creating a Facebook Page (we recommend reading all the steps before you begin):

1. **Go to** www.facebook.com/pages/create.

2. **Select the business type that best describes your business.**

   You can choose among six types of Facebook Pages (see Figure 4-6):

   - **Local Business or Place:** These Pages are meant for businesses that would benefit from a strong local market presence: a museum, a pizza shop, or a movie theater.

   - **Company, Organization, or Institution:** These Pages are meant for large national businesses, which could include nonprofit organizations and large companies. Apple and Dell are good business-to-consumer examples; Avaya and Oracle are good business-to-business examples.

   - **Brand or Product:** These pages are meant for large brands. Think Starbucks and Coca-Cola.

   - **Artist, Band, or Public Figure:** These Pages are good for politicians, artists, TV celebrities, or musical groups, such as Jimmy Kimmel, Barack Obama, and Lady Gaga.

   - **Entertainment:** These Pages are meant for brands and companies in the entertainment industry, such as Broadway shows and cable TV networks.

- **Cause or Community:** Community Pages are intended for Facebook users who like a topic or experience and are owned collectively by the community connected to it. Because you want to have administrative control of your business presence on Facebook, we don't recommend using a Community Page as a primary way to market on Facebook.

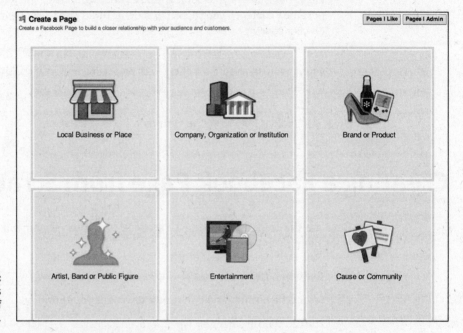

3. **Type your business name in the Company Name field to secure your organization's name on Facebook.**

WARNING

When you name your Page, it's much more difficult to change after you've acquired 100 fans. (After you have 100 fans, you can request a name change by clicking a "request change" link next to your page name on the basic information tab, but it's up to Facebook whether to grant the request.) So, choose a name that you want your fans and customers to associate with your business (see Figure 4-7). In most cases, this name will be the name of your business.

If you select a Local Business or Place, you also need to enter your address and phone number.

FIGURE 4-7:
Select the name
and category of
your Facebook
Page.

4. **Select a category for your Page.**

Depending on the Page type you select (refer to Figure 4-6), you have a variety
of choices regarding your Page category. Choose a category based on how
your customers think about your business rather than how you think about
your business. A museum of science would choose Museum as its category
even though its executive director might think of the museum as being a
nonprofit organization, which is another category choice. Choosing a
customer-oriented category makes it easier for users to find your business on
Facebook.

Although you can always change the category of your Facebook Page, try to get
it right from the start.

REMEMBER

5. **Click the Get Started button.**

When you click Get Started, you automatically agree to the Facebook Pages
Terms. Read the terms for Pages at https://www.facebook.com/
page_guidelines.php.

Congratulations! You've just created your Facebook Page, as shown in Figure 4-8.
The next sections show you how to upload and add your picture and cover image,
and add items to make your Page enticing to new customers.

You may have some differences in what you see based on the category you've chosen.

TIP

Uploading your profile picture

Your next step in creating a new Page is uploading a profile picture. A good way to
start making your Page unique is to upload your company logo or a photo of your
product. This picture represents your business on Facebook, so make it a good one.
If you're a services company, you can have photos of happy people using your service.

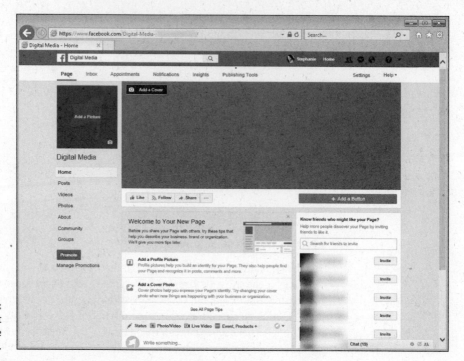

FIGURE 4-8:
This is what
your new Page
looks like.

 You can upload photos in JPG, GIF, or PNG formats only. Pictures should be 180 pixels square and are resized to 160 pixels square.

REMEMBER

To upload the first picture for your Page, follow these steps:

1. **Click Add a Picture (see Figure 4-9).**

   You are shown three choices: Choose From Photos, Take Photo, and Upload Photo.

FIGURE 4-9:
Choices for
adding a profile
picture to your
new Page.

2. **Make your choice and browse to the picture you're looking for; then click the Open button to start the process. (You can also double-click the picture in your browser to open it.)**

   After choosing the picture, you see a pop-up screen, shown in Figure 4-10, that asks you to add a description, resize, crop, or edit to get the picture the way you want it.

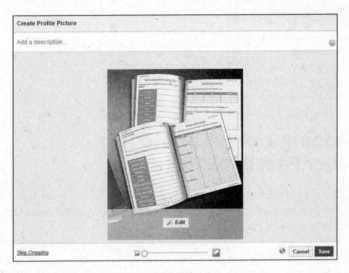

Editing your Facebook Page's profile picture

When you first create your Page, you are asked to upload a picture or video to be used as your profile picture. To change it, simply follow these steps:

1. **Mouse over your profile picture and click Change Picture.**

2. **On the drop-down menu, your choices are Choose From Photos, Take Photo, Upload Photo, or Remove, as shown in Figure 4-11.**

   Make your selection, and a pop-up window appears.

3. **In the pop-up window, select the new profile picture from your desktop.**

   Again, as you did when adding your first picture you have the option to add a description, edit, and crop.

4. **When you have made your changes, click Save.**

   Your new profile picture automatically replaces the previous profile picture.

FIGURE 4-11:
Options for
changing your
profile picture.

Adding a cover photo to your Facebook Page

The most powerful way to engage Facebook users is to use images. Facebook allows you to upload a cover photo, video, a photo/video or slideshow that appears at the top of your Facebook Page.

Think of your cover image as the primary way to create a powerful first impression when someone visits your Page. You can also use it as another tool to engage your most passionate fans.

To upload a cover image, click the Add a Cover camera icon. You will see the following choices, as shown in Figure 4-12: Choose From: Photos, Choose From Videos, Upload Photo/Video, and Create Slideshow.

FIGURE 4-12:
You have several
formats that you
can choose for
your cover.

Adding a button (CTA) on your Facebook Page

A key way to engage your audience on Facebook is to make it easy for people to take some action to interact with your community. You want to encourage them to click links and buttons and, you hope, buy your products or services. A good approach is to use a call to action (CTA) button, which Facebook provides under your cover photo or video, to the right. For example, Stella & Dot (https://www.facebook.com/stelladot/), an entrepreneurial jewelry company, put a Sign Up button on its Facebook Page, as shown in Figure 4-13. When users click the button, they're taken to the company's website, where they learn about joining the company.

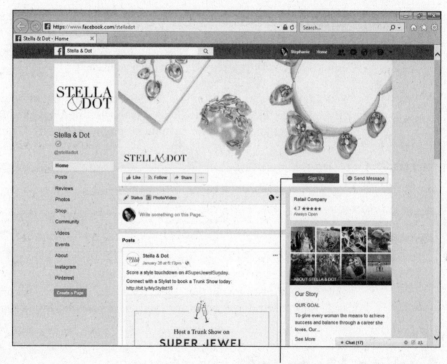

FIGURE 4-13: Stella & Dot has a Sign Up button on its Facebook Page.

Click Sign Up

Facebook offers several prepopulated button options to choose from, including the following categories:

>> Book with you

>> Contact you

>> Learn more about your business

>> Shop with you or make a donation

>> Download your app or play your game

>> Join your community

As you can see, these choices invite action and are easy to set up. Make sure to select one to include for when your Page goes live. Then monitor the response with Insights to see how well it works.

REMEMBER

The Call to Action (CTA) options will be different for your Page, depending on the Page category you have chosen.

Limiting access to your Page until launch

Before you go live with your Page, you may want to consider limiting access to admins only until you're ready to launch your Page.

You limit access by choosing the Settings tab at the top of your Page and then clicking Page Visibility in the General tab. Selecting Unpublish Page will hide it from all users, including your customers and prospects (see Figure 4-14).

FIGURE 4-14:
You can keep your Page hidden from view by keeping your setting as Page Unpublished.

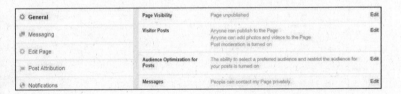

Only the administrators of the Page can view the Page while it's unpublished. Your Page won't be visible to users until you change this setting to Page Published.

Adding More Information about Your Business

The About tab contains detailed info about your business. Which details appear in these areas depends on which category and business type you choose when you create your Page. To add or edit information about your business, simply choose the About tab on your Facebook Page. (See Figure 4-15.)

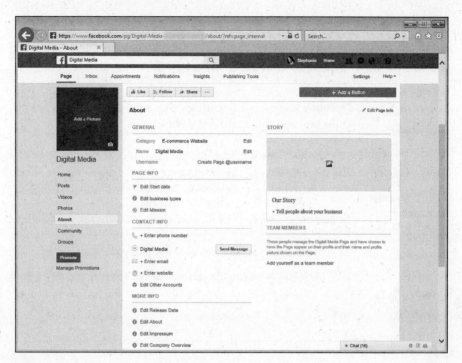

Here's a general rundown of some of the various sections within the About section including:

>> **Contact:** Here you enter your basic contact information, such as a phone number, email, and website URL. For bands, for example, this information would include band members' names and the type of music the band plays.

>> **Company Overview and Description:** Add your company's boilerplate text about who you are and what you do. Or you can add content that's more social and less "corporate" to give your Page more personality.

>> **Page Info:** Add your mission statement. You don't have to enter one if you don't have one, or you can make up something provocative.

>> **Products:** Add a listing of your products or services.

>> **Our Story:** This section asks you to tell people about your business.

Be sure to click the Save Changes button when you finish entering information or editing an item within the About tab.

REMEMBER

Facebook Pages are public, and these fields can help you with the SEO of your Page. Fill them with content that contains the keywords under which you want to be found by a search engine.

Adding Tabs to and Removing Tabs from a Facebook Page

Facebook allows you to configure or rearrange your Page tabs, which include a Video tab, an Events tab, and a Photos tab.

REMEMBER

The Tabs you see will vary depending on what kind of Page category you choose. You can also change the design template for your Page by clicking the Edit button in the Templates section above the Tabs (see Figure 4-16).

To add these tabs to your page or remove them, follow these steps:

1. **Choose the Settings link at the top of your Page.**

2. **Click Edit Page (on the left side of the screen) and scroll down to Tabs.**

Template section

FIGURE 4-16: You can add, revise, or remove Tabs on your Facebook Page in the Tabs section of your Page.

Tabs

3. **Click the Settings button to the right of the tab and make your changes.**

A pop-up window appears.

4. Add or remove the tab by selecting the appropriate option.

You can also change the order of your Facebook Page tabs views by positioning your mouse on the dotted area to the left and dragging each tab into the desired order.

5. Click Save.

TIP

Make sure that you remove any unused tabs on your Page to create a good impression for Facebook users. If someone visits your Page while you're displaying the Events app but haven't published any events, for example, Facebook users see the message This page has no Events. This isn't the kind of impression you want to make on people who visit your Page.

Adding more apps to your Facebook Page

In addition to the apps that are included with your Facebook Page (Photos, Videos, Notes, and Events), you can choose among thousands of free and premium apps. These apps allow you to add further functionality — such as promotions, videos, and e-commerce — to your Page. One way to do this is to search Facebook for an app and add it to your Page by following these steps:

1. Type the name of the app in the Facebook search bar at the top of the screen.

If you don't have a specific app in mind, simply search for the type of app you're looking for. Type the phrase *contact* to search for contact form applications, for example, and then select any apps that appeal to you.

2. In the search results, click the Use Now button for the app you want to use, as shown in Figure 4-17.

In some cases, you will be taken directly to a permissions box.

FIGURE 4-17:
Facebook allows you to search for additional applications for your Facebook Page.

3. Follow the prompts to add the app to your Page.

These prompts are different for each application.

For more on applications, see Chapter 6.

Adding Page Administrators

Facebook Pages allow businesses to add multiple administrators (see Figure 4-18). We recommend adding other admins to the Page, for several reasons:

>> Additional administrators can share the workload of managing a Facebook Page.

>> Having additional administrators on the Page helps ensure that someone replies to comments quickly. The last thing you want is to be left waiting for the only administrator of your Facebook Page to come back from vacation.

>> Additional administrators can help promote your Facebook Page through their personal networks.

Adding admins to your Facebook Page takes just five steps:

1. **Choose the Settings tab at the top of your Page and then the Page Roles tab on the left.**

2. **Enter the email address or name of the person whom you want to add as an admin.**

3. **Select one of the five levels of administrative access you'd like this user to have:**

    • **Admin:** Can manage admin roles, send messages and create posts as the Page, create ads, and view Insights

    • **Editor:** Can edit the Page, send messages and create posts as the Page, create ads, and view Insights

    • **Moderator:** Can respond to and delete comments on the Page, send messages as the Page, create ads, and view Insights

    • **Advertiser:** Can create ads and view Insights

    • **Analyst:** Can view Insights

    • **Live Contributor:** Can go live as the Page from a mobile device

4. **Click Add.**

5. **In the pop-up window, enter your Facebook password to confirm the addition of administrators.**

REMEMBER

Manager roles have full control of your Page, so make sure you know the people whom you make managers very well!

FIGURE 4-18:
Adding adminis-
trators can make
managing
Facebook Pages
easier.

Getting the Most from Facebook Marketing Resources

Probably one of the best resources on Facebook for marketers is the Facebook IQ Tools — Resources Page (https://www.facebook.com/iq/tools-resources). This Page includes several useful links for marketers and includes the following areas:

>> **Several Facebook Insight analytic categories:** These sections include Insights to Go, Cross Border Insights Finder, Audience Insights, and Insights Partners. The sections provide detailed information about each of these Insight programs.

>> **Creative Hub:** Here you can mock up your ads and get feedback from real users.

>> **Facebook Business:** This area links to a plethora of information about creating ads and Pages.

>> **Instagram Business:** Here you are served the latest information about marketing and growing your brand with Instagram ads.

>> **Facebook Blueprint:** In this section, you find detailed information about all the marketing tools and services in the form of free online courses.

>> **Stay in the Know:** Here you can sign up to get an email delivered to your Inbox that contains updated insights from Facebook IQ.

In addition to Facebook, you should check out amazing websites, including the following:

>> **Social Media Examiner:** This website helps businesses use social media tools like Facebook, Twitter, Google+, and LinkedIn to connect with customers, generate more brand awareness, and increase sales. The site is helmed by Michael Stelzner and articles are written by Facebook marketing thought leaders such as Mark Schaefer and Amy Porterfield. Go to www.socialmediaexaminer.com.

>> **Mari Smith:** Another amazing online resource for Facebook expertise is the website of Mari Smith. Her fans have called her the Queen of Facebook because of her comprehensive approach to learning and her exuberant style. Go to https://www.marismith.com/.

Understanding Facebook's Terms and Conditions

If you're a business owner, one thing that you care about, in addition to marketing your business, is protecting your business. This is why you need to understand Facebook's terms and conditions, at www.facebook.com/terms.php.

These terms and conditions set guidelines on the following areas:

>> You're responsible for the content you post on Facebook. Any copyright violation or other legal consequences are your responsibility.

>> Anyone younger than 13 can't use Facebook.

>> You can't misrepresent your relationship with Facebook to other people.

>> You can't spam users on Facebook.

>> Facebook reserves the right to delete any of your content and even delete your account if you violate the terms of service.

You have nothing to worry about if you read the terms of service and practice common-sense business ethics. If you already do (and we hope you do), the terms and conditions should be of little concern, and you can focus your efforts on building your business with Facebook!

Chapter 5

Configuring Admin Settings for Your Page

After you create a Facebook Page (see Chapter 4 for details), you're almost ready to start building a solid fan base of prospects and customers. But before you start posting content to your Page and promoting your Page through other channels, you should know how to make the most of it. You want to minimize spam and negative comments, for example. You should also know how to post as your Page and as your profile — and when one or the other is best. Another essential task is to make sure that your Page is configured to get the most exposure in News Feed. If your business has lots of events, for example, you want to ensure that people attending can easily post their event pics to your Page.

In this chapter, you learn how to configure moderation and posting settings for your Page. You also learn how to restrict specific groups of Facebook fans from seeing your Page. Finally, we show you how to post on other Pages as your Page, and how to switch between your personal profile voice and your Page voice on your Page.

Configuring Your Page for Maximum Engagement

In addition to sharing, commenting on, and liking your Page updates, Facebook users can post their own updates on your Page and tag photos from your Page, provided that you've configured it to allow fans to do so. Facebook users can also mention your Page in updates, even if they've never liked your Page or engaged with any of the content on your Page. All of this means increased exposure for your business among the members of your Facebook community and their friends. How does all of this happen on Facebook? When Facebook users take any action related to your Page, it creates a story in the News Feeds of their friends. Think of it as social word-of-mouth marketing. (See Figure 5-1.)

FIGURE 5-1:
Tagging the Kid President's Page so that friends see it in their News Feeds.

If you choose not to allow fans to share content on your Facebook Page or to tag photos, you limit the extent to which fans can connect with you on Facebook, and you also squelch the natural word-of-mouth power that Facebook has.

To configure your Page so that fans can post content and tag photos, simply follow these steps:

1. **Log in to Facebook and go to your Facebook Page.**

2. **Click Settings on the admin navigation bar at the top of your Page.**

3. **On the General tab, select the Visitor Post option (shown in Figure 5-2) and then click Save Changes to save this selection.**

4. **On the General tab, select the Tagging Ability option and then click Save Changes to save this selection.**

Page Visibility	Page unpublished	Edit
Visitor Posts	● Allow visitors to the Page to publish posts	
	✓ Allow photo and video posts	
	✓ Review posts by other people before they are published to the Page [?]	
	○ Disable posts by other people on the Page	

Save Changes   Cancel

FIGURE 5-2: Enabling visitor posting for your Facebook Page.

REMEMBER

If your business is new to social media marketing, allowing anyone on Facebook to post content on your Page may seem scary. This feeling is understandable but often unwarranted. You'll find that engaging criticism directly on your Facebook Page creates a positive image for your brand. Of course, you'll have to make the decision of whether to allow fans to post content based on your own circumstances. During the 2012 presidential election, neither Barack Obama nor Mitt Romney allowed Facebook users to post content on his Page. From a strategic standpoint, this made sense, allowing each candidate to keep tight control of his social media messaging all the way up to Election Day. You're probably not planning to run for President, but in some rare instances, keeping tight control of your messaging makes sense.

Allowing Threaded Comments on Your Page Updates

Within the General section of your Page Settings, you can allow people to reply to comments on your Page updates. To activate this feature, simply select Allow Visitors to the Page to Publish Posts and then click Save Changes.

Enabling replies to comments allows people to reply to individual comments within a Page update, as shown in Figure 5-3. This setting creates a richer discussion experience that motivates people to return again and again to individual updates on your Page.

FIGURE 5-3:
Threaded comments on the National Wildlife Federation Facebook Page.

Limiting Who Can See Your Page Content

You can also choose to prevent users of a specific age or who live in a specific geographic location from seeing your Page content. Liquor stores, for example, may want to exclude minors from seeing their Pages, and any company that sells a product banned in specific countries would use this option.

To limit users who can see your Page content, follow these steps:

1. **Log in to Facebook, and go to your Facebook Page.**

2. **Click Settings on the admin navigation bar at the top of your Page.**

3. **On the General tab, click the Country and Age restrictions, and select any restrictions you'd like to make:**

   - Enter a country in the Country Restrictions text box and select the appropriate check box to hide your Page from this country or to restrict viewing to this country.

   - Select an age group from the Age Restrictions drop-down menu (see Figure 5-4). People younger than the age you select won't be able to see your Page or its content.

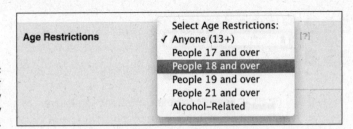

FIGURE 5-4:
You can limit your
Page visibility
based on country
and age.

Configuring Profanity and Moderation Settings

A common concern that many Page managers have is dealing with disrespectful or hateful commenters. The fact that all Facebook Pages are public and any Facebook user can comment on your Page makes dealing with this problem even more difficult.

Fortunately, all Facebook Pages have two features that automatically block offensive language and profanity on your Page:

>> **Profanity Filter:** Within the General section of your Page Settings, this option blocks profanity based on your preference. You can set it to Off, Medium, or Strong.

>> **Page Moderation:** This option is also located in the General section of your Page Settings. Simply list terms that aren't profanity but are still offensive to your specific community. The word *retard,* for example, would be offensive to an organization that deals with developmentally delayed adults but completely acceptable in a discussion of classical music, in which the term instructs a player to slow down.

If things get out of hand, you can delete comments posted by Facebook users and even ban users if they cross the line:

>> **Deleting comments:** As Page manager, you have the option to delete any comment you want. Simply click the X to the right of a comment, click Delete, and select Delete in the pop-up window.

>> **Banning users:** Some Facebook users may continue to badger your Page even after you delete their comment. In this case, you can ban such a user by clicking the X to the right of a comment, clicking Delete, and selecting Delete and Ban User in the pop-up window.

Posting as a Page versus Posting as a Profile

Facebook Pages allow admins to post content as the Page or as a profile. This feature gives admins the flexibility to express both the brand voice and their personal voice. Admins of the National Wildlife Federation Facebook Page, for example, are invested and interested in conservation issues outside their job descriptions. They participate in nature-related activities on the weekends and after work because they sincerely care about protecting wildlife. As Facebook admins, they can post updates on recent legislation that affects wildlife conservation and follow up those posts with personal comments made as private individuals.

Switching between posting as a profile and posting as a Page

When you log into Facebook as a person and visit your Facebook Page, you automatically assume the voice of your Page when posting content to your Page and replying to commenters on your Page.

If you want to switch your voice to your personal profile and post as a person on your Page, simply click the Change to *Your Name* link, shown in the top-right corner of Figure 5-5.

FIGURE 5-5:
Facebook Pages allow admins to switch between posting as their Page or posting as a profile on their Page.

Drop-down arrow

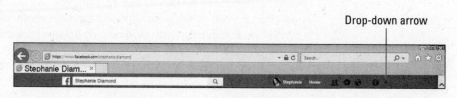

The feature that allows you to switch between voices on your Page is limited to your own Facebook Page. But what about posting on other Pages as your Page? The default setting for all Facebook users is that on Facebook Pages that they don't administrate, they post as people, not as a Page.

The following section goes over switching your identity throughout Facebook to your Facebook Page.

Posting as a Page on other Pages

Facebook lets Facebook admins completely log out as a profile and log in as a Page. This feature gives marketers the ability to build a presence throughout Facebook by commenting on, liking, and sharing content from other Pages — as their Page.

To log in as your Page, simply click the down-arrow icon at the top of the Facebook Page, and select the Page that you'd like to log in.

After logging in as a Page, you can comment on, like, and share updates from other Pages, as well as post updates on other Pages.

When you're logged in as your Page, you can also view your Page's News Feed. Your Page's News Feed, which is different from your profile's News Feed, shows you the latest updates from all the Pages that you've liked as a Page. You can also comment on, like, and share these updates directly in your Page News Feed in the same way you would if you were logged in with your personal profile (see Figure 5-6).

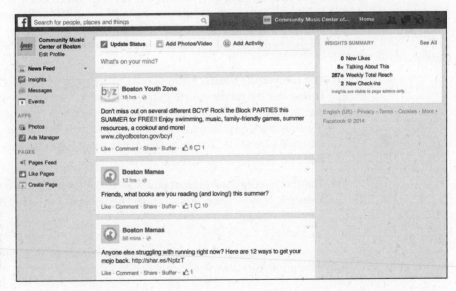

FIGURE 5-6: When logged in as a Page, you can view the latest updates from Pages you've liked as a Page.

When logged in as your Page, note that at the top-right of Facebook's menu bar you can view the latest notifications about fan activity, including notifications about new fans, and you can even see a high-level overview of your Page Insights.

Posting as a profile as a personal choice

Deciding whether Facebook admins should post as their personal profile is a choice that you should make, not your boss. The reason is that when someone posts on a Page as a profile, that person is potentially opening herself to friend requests from fans, which may be unwanted. Managers should always respect the privacy of your personal profile.

That said, if an admin is a recognized thought leader, trusted pundit, or well-known member of your Facebook Page community, allowing him to post as a profile will only enhance the relationship fans have with your organization.

Knowing the difference between being helpful and spamming

Just because you can post on another Page as a Page doesn't mean that it's always the smartest thing to do. Many Facebook marketers make the common mistake of posting to another Page in an attempt to promote their business, but the result is that they come across as spammers. As with email and other social networking platforms, Facebook users have only a certain tolerance for spam. Two factors can determine whether your post on another Page will be perceived as spam:

>> **The community doesn't know you.** As a Facebook Page marketer, you may believe that the content you're posting on another Page is obviously useful. An owner of a pet-supply store running a promotion on cat food may think there's nothing harmful about posting info about the promotion on a local animal shelter's Facebook Page. Still, many of that Page's fans will perceive that post as being unwanted and self-promoting.

>> **The community doesn't trust you.** If Facebook fans on another Page don't know you, they probably don't trust you because you haven't established a bond with them.

The obvious solution is to become a trusted member of that Page's community before even thinking about promoting your own agenda.

One way to do this is to reply to posts on that Page in a way that contributes to that post's topic and supports the Page's agenda.

In the pet-supply-store example, the store owner could improve his standing on the animal shelter's Facebook Page by replying to, say, a post about a new dog up for adoption; in his comments, he could provide fans useful information about that breed. The more the store owner follows that strategy, the more he (and his store) will get noticed by fans of that Page.

Another way is to promote the other Page's agenda on your own Facebook Page by mentioning that Page in status updates, as shown in Figure 5-7.

John Haydon - Digital Marketing shared a link via Janet Fouts.
July 7

*BIG NEWS FOR GEEKY GIRLS!

DonorsChoose.org is rewarding teachers with money when they get 4+ female students to complete a coding class. The $1 million fund is from from the Made With Code initiative from Google.

cc Social Media Examiner CharityHowTo.com TechSoup NTEN: The Nonprofit Technology Network

Google and DonorsChoose and Google Team Up To Empower Girls To Code
www.fastcompany.com

FIGURE 5-7:
Tagging other Pages in your Page updates.

Engaging Fans with Your Mobile Phone

If you're like most people, you have limited time to manage Facebook and are often away from your computer. Fortunately, Facebook Page admins have the ability to post Page stories from their mobile phones.

Posting content and managing your Page with mobile web browsers

You can post content and reply to Page updates and comments on stories from any phone with mobile web access. Entering www.facebook.com from any mobile device automatically redirects you to the mobile site.

Posting content and managing your Page with mobile apps

The Facebook Pages Manager app (iOS and Android) allows admins to manage posts, promote posts, and even schedule Page updates. Figure 5-8 shows the Pages Manager app for iPhone. Find out more about this app here:

» iTunes (https://itunes.apple.com/app/facebook-pages-manager/id514643583)

» Google Play (https://play.google.com/store/apps/details?id=com.facebook.pages.app)

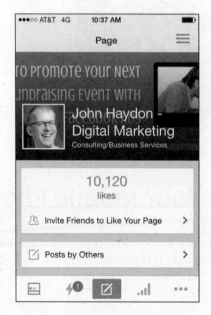

FIGURE 5-8: Facebook Page admins can use the Facebook Pages Manager app to manage their Pages.

Because these platforms are different, we don't go into detail about how to use each one. The app is very easy to use, however, and allows you to post text updates, photos, videos, and replies to fan comments.

Chapter **6**

Enhancing Your Facebook Page with Applications

I f you've ever entered a contest on Facebook or signed a petition, you've used a Facebook app. Every month, more than 1 billion people use an app on Facebook or experience the Facebook platform on other websites.

Facebook applications (apps) have become powerful tools for marketers.

When you install them on your Facebook Page, they can add a variety of features to your business's Facebook presence.

Whether you want to add a slide presentation via the SlideShare app or post content from your Instagram feed, apps can help you customize your Facebook Page.

Apps are also becoming important branding tools within Facebook. Red Bull, for example, enhances its brand with an app that lets users see tweets from their favorite athletes (see Figure 6-1).

Facebook has developed a platform for apps that's easy to use, so more and more types of industries can leverage Facebook for their businesses.

This chapter introduces you to the world of Facebook apps, shows you how to find useful applications, and discusses how to add them to your Facebook Page.

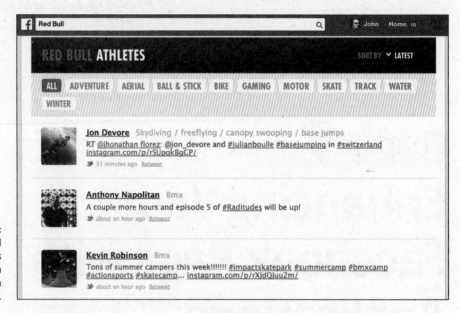

FIGURE 6-1:
Red Bull enhanced its brand with a custom application.

Understanding Facebook Applications

Facebook apps are software modules you can install on your Facebook Page that add functionality to engage your audience in ways beyond what the native apps (Photos, Videos, Events, Notes, and so on) can do.

This added functionality is displayed within a separate tab on your Facebook Page. In Figure 6-2, the Fast Company Facebook Page displays a tab for the company's Instagram feed. (For more on custom page apps, see the upcoming section "Using Third-Party Custom Facebook Page Tab Services.")

Apps can take on many forms, from video players to business cards to promotions. Facebook offers countless apps for marketers that provide business solutions and promote the business enterprise.

Some apps are designed to help you promote your website or blog, stream a live video conference, or show customized directions to your office. Also, third-party developers are licensing and selling apps that focus on the business market, including promotion apps from Rafflecopter and AgoraPulse, lead-generation apps from Woobox, and apps that encourage user participation from ShortStack and TabSite.

FIGURE 6-2:
Fast Company
enhanced its
Facebook Page
with an added
application.

Here are a few examples of some apps that can add useful marketing functionality to your Facebook Page:

» **YouTube Channels app:** If your company has sales videos, messages from the CEO, or product-demonstration videos posted on YouTube, add them to your Page for all to see. One of the best apps for this purpose is Involver's YouTube app, shown in Figure 6-3.

» **Rafflecopter:** This app helps Page admins create and manage giveaway promotions. From creating the Page template to managing, reviewing, and displaying entries, Rafflecopter makes giveaway contests a breeze. Visit www.rafflecopter.com for more info.

» **Woobox:** This app allows marketers to create sweepstakes, coupons, and giveaways for Facebook (http://admin.woobox.com/campaigns/giveaways-coupons-instantwins). Woobox also has a custom Page tab that allows you to create a fan-gate page. A fan-gate page allows admins to hide content from nonfans, as shown in Figure 6-4. When nonfans like the Page, the content is revealed. That content could be anything from articles to coupons to premium videos.

FIGURE 6-3:
The YouTube app on the Involver's Best Friends Animal Sanctuary Facebook Page.

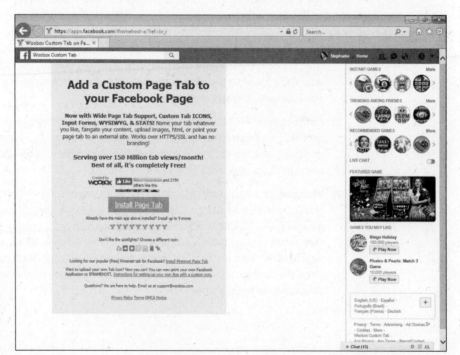

FIGURE 6-4:
Woobox's custom Page tab for Facebook that can create a fan-gating page.

Many Facebook marketers rely on apps to make their Facebook presence stand out from the competition's and to add engaging elements with which their fans can interact. (You can find more examples in the upcoming section "Choosing E-Commerce Applications for Your Page.")

REMEMBER

As we say in Chapter 3, you should clearly define the goals of your Facebook Page before investing time and money in additional apps. A nonprofit organization with the goal of raising money via its Facebook Page, for example, should consider only apps that support that goal.

A word of caution about adding too many apps: If you're like most people, you want to add the latest fancy app to your Facebook Page, but then you add one and then another, and before you know it, your Page looks like downtown Tokyo!

Two more thoughts about adding apps:

WARNING

>> **Less can be more.** Too many apps can drive away visitors who get blinded or confused by an abundance of shiny objects.

    If visitors don't know what to do, they'll leave.

>> **Nothing is permanent.** The good news about Facebook apps is that you can try them for free (even most premium apps have free trial periods) and remove them if they don't work for your goals.

Yeah, There's an App for That — But Where?

When searching for an app, you need go no further than Facebook itself. Search Facebook, peruse Facebook Groups, or check the app developer's website.

Here's how easy it is to search Facebook for an application and add it to your Page:

1. **Type the name of the application in the Facebook search bar at the top of your screen.**

   If you don't have a specific application in mind, simply search for the type of application you're looking for. Type **sweepstakes** to search for sweepstakes applications, for example.

   A list of potential matches appears.

2. **When you find the application you want, click the application's name in the search results.**

   You go to the application's profile Page.

3. **On the application's Page, click Use App.**

4. **Confirm any additional authorizations required for the app.**

   Each application has a different process.

A few active groups on Facebook are aimed specifically at marketers seeking to understand how to use Facebook Pages. One group we like is Facebook Marketing (www.facebook.com/groups/3422930005). You can use the group's search function to search for conversations about useful Facebook Page applications. (See Figure 6-5.)

FIGURE 6-5:
Searching for
Facebook apps.

Using Third-Party Custom Facebook Page Tab Services

Over the past few years, hundreds of companies have sprung up to offer online services that create custom Facebook apps. Many of these companies include a lot of marketing tools that can be added to a custom tab, such as the ones mentioned earlier in the section, "Understanding Facebook Applications."

Online custom App services typically offer a tool or wizard that you can use to create custom Facebook tabs without knowing HTML or other complicated web technologies. The price of these services can range from $0 to more than $500 per month, depending on how many Facebook fans you have, which apps you want to use, and other factors.

REMEMBER

It can be confusing to understand the difference between an app and a tab on Facebook. An *app* is a software tool that adds functionality to your Page (such as the Instagram app, which allows visitors to access your Instagram feed directly from your business Page). A *tab* works just like a divider in a loose-leaf notebook. It organizes your content into sections. The confusing part is that you can access both an app and other content from a tab.

Some of the most popular services include the following:

>> **ShortStack:** ShortStack has more than 60 widgets and applications in which users can integrate fan gates, contests, sweepstakes, RSS feeds, Twitter, YouTube, and MailChimp newsletter signups. Apps created with ShortStack work anywhere, including Facebook, mobile devices, websites, and blogs. Find out more at www.shortstack.com.

>> **Pagemodo:** With its good, professional templates, this tool makes it very easy for users to create great-looking custom tabs quickly and easily. Find out more at www.pagemodo.com.

>> **TabSite:** TabSite allows you to create custom tabs with a drag-and-drop wizard. TabSite offers unique tools such as Pin Deal, in which a fan must pin the page image to Pinterest before accessing the deal. Find out more at www.tabsite.com.

>> **Facebook Tab Manager for WordPress:** Facebook Tab Manager is a free WordPress plug-in that allows WordPress users to create Facebook Page

custom tabs by using WordPress tools for content creation and editing. Anything that can be displayed within a WordPress post or page can be displayed within custom tabs. Find out more at http://tabmgr.com.

All these solutions range in price from $0 to $499 per month, depending on variables such as the number of fans your Page has, the number of apps you want to add to your Page, and the complexity of features. The most important things to consider when deciding which company to use are the functionality and designs each company offers. All companies have a gallery and a list of clients.

Choosing E-Commerce Applications for Your Page

Brands are beginning to realize that in addition to being a powerful marketing platform, Facebook offers a huge opportunity to make money directly from Facebook users by using e-commerce applications. Also, using an e-commerce app on your Page allows you to easily measure your return on investment.

Here are a few of the most popular Facebook e-commerce applications:

>> **Ecwid:** This app (see Figure 6-6) is a shopping cart for Facebook Pages and websites. Ecwid currently has more than 40,000 Facebook stores and provides a single web-based interface that lets you manage multiple shopping carts. Find out more at https://www.ecwid.com/.

>> **ShopTab:** This e-commerce Facebook application is easy for Page admins and customers to use. It also has an app for nonprofit organizations that allows for multiple levels of donations. Find out more at www.shoptab.net.

>> **FundRazr:** This e-commerce app allows nonprofit organizations, school teams, and other organizations to collect donations on a Facebook Page. You can also sell tickets for events, manage customers, and allow fans to share campaigns with their friends. Find out more at https://fundrazr.com.

Ecwid Shop tab

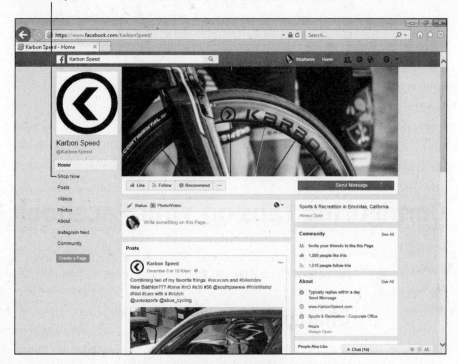

Granting Access to Applications

Facebook requires third-party apps to ask users for permission to access their email, News Feed, or other important information (see Figure 6-7).

If you have more than one Page, the app lists your various Pages and asks you to specify the Page on which you want to install the app.

If you don't want to grant the app access to your information, click the Don't Allow button. You can't use an app for which you haven't approved permissions, however.

After you click Allow and select the Page where you want the app installed, you're prompted to follow additional installation instructions specific to that application.

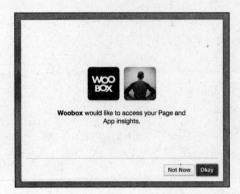

FIGURE 6-7:
Third-party apps
are required to
ask Facebook
users for
permission.

Configuring Tabs on Your Facebook Page

You can edit the tabs on your Facebook Page in several ways. You can change the tab names, change the tab images, delete tabs, and change the order of your tabs.

Changing tab names

You can change the names only of third-party tabs, not those of standard Facebook Page applications such as Photos, Videos, and Events.

To change the name of your Facebook Page tabs, make sure that you're logged in and added as a Page admin (manager role). Then follow these steps:

1. **On your Page, click the Settings tab on the admin navigation bar.**
2. **Click the Edit Page in the sidebar on the left.**
3. **Click the Settings button to the right of the tab.**
4. **Click Edit Settings link at the bottom left of this pop-up window.**

   A pop-up window appears, as shown in Figure 6-8.
5. **Enter the desired name in the Custom Tab Name field.**
6. **Click Save.**
7. **Click OK to close the window.**

Changing tab images

You can change the icons only of third-party tabs, not those of standard Facebook Page applications such as Photos, Videos, and Events.

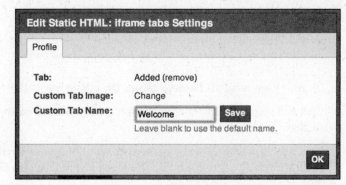

FIGURE 6-8:
You can edit the
names of many
custom and
third-party tabs.

To change the icon of your third–party Facebook Page tabs, make sure that you're logged in and added as a Page admin (manager role). Then follow these steps:

1. **On your Page, click the Settings tab on the admin navigation bar.**

2. **Click the Settings button to the left of the app.**

3. **Click Edit Settings link at the bottom of this pop-up window.**

4. **Click the Change link next to Custom Tab Image (see Figure 6-9).**

   A new browser tab opens, prompting you to upload an image. The tab image dimensions are 111 pixels wide by 74 pixels tall (refer to Figure 6-9).

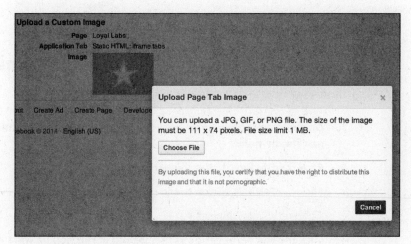

FIGURE 6-9:
Editing a
tab's icon.

5. **Upload the image.**

6. **After you upload the new image, close the browser tab and click OK.**

Changing the order of tabs

You can also change the order of tabs by following these steps:

1. **On your Page, click the Settings tab on the admin navigation bar.**

2. **Click Edit Page in the sidebar on the left and then scroll down to the tabs section.**

3. **Rearrange the tabs by dragging them (place your mouse on the two vertical dotted lines to the left of the name and move them into the desired order; see Figure 6-10).**

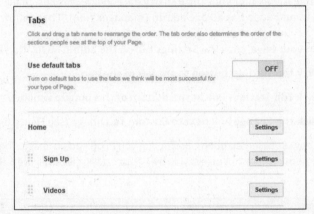

Tabs

Click and drag a tab name to rearrange the order. The tab order also determines the order of the sections people see at the top of your Page.

Use default tabs   OFF

Turn on default tabs to use the tabs we think will be most successful for your type of Page.

Home   Settings

⋮⋮ Sign Up   Settings

⋮⋮ Videos   Settings

Removing a tab from your Facebook Page

If you want to delete a tab from your Page, follow these steps:

1. **On your Page admin panel, click the Settings link on the admin navigation menu.**

2. **Click the Edit Page in the sidebar on the left.**

3. **Click the Settings button to the right of the tab.**

   A pop-up window appears.

4. **Click the Edit Settings link at the bottom of this pop-up window.**

5. **Click the Remove link (in parentheses after Added; see Figure 6-11).**

6. **Click Save.**

7. **Click OK to close the window.**

Remove link

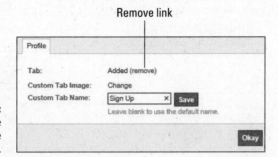

REMEMBER

You can't remove some Facebook tabs, such as Photos, from your Page. These core apps are instrumental to the Facebook experience, and Facebook developed them internally.

Creating Custom Facebook Tabs with HTML

If you're well versed in web technology and want to design your own custom tabs from scratch, you can do so in two ways:

» Use the Static HTML: iframe tabs application.

» Create a custom web page through an iframe application and add it to your Page.

The next two sections describe these techniques in more detail.

Using the Static HTML: iframe tabs application

If you know even basic HTML, creating a custom tab is easy with the Static HTML: iframe tabs application (`https://apps.facebook.com/static_html_plus`). You can easily create custom tabs from a variety of apps included with Static HTML (see Figure 6-12).

FIGURE 6-12:
The Static HTML:
iframe tabs app.

This app lets you build any content you want inside your tab. You can easily add videos, PayPal buttons, and images. You can add a variety of features and functionality by way of apps in the editor, and even use HTML, JavaScript, or CSS.

One of the best things about the Static HTML: iframe tabs app is the amount of support it has from the community of thousands of Facebook Page managers who use the app.

Designing a custom tab: Tips and recommendations

Creating tabs can be tricky business. Still, the following list of recommendations should help you through the process:

>> **Be clear about your goals.** If you're going to invest the time and money to create a custom tab, make sure you understand why you need the tab. Be very clear about your goal. Are you looking to acquire more email subscribers? Or are you looking to promote your Instagram presence on Facebook?

>> **Include one call to action.** Like so many people these days, Facebook users are very busy. Respect their time by asking for only one action. Calls to action

are often useful in achieving certain goals, but you can "go to the well" too often. Too many calls to action may just be white noise to your audience, which lowers the chances that any given user will take the action that aligns with your goal. For example, including your Twitter stream on a custom tab right next to an email opt-in form lowers your ability to acquire more emails. That's because following someone on Twitter is easier than joining an email list, and people are easily distracted.

» **Design for mobile.** More and more people use Facebook via mobile devices, such as smartphones and tablets. Before you promote your custom tab to the world, make sure it looks beautiful on all devices. Present text and images in a way that is easy to see and easy to use.

» **Use powerful images.** Generally speaking, people take action on social media because they are moved emotionally. And nothing speaks the language of emotion better than pictures (pictures, after all, say a thousand words). Research suggests that images of people produce the most powerful emotional impact. Find a picture that reflects the emotion you want people to feel after they interact with your Facebook app.

» **Make buttons stand out.** You can increase the likelihood that people will take action within your custom app if you make your call-to-action buttons stand out. It doesn't matter what color you choose, as long as the button stands apart from the other colors within the custom app.

» **Use a mobile URL.** Most third-party Facebook apps include a separate, unique URL devoted entirely to mobile use. Directing mobile users to this URL ensures that the app will display correctly on their mobile device. Make sure you use this URL (a unique URL for your application) everywhere you promote your app. Remember, more and more people are accessing websites and social media from smartphones and tablets, and this trend will only continue in the future.

» **Drive traffic to your custom tab.** Facebook is not *Field of Dreams.* People will not engage with your app just because you build it. Develop a strategy to promote your app that integrates all your other marketing channels, such as email and social media.

» **Measure results.** Finally, measure the effectiveness of your app based on your original goal. If you're looking to drive traffic to your website, use Google Analytics to track visitors from your tab. If your goal is to acquire email subscribers, track the number of new signups via your app with your email marketing software. Make any needed adjustments to your campaign.

3

Engaging with Your Customers and Prospects on Facebook

Find out the differences between your Facebook profile and your Page

See how to create and publish effective updates that engage your audience.

Find out how to effectively promote your Page in stores and at events.

Discover what's working and what's not with Facebook Insights.

» **Posting with a purpose**

» **Responding to your Facebook community**

» **Using video to engage more customers**

Chapter **7**

Creating a Remarkable Presence on Facebook with Content Marketing

In the age of Facebook, businesses are realizing that in addition to the products they sell, information is one of their core offerings. In fact, information may just be the most important one. Facebook marketing starts with giving valuable and interesting information to your customers; information is the new marketing currency.

This is why a content strategy is probably the most important strategy for marketing on Facebook. A *content strategy* consists of the plan, goals, and tactics you'll use to decide what content to post on your Page, when to post it, and how to measure its effectiveness.

In this chapter, you find out why content is important and how to create remarkable content. You also see how to reply to comments people post to your Facebook updates.

Understanding How Content Marketing Works on Facebook

To understand how content engages Facebook users, you must understand the News Feed. In Figure 7-1, you can see that updates and stories from a friend of one of the authors and Pages that he has liked are displayed on his News Feed — the primary place where Facebook users interact with friends and brands.

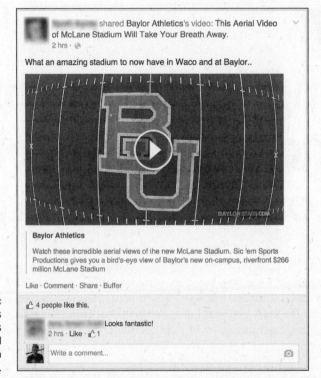

FIGURE 7-1: Facebook users view updates from friends and Pages primarily in their News Feed.

Understanding the difference between your website and your Facebook Page

When you publish content on your website, visitors must go to that specific web page (a single location) to view that content. This content can be a simple web page or a blog post.

But when you publish a Facebook update on your Facebook Page, fans don't view your story in a single, static location; they view it in their News Feed (shown in

Figure 7-2), where it must compete for attention with other businesses (Facebook Pages) and friends. In fact, less than 5 percent of a Facebook Page's fan base actually visits the Page. All the action (liking, commenting, sharing) exists in the News Feed.

To reinforce the fact that the News Feed is home base for Facebook users, a comScore Mediabuilder study also shows that Facebook users spend 27 percent of their time in the News Feed, as shown in Figure 7-3.

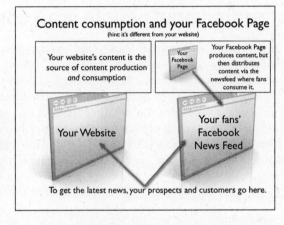

FIGURE 7-2:
Content on Facebook is consumed differently from content on a traditional website.

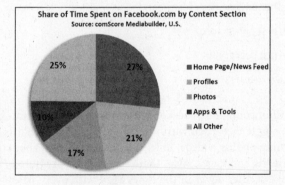

FIGURE 7-3:
Users spend 27 percent of their total time on Facebook on their News Feed.

There are three reasons that Facebook users make the News Feed their home base on Facebook:

>> **The home page:** The News Feed is the first thing all Facebook users see when they log in to Facebook, enabling them to view and engage with updates from friends and Pages they've liked without having to visit individual personal Timelines or Pages.

>> **A central place to share:** At the very top of the News Feed, Facebook users can post photos, videos, status updates, and links.

>> **Filtering:** In their News Feed, Facebook users can choose to filter content by friend lists and interest lists. They can choose to view only stories from close friends, for example. When they filter by friend lists, they still see stories about your Page that friends on that list have created (by liking or commenting on posts, liking your Page, and so on).

Understanding how people scan content

We all have a high school friend (call her Maria) who found us years later on Facebook and who now posts firehose barrages of pictures, videos, and comments about her latest crochet creations to our Facebook Page. Because we're nice people, we don't want to offend her by unfriending her. Instead, over time, we've tuned out Maria's Facebook updates. The ability to tune out undesirable messages isn't new, but it's a factor that you need to consider when publishing content for any channel (website, email, direct mail, Facebook, and so on). Instead of reading a 1,000-word article on your website, your prospects will probably just

>> Scan the title.

>> Scan the subheadings.

>> See whether anyone has recommended your article.

>> Scan the first paragraph.

>> Scan the last paragraph.

>> Look at the pictures.

How people filter content on Facebook includes these same strategies, but instead of viewing a single web page with a few related articles (that is, your website), they're scanning photos, videos, links, and status updates about unrelated topics from both friends and Pages. Also, there's the added pressure of all this content getting pushed farther down in the News Feed with every passing moment. You can begin to see that being concise, relevant, and interesting are key success factors in getting the attention of customers and prospects on Facebook.

Understanding how Facebook's News Feed algorithm affects visibility on Facebook

Just because someone becomes a fan of your Page doesn't mean that she's seeing your Page content in her News Feed. This fact bears repeating: *Someone who becomes a fan of your Page doesn't automatically see your Page content in her News Feed.* A sneaker company that attracts new fans in exchange for a 20 percent discount but fails to post updates that are interesting and engaging to fans will find a hard time nurturing and growing a vibrant fan base. Its Page updates will disappear from its fans' News Feeds because of the Facebook News Feed algorithm.

The *News Feed algorithm* is ever changing. It's what Facebook uses to determine how content ranks within a user's News Feed. In general, updates that aren't interesting or useful to Facebook users likely won't appear in their News Feeds. In 2018, Mark Zuckerberg announced that Facebook's algorithm will favor friends and family, thereby pushing Page content out of view.

In general, to determine whether a Page post shows up in the News Feed, Facebook's algorithm considers these main factors:

>> **Whether you've interacted with a Page's posts before:** If you like every post by a Page that Facebook shows you, Facebook shows you more posts from that Page.

>> **Other people's reactions:** If everyone else on Facebook ignores a post or complains about it, the post is less likely to show up in your News Feed. Conversely, if a post has an extraordinarily high rate of engagement, Facebook considers the post more authentic and pushes that update to more of your Facebook Page fans.

>> **Your interaction with previous posts of the same type:** If you always like photos, there's a better chance that you'll see a photo posted by a Page.

>> **Complaints:** If that specific post has received complaints from other users who saw it, or if the Page that posted it received lots of complaints in the past, you'll be less likely to see that post.

>> **Popular videos:** Facebook will display videos that are popular based on time watched and whether they were completed.

>> **Timely posts:** If a topic is hot at the moment, Facebook will be more likely to display it in your News Feed immediately.

>> **Click-bait:** Facebook is cracking down on click bait. *Click-baiting* occurs when a link is posted with vague or sensationalistic headlines that encourage people to click without telling them what they'll see when they reach the advertised page. They don't want you to see content in your News Feed that will waste your time.

The bottom line is that Facebook wants to make the News Feed useful to Facebook users so that they keep coming back. Return visits mean more advertising revenue for Facebook (its ultimate bottom line).

Understanding that Facebook users can hide all posts from your Page

Just because a user liked your Page doesn't mean that he's reading your posts. When a user sees your post in his News Feed, he can omit your posts from his News Feed but remain a liker of your Page. To do this, he simply clicks the three-dot sign on the right side of the page and is shown several options, including Hide Post. If the user clicks that option, he sees fewer posts like yours.

You can find out how many people (but not specific names) have hidden your Page's posts in your Insights dashboard.

To view how many people have hidden your posts, follow these steps:

1. **Log in to Facebook, and visit your Page.**

2. **Click Insights in the admin navigation menu.**

3. **Click the Reach tab and scroll down to the Hide, Report As Spam, and Unlikes report (shown in Figure 7-4).**

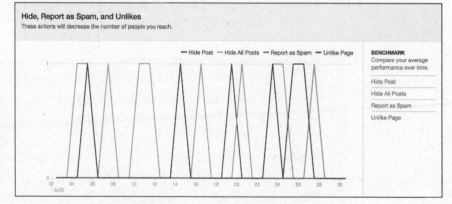

FIGURE 7-4: You can see how many people have hidden your Page posts in Facebook Insights.

Creating compelling content for your Facebook Page

According to the 2016 State of Digital Content from Altimeter (http://www.prophet.com/thinking/2016/10/state-of-digital-2016/), brands found Facebook (71%) and Email (62%) to be the most effective channels for generating engagement for their content. Creating, aggregating, and distributing information via your Facebook Page help build trust between you and your customers. If that information is off topic or irrelevant, however, it can weaken that trust. Being useful, authentic, and relevant is the key.

If you sell antiques, for example, don't post about your fly-fishing trip just because it's a hobby of yours. On Facebook, you can easily find out what sort of content your customers are looking for. You can always ask your customers directly about the types of content they want so that you can make your Page more useful to them.

Keep in mind that creating relevant content that resonates with your audience is part science, part art:

» On the science side is *Facebook Insights,* which is a set of metrics that quantifies how people interact with your content. If something works based on the response it receives, by all means produce more content similar to it. (Chapter 10 discusses Facebook Insights at length.)

» On the art side of the equation, your content strategy requires an element of creativity. Even if you simply repurpose other people's content, such as by sharing another Page's most popular updates (see Figure 7-5), you must be artfully selective to determine what's worth sharing with your customers.

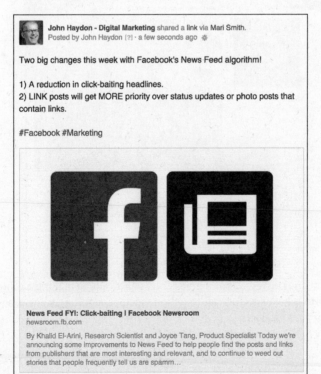

John Haydon - Digital Marketing shared a link via Mari Smith.
Posted by John Haydon [?] · a few seconds ago ☀

Two big changes this week with Facebook's News Feed algorithm!

1) A reduction in click-baiting headlines.
2) LINK posts will get MORE priority over status updates or photo posts that contain links.

#Facebook #Marketing

News Feed FYI: Click-baiting | Facebook Newsroom
newsroom.fb.com

By Khalid El-Arini, Research Scientist and Joyce Tang, Product Specialist Today we're announcing some improvements to News Feed to help people find the posts and links from publishers that are most interesting and relevant, and to continue to weed out stories that people frequently tell us are spamm...

FIGURE 7-5:
Pages can share updates from other Pages.

Knowing your audience

Before you can deliver content that's relevant to your customers' lives, you need to understand your audience. Who are these folks? What interests and motivates them?

Ponder these questions when deciding whether your content is on message and relevant to your audience:

>> Does the content address your audience's questions, concerns, or needs?

>> Does it inspire or entertain your intended audience?

>> Does it help users complete a specific task?

>> Will it help influence a decision?

Figure 7-6 shows an example from Square that seeks to help its small-business customers increase sales.

FIGURE 7-6:
Square publishes useful updates to educate small-business owners.

REMEMBER

Content and conversations significantly contribute to making a *conversion* — getting a user to take a specific call to action, such as signing up for a newsletter or even buying your products.

Staying on message

According to the traditional marketing model, from awareness and knowledge come desire and action. With Facebook, however, the rules have changed. Everyone and everything is connected, so any engagement you do through your Page doesn't go away.

After you post something on your Page, fans may take your advice, or they may pass on the videos you uploaded to others. Therefore, you have to maintain a common message or theme throughout all your updates to ensure that you always accomplish the goals you set for yourself in your Facebook marketing plan, whether those goals involve brand awareness, increasing sales, or both.

TIP

Get fans to share their tips as well.

An easy way to stay on message with your Facebook fans is to develop a content calendar based on topics for each day of the week. An auto repair shop, for example, might post on the following schedule:

>> **Monday:** Safe-driving tips

>> **Tuesday:** Do-it-yourself repair tips

 Tell fans to ask questions in the comments.

>> **Wednesday:** Discounts and specials

>> **Thursday:** Recommendations for weekend day trips

 Get fans to share their favorite driving destinations as well.

>> **Friday:** Show and tell

 Get fans to post pictures of their cool cars.

REMEMBER

Publish content based on what your customers need or want, not what your company needs or wants. Again, Facebook is 100 percent about WIFM (what's in it for me?).

Defining Your Posting Goals

Compelling content doesn't magically appear. It requires planning, creativity, and an objective. Content without a goal doesn't help you sell more products, build awareness for your cause, or promote your brand.

Your content needs to align with the business goals of your organization. Some basic goals may include

>> Driving traffic to your website

>> Enhancing your brand

>> Improving customer service

>> Generating leads

>> Increasing ad revenue

>> Adding e-commerce to your online marketing efforts

If your content strategy includes incentives such as coupons, giveaways, and promotions, you need to translate that strategy into a very clear and straightforward call to action (or goal). You may have several converging goals behind your posts, such as to let people know about an event as well as provide an incentive for those who RSVP to attend.

The following section examines some motivational goals to consider when you publish content to your Facebook Page.

Getting Fans Engaged

Engagement is the name of the game on Facebook. By *engagement*, we mean soliciting a response or action from your fans. This action could be commenting on a post, liking something, contributing to a discussion topic, or posting photos and videos. You want fans to interact with your Page for several reasons:

>> You can build a relationship with fans through dialogue and discussion.

>> The more activity is generated on your Page, the more stories are published to your fans' News Feeds, which drives more awareness of the original action and creates a viral marketing effect.

How do you get your fans to engage with your Page? The answer depends on your audience and the subject matter of your Page. Here are some helpful hints for encouraging fan engagement through your content:

» **Show your human side.** All work and no play makes for a very dull Page. People like to share the more human side of life. Many people take part in Take Your Child to Work Day or even Take Your Dog to Work Day, for example. If you participate in one of these events, post a picture of your child or pet and then add a note that they're doing a great job of helping Mom or Dad at work. Ask your fans whether they're taking advantage of this opportunity, and encourage them to post pictures as well.

» **Ask your fans what they think.** Be direct: Ask fans what they think of your organization, new product, or position on a topic. Fuddruckers – North Andover, a restaurant in Massachusetts, regularly asks its fans to share their thoughts on their favorite food (see Figure 7-7).

» **Tell your fans how much you appreciate them.** Don't underestimate the goodwill gained by saying thanks. Thanking your fans for their questions or complimenting them on their comments can go a long way in social media circles. The clothing retailer Lands' End is known for its exceptional customer service, and its fans aren't afraid to tell everyone about it!

» **Highlight a success story.** Another tactic that appeals to vanity is highlighting a fan's success. She'll be sure to thank you for the attention, and your other fans will appreciate hearing about one of their own making good. Many companies on Facebook run a Fan of the Month promotion and foster engagement by soliciting entries.

» **Share your tips and insights.** People are always looking for information that helps them do their jobs better. Don't underestimate your knowledge and what you have to share that's valuable. Sharing helpful tips is some of the best engagement around. Social Media Examiner does a great job providing a steady stream of tips to its Facebook fans, as shown in Figure 7-8.

» **Provide links to relevant articles and research.** You don't have to be a prolific writer to be valuable to your fans. By posting links to relevant articles, videos, resources, and research, you build your credibility as a content aggregator.

REMEMBER

For more on engagement, see Chapter 9.

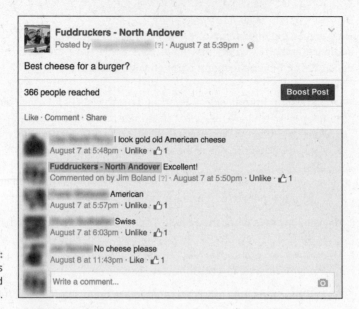

FIGURE 7-7:
Fuddruckers asks fans about food preferences.

FIGURE 7-8:
Social Media Examiner gives its fans a steady stream of tech tips.

Saving Time Creating Visual Content

Most marketers are finding that visual content is becoming more and more important to their overall content strategy. The challenge for many marketers is that creating compelling, interesting, and attractive visual content is very difficult. Following are a few recommendations for creating visual content quickly and cheaply:

>> **Canva** (www.canva.com): If you need to churn out visual content that's beautiful (or at least branded), Canva is your tool. It has templates for Facebook covers, social media posts, posters, blog graphics, and more.

>> **PicMonkey** (www.picmonkey.com): PicMonkey is an online editing tool that offers many of the basic features of Adobe Photoshop: cropping, resizing, adding text, and so on. It's also very easy to use, and it's mostly free.

>> **Piktochart** (www.piktochart.com): What you'll love about Piktochart is its wide variety of infographic templates and themes. Instead of starting from scratch, you're starting with 75 to 80 percent of a final product.

>> **Easel.ly** (www.easel.ly): This website features thousands of free infographic templates and design objects that you can use to create visual content. Like Piktochart, the site has drag-and-drop design elements. Base your content on existing templates or start from scratch with something original.

Understanding the Importance of Video Content for Marketing

"In five years, most of Facebook will be video." Mark Zuckerberg uttered those words in 2014. As of 2017, that prediction was becoming a reality. Video is showing up across the Facebook platform. According to Socialbakers, video reached more fans in 2015 than any other kind of content on Facebook, and this is even more true in 2018.

So where can you post your marketing videos? Everywhere! Some of the places you can post videos include:

>> Your Facebook Page cover

>> Ads, both desktop and mobile

>> Timeline posts, both desktop and mobile

>> Facebook Stories

>> Instagram Stories

>> Live videos (streaming)

>> 360-degree videos

Facebook makes uploading videos to these venues easy and provides Insight data so that you can evaluate your videos' effectiveness (see Chapter 10). You can also control who sees your videos by adjusting the privacy settings.

TIP

For best results, Facebook recommends that you upload your videos using either an MP4 or a MOV format.

After you have videos uploaded to your Facebook Page, you can access them for cross-posting and sharing from the Publishing Tools link at the top of your Page, as shown in Figure 7-9.

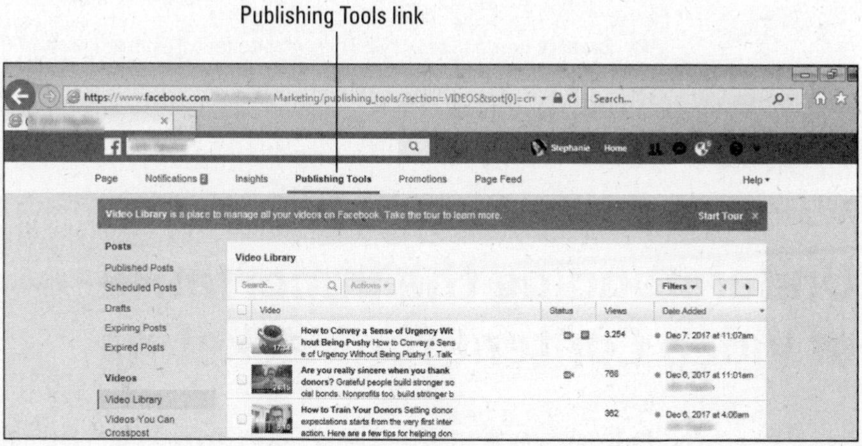

Publishing Tools link

FIGURE 7-9:
Accessing your Video Library from the Publishing Tools link.

Chapter 8

Growing Your Facebook Page's Fan Base

After you've created a Facebook Page that has all the elements you need, you can begin promoting it. The power of using a Facebook Page for marketing exists in the Facebook social graph: the network consisting of hundreds of billions of friendships, Pages, and Page updates. But at the point where you might lack any presence on Facebook, you have to use resources outside Facebook to promote your Page.

In this chapter, we show you how to begin with existing marketing assets (such as direct mail, email lists, and your website) for a strong initial push to send your Page into the Facebook stratosphere. We tell you why your Page needs content that's optimized for Facebook users and why that content must be unique. We also give you strategies such as using incentives and hidden content (accessible only by fans) to build your Facebook Page fan base. Finally, we tell you how to use other channels, such as blogs and YouTube, to promote your brand-new Facebook Page.

Mapping a Launch Strategy for Your Facebook Page

Many marketers refer to the initial stage of a promotion as the *launch,* whether the product is a book, the newest model of a car, or an event. At a launch, you might announce a widely covered and highly anticipated product, such as the latest iPhone, or distribute free samples to promote the opening of a local restaurant. But in all cases, a launch is the beginning; it's the takeoff.

Launch is an appropriate word for creating a Facebook Page. It's even similar to the basic stages of launching a rocket ship:

>> **Preparation:** Like a rocket ship, your Facebook Page presence requires a strategy to steer its course. It also needs a main image, applications, and a Welcome tab to provide function and features for Facebook users.

>> **Countdown:** Set goals for your Page, and estimate a deadline for launching it to essentially force yourself to prepare everything for success.

>> **Initial thrust:** When you start with no Facebook fans, you have to fight gravity to thrust your "vehicle" up and away from Earth, using assets such as a huge email list or an announcement at a conference about a special attendees-only promotion on your Page. Throughout this chapter, we show you several strategies for leveraging existing marketing assets.

>> **Second-stage thrust:** After you've acquired a fair number of fans of your Facebook Page and achieved a healthy amount of engagement on it, you can fire off a second round of "thrusters," such as featuring Facebook-sponsored ads that leverage your fans' friend networks or conducting a cross-promotional campaign with another Facebook Page.

>> **Orbit:** At this stage, slightly ahead of a tipping point, you must simply navigate and continuously refresh your attitude and creativity so that fans stay interested.

Fostering a Sense of Enchantment on Your Facebook Page

To create a Facebook presence, you must establish a vibrant brand identity, in the form of a Page, publish content that inspires conversation, and respond quickly and thoroughly to comments from fans.

In other words, to create a Facebook presence, create enchantment with your Facebook Page so that fans are naturally inspired to share your Page with their friends.

How can you achieve this goal? Well, it's not easy, but it's doable if you understand that all marketing ultimately boils down to developing a brand identity that people know, like, and trust:

>> **Know:** You clearly communicate who you are, the benefits your business offers, and how you can be reached. All this information should be included in your Facebook Page profile and within the content you publish, such as by adding your logo or your brand on all photos and cover images.

>> **Like:** Ultimately, people do business with people they like. If price, features, and benefits are indistinguishable, customers usually choose the brand they like the most. Facebook can't make people like your Facebook Page or its content unless they like you in real life.

>> **Trust:** People do business with people they trust. It's an absolute requirement! You build trust by being responsive, cheerful, and dependable.

Peet's Coffee and Tea (`https://www.facebook.com/peets`) is known for its desire to be socially responsible and also give back to its customers. To get customers to engage and trust the company, it provides coffee rewards to loyal customers ("Peetniks"). It also creates charitable campaigns, as shown in Figure 8-1. Through these and other strategies, the organization has developed a base of fans who know, like, and trust Peet's Coffee and Tea.

So, after you have worked to get your customer to know, like and trust you, what do you do next? Altimeter analyst Brian Solis says that you need to create an experience that customers "have, remember, and share" (`http://www.briansolis.com/2017/10/customer-experience-defined-experience-customers-remember-share/`). When customers have a meaningful experience, they remember it. It fosters loyalty and repeat engagement, as well as encourages them to share it with others, thereby becoming an important influencer for your company. As you know, sharing is the gold standard for Facebook marketers. If you focus on creating outstanding, customer-centric experiences, you will find that your investment in these experiences will deliver great rewards.

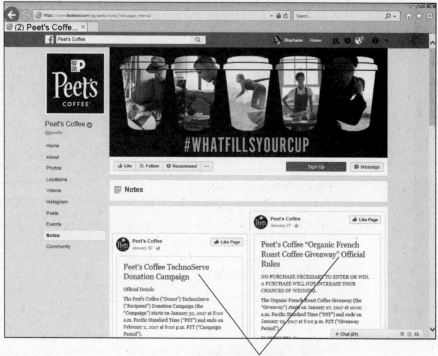

FIGURE 8-1:
Engaging
Facebook users
with rewards and
donations.

Donations and giveaways

Answer a few questions to help set your Facebook Page apart from your other marketing channels:

» How can you bring the unique voice of your business to life in a compelling and personal way?

» In what specific ways do current customers like to connect with your business? What content do they find useful, valuable, or interesting?

» In addition to building awareness for your business, how important is it for you to use Facebook to drive sales?

The more clearly you can answer these questions, the clearer your brand messaging will be to Facebook users.

Preparing Your Facebook Page for Launch

Before you launch your Page, it should be ready to make a good first impression, which is often the *only* impression you get to make. Follow these tips for your Page:

>> **Pick an appropriate name for your Page.** You can boost the ranking of your Page in search engines by choosing a Page title that includes the name of your brand.

>> **Display an attractive avatar or a main image that reflects your brand.** This image is displayed in a variety of sizes (and as small as 32 pixels square), so keep it simple. Omit the name of your business, in fact, because the page name appears wherever your Page avatar appears on Facebook (in News Feeds, Timelines, and hovercards, for example).

>> **Add a cover image or video that tells a story.** Make sure that it tells a story involving your business, but try not to be too "salesy." A restaurant, for example, could show a festive Friday night in the dining room.

>> **Create a username at** `http://facebook.com/username`.

>> **Add compelling posts to your Page.** New fans should see content to like, comment on, and share after they arrive.

Enhancing Your Facebook Page with Content before Launch

Before you promote your Facebook Page, you have to seed it with photos, videos, and links that new fans can share, comment on, and like.

Again, when fans engage with your Page stories, *their* friends see that activity. Via this fundamental connection, awareness about your business slowly (but surely) penetrates the vast network of Facebook users.

Two charts within the Insights application show both the relationships among Facebook users who engage with Page updates and how their friends see that engagement. The Reach report contains two charts that show how engagement influences reach.

Figure 8-2 shows the number of Facebook users engaging with your Page (Likes, comments, shares) and how that engagement creates more reach.

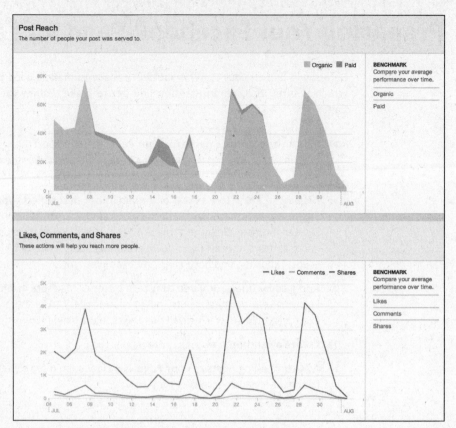

FIGURE 8-2:
Fans who engage with your Page content create viral reach.

Adding a Compelling Reason for Users to Like Your Page

Users are unlikely to like a Page for the simple pleasure of liking it. Telling customers and prospects that you're now on Facebook isn't a compelling reason for them to like your Page. Facebook users are people like you and us; they need a good reason to like it. The exchange of value has to be clear. Why should they like your Page? Do they like you and your business in real life? If not, being on Facebook won't fix this problem.

Here are a few ideas to help you start developing compelling reasons for Facebook users to like your Page:

>> **Offer a discount.** In exchange for people liking your Page, create a custom tab to display and manage a discount (see Chapter 6).

>> **Focus on the community.** Communicate the value of the community of Facebook users and share it on your Page. Buffer (http://buffer.com), an online app, conducts meetups with its users around the country and displays its fan photos, as shown in Figure 8-3.

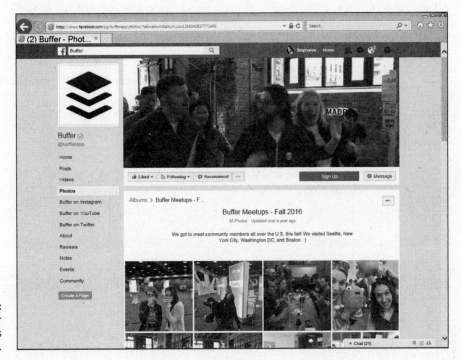

FIGURE 8-3:
Fans of Buffer displayed on its Facebook Page.

>> **Offer exclusive content.** The best way to offer value may be to publish content that can't be found on your website, in your Twitter feed, or on any other channel. The Museum of Fine Arts in Boston frequently posts behind-the-scenes photos of exhibits being assembled.

>> **Highlight contrast.** Research your competitors' efforts, and offer a benefit that's unique by comparison. A hair salon might post short how-to videos on quick, do-it-yourself trims that you can do in a pinch.

>> **Post Timeline contests.** Facebook allows marketers the opportunity to conduct contests in updates by offering a giveaway to anyone who likes or comments on a specific update.

Adding photos and videos

You can upload an unlimited number of albums, and as many as 1,000 photos per album, to your Facebook Page. You can reorder photos, rotate them, and acknowledge Facebook members by *tagging* (identifying) them in photos. I explain how to tag photos in the later section "Tagging photos to promote your Page to your friends."

To upload a single photo or video, follow these steps:

1. **Click the Photo/Video link in the Publisher.**

   A box pops up, giving you the option to upload photos/videos or to create a photo album.

2. **Click the Upload Photos/Video link (see Figure 8-4) and navigate to the image on your computer.**

FIGURE 8-4: Uploading new photos for a Page.

3. **Double-click the photo or video when you locate it on your computer.**

   Facebook automatically uploads the photo or video.

REMEMBER

   To inject personality into your Page, add images and photos that communicate who you are and what your business is about. Select photos that you want customers to see, not the holiday party at which everyone had a few too many cocktails.

4. **If you're uploading a single photo, describe the photo.**

   After you select a photo or video, write a short but compelling description in the Say Something About This field above the file.

5. **Click the Publish button.**

   When you upload a video, you have to wait. Facebook needs time to upload the file and displays a process bar while the video uploads.

6. **When the video finishes uploading, edit the title and description.**

   You can tag the Page in the video, add a location and title, and write a description, as shown in Figure 8-5.

7. **Click Save to publish the video on your Page Timeline.**

FIGURE 8-5:
Editing the details
of a video.

Adding photo albums

Facebook lets you create photo albums that contain multiple photos, which is an excellent way to organize content based on specific topics for your fans to enjoy. The National Wildlife Federation has created several albums containing photos submitted by fans, including the one shown in Figure 8-6.

To create a photo album, follow these steps:

1. **Click the Photo/Video link in the Publisher.**

2. **Click the Create Photo Album link (refer to Figure 8-4).**

   Facebook opens a new window, prompting you to select photos to upload.

3. **Select photos on your computer and click Save.**

   It would be useful to add a description to each photo so that photos are easier to find.

4. **Add a title, location, and description to the album.**

   You can rearrange the order of photos in the album by dragging them to new locations in the album.

FIGURE 8-6:
A photo album is
a useful way to
get fans engaged.

TIP

On an Android or iOS device, you can take a photo or video and immediately upload it to your Facebook Page by using the Facebook Pages Manager app.

TIP

You can download the iOS version at `https://itunes.apple.com/us/app/facebook-pages-manager/id514643583` and the Google Play version at `https://play.google.com/store/apps/details?id=com.facebook.pages.app`.

Adding milestones

The Facebook Pages *milestone* feature lets users easily view important moments in your business's history. Examples of milestones are opening a new store, releasing a new product, and winning an award.

To view a company's milestones, users will click your About tab to the left of your Timeline. They'll see your milestones listed by date, which lets Facebook users quickly navigate to different years in your Page Timeline, as shown in Figure 8-7.

To add milestones to your Page, follow these steps:

1. **Click the Events, Products, Job+ link in the Timeline and then click add a Milestone to your page (see Figure 8-8).**

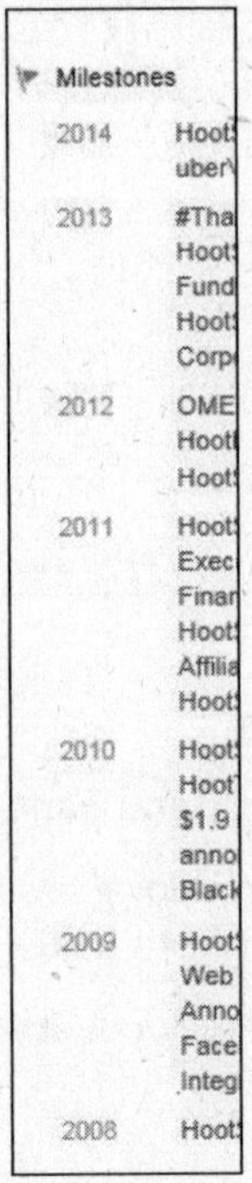

Milestones

2014   Hoot
        uber\

2013   #Tha
        Hoot
        Fund
        Hoot
        Corp

2012   OME
        Hoot
        Hoot

2011   Hoot
        Exec
        Finar
        Hoot
        Affilia
        Hoot

2010   Hoot
        Hoot
        $1.9
        anno
        Black

2009   Hoot
        Web
        Anno
        Face
        Integ

2008   Hoot

FIGURE 8-7: Facebook users can navigate to specific milestones in your Timeline.

Milestone   Event, Products, Job +

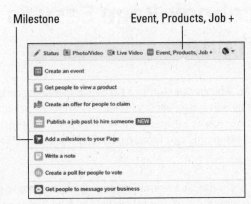

FIGURE 8-8: Create milestones directly in the Timeline.

2. **In the pop-up window, add an event title and a photo, date, location, and description, as shown in Figure 8-9.**

   Add the title of the event, such as Opened for Business, along with the opening date, a location and description, and a photo. The dimensions of a milestone photo are 843 x 403 pixels.

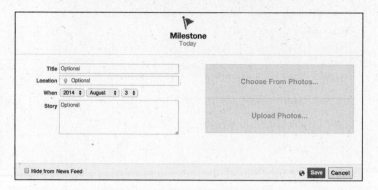

FIGURE 8-9:
Milestones
should include an
event name,
photo, date, and
location (if
applicable).

3. **Save the milestone by clicking the Save button.**

4. **(Optional) Hide the milestone from News Feed, if you want.**

   Select the Hide from News Feed check box if you're adding several milestones at a time and don't want your fans to see it in their News Feeds.

   After you save the milestone, fans will see it when they look at your About page.

Making Your Facebook Page Easy to Find in Search Engines

Anyone, regardless of whether person is a Facebook member, can find and access your Facebook Page by using Facebook's internal search feature or search engines such as Google and Microsoft's Bing. A Facebook Page can improve your search engine rankings so that people can more easily find both your Facebook Page and your website.

All Facebook Pages are public, so search engines such as Google include them in search results. Build a positive image for your brand and engage readers so that they engage with you and return to your Page often.

By publishing a steady stream of links to your company's blog posts and other pages on your company's website within Facebook, you allow search engines to find you more easily. This process is known as *search engine optimization (SEO)*. Simply by having a Facebook Page, you increase the number of relevant links to your site — and, therefore, your site's SEO.

Adding links to your Facebook Page is only a start. Those links should include relevant keywords related to your business. Additionally, the content within the linked article should have relevant keywords. An auto repair garage, for example, would post links to articles about do-it-yourself auto-repair tips on its Facebook Page.

Here are seven ways to optimize your Facebook Page for both Google and Facebook search:

>> **Decide on a page category.** Select the best possible category for your Page. You can edit the category in the Page Info admin panel.

>> **Refine the subcategories on your Page.** If you have a Facebook Place (a local place or business), you can add or update as many as three subcategories within the Page Info admin panel.

>> **Complete your address.** Graph Search allows users to search for local nonprofit organizations that their friends like, for example, so supply the complete and current address.

>> **Fill out the About section.** The information you share in this section helps people find your Page in search results — both on Facebook and search engines, particularly if you insert keywords at the beginning of specific fields.

>> **Tag photos.** A photo is a primary content type that's displayed in Graph Search results. Tag every photo with your Page name and any location that's associated with the photo.

>> **Pay attention to photo descriptions.** Include appropriate keywords in the description of each photo or video you post to your Page. A photo of an adoptable dog at an animal shelter, for example, should have the breed of dog and the words *for adoption* in the description.

>> **Create a username.** If you haven't done so already, create for your Page a custom URL (in the format www.facebook.com/username) that includes the name of your organization to improve its SEO for both Facebook and Google.

For in-depth coverage of SEO (there's way too much information about it to cover in this book), check out *SEO For Dummies*, 6th Edition, by Peter Kent (Wiley).

REMEMBER

Your Page should contain many instances of the keywords that can help it appear at the top of the list of results in search engines. If you're a professional photographer, add keywords such as *wedding photography* and *photography in Atlanta* to help track down the people who are in the market for those specific services. Use these keywords on the Info tab and in any notes you post. Also, provide all necessary contact information, such as your address and your company's website and blog addresses.

Networking with Friends to Launch Your Facebook Page

As we mention at the beginning of this chapter, one challenge of launching a brand-new Facebook Page is users' lack of awareness of your Page within Facebook. Often, the first step that many administrators take in launching their Pages is leveraging their existing networks of friends, such as personal connections developed via email and personal Facebook profiles.

Encouraging your friends to share your Page with their friends

The Share button, which appears at the bottom left of the cover image on every Facebook Page (see Figure 8-10), lets people invite their Facebook friends to check out your Page.

Follow these steps to post an update about your Page to your Timeline:

1. **Click the Share link on the left side of the Page.**

   The Share This Page dialog box appears.

2. **Write a compelling message about your Page.**

   Though the message can be as long as you'd like, keep it short and sweet. Be sure to add a call to action, such as "Share this Page with your friends!"

3. **Click the Post link.**

   A story is published in the News Feeds of many of your friends and on your personal Timeline.

FIGURE 8-10: The Share feature on a Page.

Promoting your Page to friends with the Invite feature

People who have become friends with you on Facebook may not realize that you've set up a Page specifically for your business. Facebook makes it easy for you, as a Page admin, to let people in on the good news. Follow these steps:

1. Click the Invite Friends link from the . . . (ellipsis) button below your Facebook cover.

The Invite Friends dialog box appears, as shown in Figure 8-11.

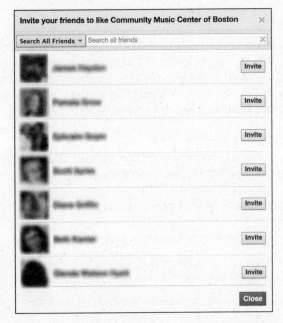

FIGURE 8-11: Sharing a Page with friends by using the Invite Friends feature.

2. Scroll through your friends' pictures and click the Invite button of each person you want to invite, or type a friend's name in the Search All Friends box at the top to find a specific friend quickly.

3. Click the Send Invites button at the bottom of the dialog box.

The Success dialog box appears, letting you know that your recommendations have been sent. Get ready for all the new Likes to roll in!

People to whom you promote your Page who aren't already Facebook members must join Facebook to be able to like or comment on your Page.

Using Tagging and Mentions on Facebook to create engagement

Facebook lets you tell people and businesses you are talking about them by using two different methods: Tagging and Mention (the terms are often used interchangeably, but they have differences). We discuss the different ways to use them in the following sections.

Tagging

Tagging Facebook users can only be done from your personal profile. If you tag a person by identifying her in a post ("I'm with this person") or a photo ("I'm identifying this person"), she receives a notification. You can tag only a person you are connected to on Facebook. Using this method, you can alert your friends that you're saying something about them and hopefully encourage them to engage and share.

When you tag a user in a photo or post, that person can hide it from his Timeline by clicking the Remove Tag link next to the profile name.

To tag a photo or person on your personal profile:

1. **Click the What's on Your Mind area in your Timeline.**

   A screen pops up, showing you tagging choices, including Tag Friends and Tag Events. (The Tag Events choice is not shown in the figure.)

2. **For this example, click Tag Friends, shown in Figure 8-12.**

   You see a space under your post that says "With."

3. **Start typing the name.**

   A list pops up, allowing you to choose the friend you are talking about.

4. **Click the person's name.**

   The name is inserted into the post. Finish the post as you normally do.

5. **Click Post.**

You can also go to a photo on your profile or another person's profile and tag a photo by clicking the photo and then clicking the Tag link at the bottom of the photo. The person is then notified.

This pops open for you to type in a name

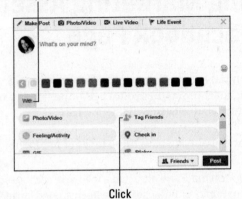

FIGURE 8-12:
Tagging a friend
on a Facebook
profile.

Click

REMEMBER

The ability to tag specific Facebook users depends mostly on how their own privacy settings are configured.

Mention

A mention can only be done from your Page. Mentions are used to comment about a Page or people you aren't connected to. You mention a person or Page using the @ sign. When you mention a business Page or person, the person or Page receives a notice.

To mention Pages or a person, log in as your Page by following these steps:

1. **Click the arrow icon in the top-right corner of the page.**

   The Use Facebook As drop-down menu appears, displaying all the Pages you manage.

2. **Choose the Page that you want to log in as.**

   When you're logged in as your Page, you can mention Pages or Facebook users.

3. **Start creating a new post or commenting on an existing post by entering the @ sign.**

   A list of choices pops up.

4. **Click the Page or name and it is inserted into the post.**

   Finish the post as you normally do.

5. **Click Publish.**

Leveraging Existing Marketing Assets to Launch Your Facebook Page

After you attract an initial boost of personal friends to your Page, as described in the preceding section, start promoting your Page — perhaps by using marketing channels and assets that you've been building for years.

Chances are good that you already have these types of marketing assets:

>> **A large following:** You may have attracted a following because you're well known in your community or because you've been around longer than anyone else.

>> **Attention:** This asset is often a matter of time and place. Restaurants can garner the most attention when people are eating in the establishment; online retailers, by way of email; and nonprofit organizations, at fundraising events.

The following sections describe how to use existing marketing assets to promote your presence on Facebook.

REMEMBER

The essential value of Facebook is getting your current customers to tell their friends about your products or services. Give your current customers reasons to engage with your Facebook Page and its content.

Your email signature

Suppose that every email you sent in the course of doing daily business included a link to your Facebook Page! Adding an anchor link in your email signature that connects with your Facebook Page is relatively easy to do in most email programs, such as Outlook, Gmail, and Apple Mail. If you want to enhance your email signature you may want to check out a service like WiseStamp (www.wisestamp.com). WiseStamp allows you to do such things as to add a Like button or provide other links in your email signature so that you can drive traffic to your channels. WiseStamp has a free version and premium plans.

TIP

Someone could become a fan of your Page based on the number of current fans your Page has. Gaining as many new fans as possible creates a kind of social validation for these future fans.

Your email list

You can promote your new Facebook Page in many ways, but the easiest way to attract new connections is to use your email list — an asset that you may have been growing over the past few years.

Facebook users share useful information with their friends and click the Like button on Pages that help them achieve that goal. If they receive an email saying "We're now on Facebook; please like our Page," they're likely to delete it unless they're hardcore fans. If they ask "What's in it for me?" and don't receive an answer, no perceived value exchange takes place.

When you're emailing your current list about your Facebook Page, keep these tips in mind:

» **Focus on the value to the recipient, not to your business.** Prospective customers and customers are always asking "What's in it for me?"

» **Write the message in the second person, using *you* and *your* to speak directly to the customer.** This approach gives the email a more personal feeling.

» **Present the benefits in a concise list of bulleted items (as we've done in this list).** Bullet points are easy to scan and read, allowing recipients to find what they're looking for fast.

» **Tell recipients that they'll meet other people who have similar interests and ideas.** They'll feel that they're joining a community, not just another Facebook Page.

» **Make messaging the same.** Don't confuse people by using different messaging in email and in Facebook content. When the messaging is consistent across your channels, the results are more effective. An email subscriber who reads an email about a recent sale will be more likely to act after seeing a Facebook update about that sale, for example.

» **Make the content different across channels.** Email subscribers may wonder why they should become Facebook fans when they already subscribe to the email list, for example. You can use email to share customer stories about your product or service and use Facebook to share photos and videos from those stories.

» **Consistently cross-promote each channel.** Within your email newsletter, for example, include links to the photo album that are related to stories covered in the newsletter.

Printed marketing materials

The best way to promote your Facebook Page in print, such as in annual appeals or newsletters, is to create a custom URL (as described in Chapter 4). A custom URL is much shorter than the default Facebook Page URL, which no one is likely to take the time to type from a printed page. Use this custom URL on every single piece of printed material that you send.

Your blog

Write a blog post that describes the launch of your Page, followed by a few posts that elaborate on the best comments on your Page updates. Include a link to your Page or the Page update (or both).

Webinars

If your business regularly holds webinars, make your Facebook Page's Timeline the place where you announce events and send people to your landing page to register for webinars.

YouTube

As you may know, YouTube is the top video-sharing website in the world. Posting videos there is a way to promote your business to millions of people. If you already have a presence on YouTube, you can leverage that asset to promote your Facebook Page. Nimble, a Customer Relationship Management (CRM) software app, uses its call to action (CTA) button to link to its large collection of software demos (see Figure 8-13). CRM software helps you manage information about each of your customers so that you can communicate with them and help them use your products.

TIP

If have a YouTube channel, make sure to link your pertinent videos in the Video section of your Facebook Page.

FIGURE 8-13:
Nimble uses its
CTA button to
send users to
demos of its
software.

Call to action button

Promoting Your Facebook Page in Your Store

When people visit your business and have a positive experience, they naturally want to share that experience with their friends (a type of word-of-mouth advertising that has been going on for eons). When you launch your Facebook Page, promote it in your store. If people check in to your place on their mobile devices, those posts provide additional exposure for your business in their News Feeds.

TIP

Use Facebook's downloadable signs to promote your Facebook presence in your store. Download them at https://www.facebook.com/business/help/149774151793586?helpref=uf_permalink.

Promoting Your Facebook Page by Using Facebook Ads

One way to acquire Facebook fans is to use Facebook Page Ads to promote your Page to the friends of your existing fans.

These ads appear in the sidebar on Facebook and in the News Feeds of Facebook users. The powerful aspect of these ads is that they leverage the social graph — the Facebook network of friends.

Facebook Ads are different from traditional online ads or Google ads in four ways:

>> They can target friends of your current fans to take advantage of the idea that "birds of a feather flock together."

>> A user's friends who have already liked your Page are displayed this way: "John, Bill, and Barbara like the National Wildlife Federation." Facebook users are more likely to take action when they see that their friends have already taken that action.

>> Users can like the Page directly in the Sponsored Story. This setup eliminates any potential abandonment that may occur when people click a link to visit your Page and then decide not to like it.

>> The names of new fans are displayed in the Likes report within Facebook Insights so that you see how these Sponsored Story ads compare with other methods of acquiring fans.

For more on using Facebook Ads, see Chapter 11.

Promoting Your Facebook Page by Using an Integrated Approach

In the typical business or non-profit organization, the marketing communications include various channels, such as direct mail, email, social media, traditional public relations, print assets, and online and offline advertising. Using these methods shows that your business or organization has made an effort to embrace a wide variety of channels, hoping to engage people from every angle.

As you may have already experienced, the results from any single promotional channel or approach are much less significant than the results from an integrated approach, in which all channels are combined into a single communications plan. To start creating an integrated plan, ask yourself these questions:

>> How do people typically find out about my business or nonprofit? (From a Facebook friend? From searching on Google? From a road sign? From a newspaper ad?)

>> What is the next step for someone to take with my business after becoming a Facebook fan? (Joining an email list? Redeeming a coupon in my store?)

>> Where do people usually begin their relationship with my business? (Searching? Joining my email list?)

>> Which channel do most of my new customers join? (Email? Direct mail?)

>> How can my customers easily tell their Facebook friends about a new purchase?

>> Where do I have a lot of natural attention? (In my store? At events and conferences?)

After you've jotted down a few ideas for the channels mentioned in this chapter, use the answers to these questions to start mapping a way for all your channels to work together as a whole.

Chapter **9**

Engaging Your Facebook Fans

After you create a Facebook Page (see Chapter 4 for details on creating a Page), you can start posting content that Facebook users will like, comment on, and share (see Chapter 7 for more on effective content strategies). The next step in this progression is engaging with Facebook users who comment on your updates, post content on your Page, or interact with your business in some other way on Facebook.

Engagement is partially a "quantity game," meaning that the amount of time and effort you spend has a huge correlation with the results you receive. In this way, using Facebook isn't too different from in-person networking. When you attend a networking event, for example, the more people you meet directly increases your potential for business. Networking is also a quality game. Continuing with the preceding example, suppose that you attend 50 events. If all you do is hand out your business card to as many people as possible and offer no additional value, all people will remember about you is the moment you interrupted them.

If, instead, you offer a solution to problems they brought up during your conversation, they'll not only remember you but also might repay the favor by referring new business to you.

In the same way, sharing useful resources and spending time conversing with your Facebook Page community is the surest way to attract new customers, increase the prevalence of repeat customers, and grow your prospect list.

In this chapter, we show you the strategies and tactics that generate conversations, as well as show you how to avoid unknowingly creating interruptions.

You also see how to manage notifications, use your Facebook Page activity log to filter various types of interactions, and create a Facebook Page community policy to set the tone and expectations with your community.

Understanding What Engagement Really Means

If you've been reading up on how to market your business with social media, you've no doubt run across the word *engagement*. Like the word *love*, engagement means less and less the more it's used.

To some people, engagement means publishing interesting and creative content with little interest in understanding or listening to one's customers or prospects. To others, engagement is all about conversation: asking questions, replying to comments, expressing appreciation to fans, and so on.

The truth is that engagement is both. You have to publish interesting content, but you also have to understand what your fans are interested in. This isn't different from what you do to nurture and develop professional relationships or the relationships you have with your customers. Other people express a need, and you respond to that need as best as you can! All the skills you've developed building professional relationships in the real world apply to Facebook as well.

What engagement means for word-of-mouth marketing

As with in-person networking events or conferences, engagement — meeting your customers, getting to know them, and inspiring them to take action — takes time and effort. Online or off, people are still people, which means that there are no shortcuts to building healthy relationships with your customers and prospects. That said, engagement means something slightly different from each party's perspective.

Engagement includes the strategies to motivate your customers to talk about your business — word-of-mouth marketing. You also want them (ideally) to trust you enough to tell you when they have a problem or when they love what you do.

You want fans to interact with your Page for two reasons:

>> You can build a relationship with your fans through dialogue and discussion. Obviously, this leads to sales to a percentage of those fans.

>> The activity that's generated on your Page as a result of these discussions creates more stories in your fans' News Feeds, which exposes your business to their friends.

TIP

Always stay on message, which means making sure that the content relates to your business in some way. And consider keeping your links on the positive side. There's no need to associate negative news with your business.

Understanding what engagement on Facebook offers you

If you view Facebook only as a place where you promote your business to selectively targeted users, you're missing the entire point.

The real strength of Facebook is word-of-mouth marketing. Suppose that you hear about a new restaurant from one of your Facebook friends. He says that he's eaten there and loves it. That recommendation carries 1,000 times more weight than an update from that restaurant's Page.

If that restaurant is smart, it will capitalize on recommendations like that one by focusing most of its marketing resources on creating an engaged fan base (one that talks about the restaurant) instead of trying to reach every Facebook user who might be a potential customer.

Understanding how Facebook users engage with your business

To create a strategy for building an engaged Facebook fan base, it's important to understand the various ways Facebook users can engage with your business.

Facebook users typically share your content from your website or engage with your Facebook Page updates, apps, and events. Here are the various ways Facebook users can engage with your business and why it's important to respond appropriately:

>> **Share content from your website.** Facebook users frequently share content from other websites. If you look into your website's statistics, you'll see how often Facebook users have shared content from your website. In Chapter 15, we go into greater detail on using social plug-ins on your website to increase the amount of content that's shared from there, but for now, just know that people will share your content — especially if you publish fresh content on a consistent basis. Marketo does an excellent job of publishing fresh content with blog posts, e-books, and webinars, as shown in Figure 9-1.

Marketo shared a link.
October 14

Poor email marketing can damage two critical things: your customer relationships and your bottom line. Here's why you need to start seeing failed customer comms as negative, not neutral events.

The Real Cost of Sending Bad Email
blog.marketo.com
Behavioral personalization is fundamentally shifting the landscape of customer communication. One of the biggest beneficiaries of this new technology is email marketing. With this shift, does the cost of sending a bad email change?

Like · Comment · Share · Buffer   ⤳ 22 Shares

👍 Ana Lucia Novak and 485 others like this.

FIGURE 9-1: Marketo publishes tactical content and how-to articles on its Facebook Page to engage fans.

>> **Like your Page.** When Facebook users like your Facebook Page, they create a story in their friends' News Feeds, which makes them aware of your business (through viral reach). When a Facebook user likes your Page, you have no guarantee that she'll receive your content in her News Feed, but her Like is an expression that she likes your organization (as opposed to liking a specific Page update; see the next item).

>> **Like a Page update.** Both fans and nonfans (essentially, all Facebook users) can like any of your Page updates. When Facebook users like your photo,

video, or text update, they create a story in their News Feeds, which creates viral reach for that specific update (because their friends see that update). This creates *viral reach,* meaning that a Facebook user sees a story in her News Feed because her Facebook friend liked, commented on it, or shared it. Her friends in turn may like, comment on, and share that update.

>> **Comment on a Page update.** When a Facebook user comments on one of your updates, that comment also creates viral reach. But liking an update and commenting on an update are very different. You have to understand that when someone takes the time to write a comment on your update, she's more invested in that interaction. In other words, likes are in some ways throwaway gestures — simple taps or mouse clicks. But a comment takes time and consideration. It's an expression, no matter how small, of deeper engagement. Taking the time to reply to comments thoughtfully goes a long way toward building an engaged fan base.

>> **Share a Page update.** Of the three types of actions that Facebook users can take on an update — liking, commenting on, and sharing — sharing is the strongest. When a Facebook user shares an update, he's essentially saying "All my friends need to see this!" Facebook's algorithm also places more weight on shares.

TIP

When Facebook users share your updates, saying thanks where appropriate is a good idea. You can tag the user in the comments on the update or say thanks in the shared update (privacy permissions permitting).

>> **RSVP to an event.** When Facebook users RSVP to an event, they create a story in their friends' News Feeds ("John is attending the national hot dog–eating competition!"). As discussed in Chapter 13, Facebook Events have their own Timelines where you can post pictures about the events and reply to comments from people who sent RSVPs.

Measuring Engagement with Facebook Insights

In one sense, engagement is the human connection between customer and business. But you can't determine whether your marketing efforts are giving you the expected return based solely on how connected they make you feel — and this is why you measure engagement.

Page mentions in status updates, replies in comment threads, and the general sentiment expressed in the actions that Facebook users take on your Page can be measured with the Insights analytics tool included with every Facebook Page. As you can see in Figure 9-2, Facebook Insights allows you to see how each post has performed.

Published ▼	Post	Type	Targeting	Reach	Engagement	Promote
09/04/2014 2:09 am	Columba Catholic College students from Charters Towers showing their support their own way!		🌐	19.7K	7%	Boost Post
09/02/2014 8:11 pm	Cloncurry, we can't wait to yarn recognition with you over morning tea this Friday! Friday 5		🌐	20.5K	6%	Boost Post
09/02/2014 4:45 am	Woorabinda community BBQ, yarn, and movie afternoon!	🔗	🌐	3.4K	3%	Boosted
09/02/2014 12:58 am	G'day Charters Towers! It's your chance to join the Journey to Recognition. Tomorrow, 10-11am		🌐	15K	4%	Boost Post
08/29/2014 3:05 am	The Journey has been collecting notes and well wishes from those we meet along the way. Nebo,		🌐	9.8K	4%	Boosted
08/28/2014 8:37 pm	This morning we had a great discussion over breakfast and a guided tour of the Juru Walk in Ayr.		🌐	13.1K	6%	Boost Post

FIGURE 9-2: Measure fan engagement received for each Page update.

The Facebook Insights table shown in Figure 9-2 helps marketers measure the following different types of engagement:

>> **Liking, sharing, or commenting on a Page story:** You can view more details about likes, comments, shares, and clicks by clicking the post in the Post column.

>> **Playing a video or viewing a photo:** You can view details about video plays, photo views, and more by clicking the post in the Post column.

>> **Viewing organic and paid reach:** You can also view details about organic, paid, and even viral reach. In the following list, three Facebook Insights reports show how engaged Facebook users are with your content. (Facebook Insights is covered in detail in Chapter 10.) Make a habit of regularly viewing these three reports on your Page.

Insights link

FIGURE 9-3: Insights is available on your Facebook Page.

To access these reports, click the Insights link on the Admin navigation menu at the top of your Page, as shown in Figure 9-3:

- **Likes, Comments, and Shares report:** Click the Reach tab within Facebook Insights and scroll down to the Likes, Comments, and Shares graph (see Figure 9-4). This graph shows you how many Facebook users have liked, commented on, or shared your Page update over a selected time range. Mousing over the lines in the graph shows you how many people were talking about your updates on a specific day.

- **All Posts Published report:** Click the Posts tab within Insights, and you see the All Posts Published report (see Figure 9-5), which shows you details on each of the posts published in the previous 90 days. Details in this report include the date you posted the update, a link to the update, the number of users engaged with that update, and the number of people whom the update reached. You can also quickly determine which updates performed best, and from this information, you can start to define trends about the content on your Page that people reacted to most.

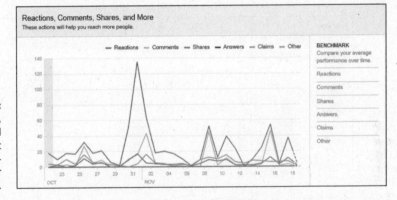

FIGURE 9-4: The Likes, Comments, and Shares report reflects engagement with your Page posts.

- **Reach report:** Click the Reach tab within Facebook Insights and scroll down to see the Reach graph. This report shows you the number of people who saw the actions displayed in the graph on the left. Reach is a direct result of engagement. Figure 9-6 shows how engagement spreads through Facebook, like a sound and its echo.

TIP

Because real engagement with fans grows over long periods of time, choose weeks or months for your ranges of data in Insights. In other words, don't bother tracking this information on a daily basis.

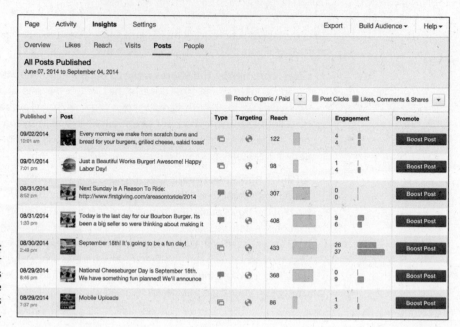

FIGURE 9-5:
See which of your
Page updates
have received the
most comments
and Likes.

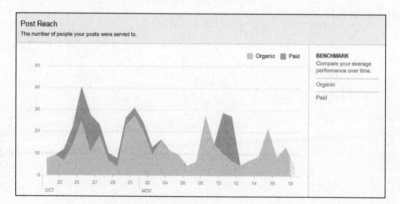

FIGURE 9-6:
See how many
people saw your
updates with the
Reach report.

Facebook uses an algorithm to determine which fans see your content in their News Feeds. One of the biggest factors in this algorithm is the prevalence of comments and Likes each of your Page stories receives. Facebook Insights shows you how you can post updates that receive more Likes and comments.

REMEMBER

When someone takes the time to comment on an update or post a question to your Page, she's identifying herself as someone who's definitely more interested in your business than the casual Facebook user who simply Likes the Page update.

Getting Tactical with Engagement on Your Facebook Page

Aside from posting content for Facebook users to engage with, you have three ways to further enhance your relationship with Facebook users by conversing with them on your Page:

>> **Replying to their comments on your updates:** Facebook users often comment on or ask questions about the updates you post on your Page. Many times — especially when they ask questions — they expect you to reply in a timely manner.

>> **Replying to their posts on your Page:** Facebook users have the ability to post content directly on your Page (or rather, they do if you've selected this setting on your Manage Permissions tab; see the section "Getting Notifications about Facebook Users' Activity," later in this chapter). They expect prompt replies to their posts, especially if they need you to answer a question.

>> **Replying to messages they send you:** If you enabled the message feature on your Page, Facebook users can send you private Facebook messages similar to the messages that they send their friends. If you enable a Messenger chatbot, fans can send you messages to which you can respond almost immediately, if you choose.

TIP

If you enable a chatbot, remember that someone will need to monitor it. If you set it up but don't respond quickly, you will have set a customer expectation that you can't meet.

Asking questions is one of the most effective ways to engage your fans, particularly if those questions are highly relevant and specific. Try some of these approaches:

>> Find a topical news story that connects to your business, and ask what people think about it. Post the question with a link to the news story for a bigger response.

>> Pose a question you get from your potential customers, and ask your enthusiasts how they would answer it.

>> Use fill-in-the-blank questions. The Life is Good Facebook Page (www.facebook.com/Lifeisgood), for example, asked this fill-in-the-blank question: "A positive life lesson I'd like to share is XX." The Page received more than 1,300 comments and more than 500 Likes in just a few days!

>> Ask a question with a one-word answer. Don't ask your audience to write a detailed evaluation of something. Some of the most popular fill-in-the-blank questions require just a one- or two-word response ("Chocolate — Dark or Milk?").

Getting Notifications about Facebook Users' Activity

To get timely notifications of activity by Facebook users, configure your notification settings in the Settings section of your Facebook Page. To configure your notification settings, follow these steps:

1. **Click the Settings link on your admin navigation bar.**

2. **Click Notifications in the left sidebar, as shown in Figure 9-7.**

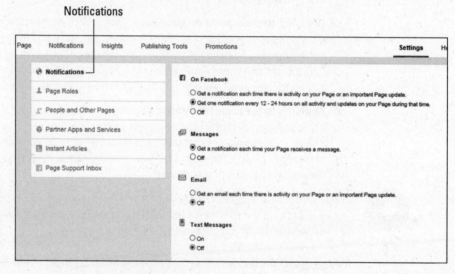

FIGURE 9-7:
Facebook Page admins can receive notifications about Page activity on Facebook and by email.

3. **Select your desired method of getting notifications:**

   - **On Facebook:** Selecting this option means that you'll receive notifications about activity by users on your Page in the same area where you receive notifications from your Facebook friends. You can also select the specific type of notifications to receive (new messages, reviews, tips, comments, posts by others, new Likes, and so on).

   - **Messages:** If you turn this on, you will receive a notification about each message you receive.

   - **Email:** Selecting this option means that you'll get an email when someone likes, comments on, or shares one of your updates; posts an update to your Page; or sends you a Facebook Page message.

   - **Text:** You will receive text messages if you turn this on.

TIP

The notifications method you choose depends on your preferences. Keep in mind that you can choose more than one type of notification and then simply deselect the ones that aren't suited to your work habits.

Viewing Your Facebook Page's Notifications and Activity Log

Your Facebook Page's Notification area shows the latest activity from Facebook users in response to your Page updates. The actions include liking, commenting, and sharing your updates. You can click each notification to see more details, reply to comments, and thank users for sharing your updates. The activity link is found below the Notifications link and is the place to see Check-ins, Mentions, and Shares by your fans. To view your Facebook Page activity log, click the Notifications link on your admin navigation bar. Then click the Activity link (see Figure 9-8) to filter your activity in the left sidebar.

Notifications

FIGURE 9-8: Accessing the activity log.

Responding to Comments and Posts

When a Facebook user asks you a question or is interested enough in what you're saying to post a comment on your update, he has invested time in the interaction. Not responding or acknowledging him in some way makes it seem as though you're ignoring him. Who wants to give money to a company that ignores him even before a sale takes place? If a user asks you a question, respond to it. If you receive a compliment, thank the person, and reinforce your commitment to creating exceptional customer experiences. If you receive a negative comment, ask how you can improve the overall experience.

In short, every time someone reaches out to engage with your Page, engage with that person in return. Failing to reciprocate can backfire or cost you revenue.

Although generally you want to respond to comments within 24 hours, in some cases — such as an irate customer who's never going to be happy with anything you say — you may be better off not responding at all. Trying to decide when to respond and when *not* to respond can be tricky, so here are some tips to help you make this decision:

>> **If you clearly made a mistake, respond and correct the situation quickly.** Apologies can go a long way if you explain that steps are being taken to correct the situation.

>> **If someone leaves a negative comment about something that never took place or is based on incorrect facts, correct him.** Always be polite, because people often don't realize that they've made an error. If you don't respond, however, this misconception could spread and escalate.

>> **Try to salvage a bad situation.** If you made a mistake and think you can put a positive spin on a bad experience or convince the customer to give you another chance, a response is appropriate to right the perceived wrong.

>> **An irate person may never be satisfied, so you may be better off not doing anything.** Sometimes, people direct their frustration with the world to you and your Facebook Page. To find out whether you're dealing with such a person, take a look at the other comments she's made. You may conclude that it's better for you not to enter a fight you're never going to win (see the next item). Instead, invest your time and efforts where you can have a positive result.

>> **Don't engage in a fight you can't win.** Sometimes a response does more harm than good. A negative comment or review can have a devastating effect on a company's online reputation. But you don't want to engage in a back-and-forth discussion that uncovers more cracks in the armor, so to speak. In these situations, take a passive role as opposed to going for the jugular.

>> **Don't let anger derail your response.** Although the saying "It's not personal; it's just business" is good in principle, it's not always good in practice. Disparaging Facebook comments can really make you angry. Rather than rattle off a negative response, have someone who's less emotional about the situation respond, or wait until your emotions calm before responding. An angry response can really damage your relationship with the customer and can have a spill-over effect on all who read it.

Running Facebook Contests

Contests and giveaways have traditionally played vital roles in consumer marketing, used by cereal companies, fashion retailers, automobile dealers, and so on. The promise of winning something of value for free is a tremendous lure. Whether they're backed by a media campaign, promoted on a product's packaging, or announced at an employee sales meeting, promotions have the power to motivate and drive engagement.

All the same incentives that served marketers before Facebook, such as raffles and drawings, still apply on Facebook. Promotions with high-value prizes tend to be more active. Even if you don't have access to costly prizes, you can still offer an appropriate reward. (Even I, John, have been known to fill out a form for the chance to win a T-shirt if it's really cool.)

Facebook currently offers an app to conduct simple contests (https://apps. facebook.com/my-contests/). You can also check out some third-party promotion apps to find a solution that works best for your promotion. Find out more about contest and promotion apps in Chapter 6.

Understanding Facebook rules for contests

The Facebook Promotions Guidelines page spells out the rules for the use of promotions on the Facebook platform. You can find the current guidelines at www. facebook.com/promotions_guidelines.php.

REMEMBER

Keep the following guidelines in mind when you're running a promotion:

>> You must use special wording (see the official guidelines). Facebook clearly states that you must include the exact wording right next to any place on your promotion entry form where personal information is requested.

>> You must tell the entrant exactly how her personal information will be used — that you're collecting her email address for marketing purposes, for example.

>> The entrant must know that the promotion isn't run or endorsed by Facebook.

WARNING

The Facebook Page terms and conditions state that you *can't* do the following:

>> Establish photo promotions that require entrants to change their profiles in any way, such as uploading a branded photo for their profile pictures.

>> Establish status-update promotions that require posting status updates for entry.

>> Automatically enter people in a promotion after they become fans. You can always link from your Facebook Page to a promotion hosted on your own website, outside the Facebook guidelines. You still need to be mindful about how you use the Facebook name, however, and it's probably best not to use the Facebook name at all in association with any promotion that's not on Facebook.

Using third-party apps for Facebook promotions

The best way to run a contest on Facebook is to use a third-party app. Many third-party apps, such as ShortStack, allow you to sort contest entries, allow users to upload photos, and even sync with MailChimp and other cloud-based services.

This approach makes sense because you acquire emails in addition to engaging Facebook users. And building your email list is essential!

Creating an effective promotion

Facebook offers a compelling environment in which to host a promotion or give-away. You can use your Page as a starting point — linking to your website for promotion entry details — or have the entire promotion contained within the Facebook community.

Promotions can be very creative and challenging, or they can require a simple yes or no answer. They can motivate users to upload a video or complete a contact form. Some promotions require a panel of esteemed judges to determine the winner; others select winners randomly. Still other promotions allow the users to vote for the outcome. An example of a Facebook sweepstakes is one by Luvs Diapers.

Users accessed the contest from the Sweepstakes tab on the left side of the Page, as shown in Figure 9-9. The winner got diapers for a year.

Although promotions are as unique as the companies that host them, we offer some tips that can improve your chances of success. Here are some best practices for creating Facebook promotions and giveaways:

>> **Offer an attractive prize.** The more attractive the prize, the more responses you'll get. A box of Cracker Jack won't garner much interest. For a prize to be attractive, though, it doesn't necessarily have to cost a lot. The best prizes tend to be those that money can't buy, such as a chance to meet a celebrity, to participate in a TV commercial, or to attend a product's prerelease party. There's no better way to get people to try your products or services than to offer them as prizes!

>> **Use your existing customers and contacts to start the ball rolling.** Getting those initial entries is always the toughest part of running a Facebook promotion, so you need to reach into your network of family and friends. Reach out to your mailing list of customers with a friendly invitation. Promote the promotion on Twitter, Pinterest, LinkedIn, Instagram, Myspace, and (of course) your Facebook Page. Wherever you have contacts, use whatever social network, email exchange, or messenger service you have to get them to participate.

>> **Cross-promote via your website.** You need to promote your Facebook promotion across all your channels, including your website, to gain maximum participation. Adding a promotional banner with a link to your Facebook Page is a good start, but you can do much more to promote your promotion. Issue a press release via one of the many news wire services. Add a message to your phone answering system. The possibilities are endless.

>> **Keep the promotion simple.** Don't make the rules too complicated. The fewer the questions on a form, the higher the rate of completion. Keep the first prize a single, valuable item and have several smaller second-place prizes.

The fewer the clicks to enter the promotion, the better.

REMEMBER

>> **Don't set the bar too high.** If you ask participants for an original creation, keep the requirements to a minimum. Don't place a minimum word count on an essay promotion, for example, and don't require a video for the first round of submissions, because videos are a lot of work.

>> **Run promotions for at least one month.** Things like word-of-mouth marketing require time. The more time you spend promoting the promotion, the more entries you get. The more you build up excitement by keeping the promotion in front of your fans, the more often they take note of it and look forward to the big day when the winner is announced!

>> **Integrate your promotion with a media campaign.** Facebook Ads are ideal complements to any promotion. By combining a Facebook Ad campaign with a promotion, you maximize viral effect and amplify the number of engagements. (See Chapter 11 for more on Facebook Ads.)

>> **Make your promotion fun, interesting, and unique.** The main thing to keep in mind when planning a Facebook promotion is that members want to be entertained. Promotions should offer an outlet for self-expression, engage members, encourage them to share with friends, and communicate something unique about your brand.

>> **Make it fair and transparent.** Clearly explain how your winner will be selected. Include all details about the selection process. If you plan to judge a photo contest based on creativity, artistic statement, or image quality, include these criteria in your rules:

● **Explain how prizes will be awarded:** You also want to explain how you'll contact the winners. How many days does a winner have after she's notified to reply and accept her prize, for example?

● **Reserve the right to change the rules:** State that you have the right to change the winner-selection process at any time, just in case you run into an unforeseen issue.

>> **Use third-party apps to engage your Facebook community.** A few notable apps can help you manage your Facebook community. These apps include features such as advanced scheduling, publishing quizzes, list-building actions, and content curation. Following are our three favorite (and most strongly recommended) apps for managing a Facebook community:

- **AgoraPulse:** AgoraPulse is a social media management platform that focuses on Facebook and Twitter. It includes marketing apps (Quiz, Instant Wins, Contests, Sweepstakes, Coupons, and so on), moderation and management tools for Facebook and Twitter, and post scheduling. The app lets you identify your most engaged fans, compare your performance with that of competitors, and export reports into a Microsoft PowerPoint presentation.

- **ActionSprout:** ActionSprout lets you acquire emails in the News Feed by using Facebook actions that allow Facebook users to share their email with ActionSprout when they click a specific action. You can publish an update encouraging your Facebook fans to "Stand For" a particular issue or topic, for example. When a user clicks Stand For in the update, he joins your email list. You can automatically email Facebook users who engage with the app as well as download emails into your customer relationship management software (CRM).

- **Post Planner:** Post Planner allows you to schedule posts to multiple Pages, repeat posts, and even curate the most viral content from other Facebook Pages. Post Planner lets you put a share bar above your shared posts so that you can build your email list, get more Twitter followers, and even promote a product or service. In my (John's) Post Planner share bar, I encourage Facebook users to join my email list, whether I'm sharing my own content or content from another website (see Figure 9-10).

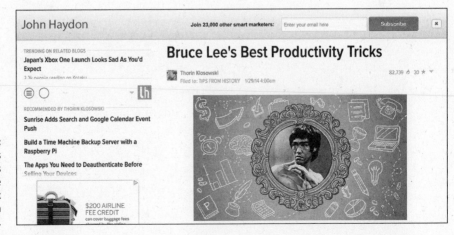

FIGURE 9-10:
Post Planner's share bar allows you to acquire emails via link posts shared on Facebook.

ADOPTING THE FARMER'S ATTITUDE

Farmers know that results require hard work and patience. Depending on the season, farmers pull weeds, fertilize soil, plant seeds, and so on. These are demanding jobs, but none of them can make the harvest come any faster. Farmers understand that nature is governed by strict laws of cause and effect. You reap what you sow, but only in due course. Facebook — or any other social media platform — works exactly the same way. Scratch that — all human relationships and worthwhile endeavors work the same way. Be patient! Results will come in time.

Chapter **10**

Improving Your Marketing Strategy with Facebook Insights

acebook Insights is an analytics tool for your Page that helps you make better marketing decisions with Facebook. It shows you what your fans like to talk about so that you can publish content that continues to engage them. Insights also helps you spend your Facebook advertising dollars more wisely by targeting Facebook users who are similar to your most engaged fans.

Most important, Insights helps you discover the strategies that work for your specific Facebook Page community. These strategies are better than any you'd get from relying on your gut or, worse, the best practices you read on some blog.

In this sense, Facebook Insights is your personal GPS for your Facebook Page, telling you exactly what you need to do to arrive at your destination. The destination, of course, is each marketing campaign objective.

In this chapter, we show you how to improve your Page by using the information Facebook Insights provides. We explain what the metrics are and how to use them to reach your goals. We also offer tips on how to integrate third-party analytics into your Page.

Getting Analytical with Facebook Insights

As you proceed with your Facebook marketing journey, you begin to get a sense of what's working and what isn't working. You see that some of your Page updates get a lot of Likes and comments, while others get only crickets.

Based on these simple observations, you'll get hunches about what kind of Page stories work, and you may eventually get better at posting stories that effectively engage your fans.

Although this type of nonanalytical analysis — thinking with your gut — is an effective way for beginners to see how Facebook users respond to content, it doesn't provide the data you need to be truly successful as a Facebook marketer. The following list, for example, includes some questions you won't be able to answer with your gut:

>> What were the most engaging updates within a specific period?

>> Do your fans prefer videos or photos?

>> How many times are you reaching fans each week?

>> What other websites sent traffic to your Facebook Page?

>> How many fans hid your Page stories on their News Feeds?

We're not saying you shouldn't listen to your intuition, because we both know that following your gut can give you great information. *Confirming* your intuition with statistics, however, is just smart business.

Additionally, with Insights you can identify trends within your Facebook Page — such as where most of your engaged users are located, their ages, and their genders — that you'd never see by scrolling down your Page. Understanding trends helps you adjust your content strategy based on what's really working instead of basing it on best guesses and random shots in the dark. Additionally, this information can help you target Facebook Ads much more effectively.

Using Facebook Insights

The next few sections show you how to access and use Facebook Insights.

REMEMBER

Keep in mind that only Page admins (all roles) can access Insights.

Understanding the two types of Likes your Facebook Page receives

Before you dive into analyzing how effective your Facebook Page efforts are, you need to understand that your Facebook Page can have two types of Likes:

>> **People liking your Page** by becoming fans or connections of your Page. Facebook users can *Like* (become a fan by clicking the Like button) and *Unlike* your Page.

>> **People liking your content** by clicking Like after reading a specific post or Page story that you publish. Facebook users can also stop a single story or all stories from your Page from appearing in their News Feeds.

Accessing Page Insights

You can access Facebook Page Insights in three ways:

>> **Directly on the Page:** To access Facebook Insights, log in and then click the Insights link on the admin navigation bar at the top of your Facebook Page (shown in Figure 10-1).

FIGURE 10-1:
Access Insights on the admin navigation bar of your Page.

>> **From the Facebook Insights web page:** If you manage more than one Page, you can bookmark the All Pages screen — where all your Pages are listed — for future reference (see Figure 10-2). Go to https://www.facebook.com/insights and select the Page you'd like to analyze.

FIGURE 10-2:
Access Insights
on the Facebook
website.

>> **From the Pages Manager app:** If you use the Facebook Pages Manager app
(for Android and iOS), you have access to a scaled-down version of Insights
right within your mobile device (see Figure 10-3).

FIGURE 10-3:
Access Insights
on your mobile
device with the
Facebook Pages
Manager app.

Exploring Facebook Page Insights

Facebook Insights provides critical data about activity on your Page, such as people liking your Page, and about activity related to your Page updates, such as when users comment on or like one of your Page updates.

Facebook Insights displays data on 15 tabs:

REMEMBER

The tabs you see may be different depending on the category you chose for your business Page.

>> **Overview:** An overview of how your Page is performing day to day.

>> **Promotions:** This report shows you how well each of your ads performed including boosted posts and other types.

>> **Followers:** A report that shows you the net followers of your page that week and where the follow occurred.

>> **Likes:** Reports about the Facebook users who like your Page.

>> **Reach:** A report about the Facebook users who see your Page content.

>> **Page Views:** This report provides details about how many times people viewed your Page.

>> **Page Previews:** A report that tells you the amount of times someone hovered over your Page or other content but didn't click.

>> **Actions on Page:** A report about the different things your followers did on your pages, for example, how many clicked an action button.

>> **Posts:** A report about how Facebook users are engaging with your Facebook Page updates.

>> **Events:** Details about the number of people you reached at your events.

>> **Videos:** A report about how your videos are performing.

>> **People:** Demographic reports on the people you reach, the people who like your page, and the people who engage with your content.

>> **Local:** This report tells you what happened in the area around your business.

>> **Shop:** If you have an online shop, you can see a report about your sales.

>> **Messages:** A report about the conversations you've had with your fans on Messenger.

In the next few sections, we discuss these tabs in greater detail.

Understanding the Overview Report

The Overview report is the first tab you see when you click Insights. This report shows the Actions on your Page, total Page Likes (fans) that you've acquired over the past week, how many people saw your posts or previewed them over the past week, how many people engaged with your updates over the previous seven days, and several other measures, detailed below. You can see stats about your most recent posts and promotions, as well as stats about other Pages you watch, which allows you to compare the performance of your Page and posts with similar Pages on Facebook.

The default date range for the Overview report is a seven-day period ending with the present date, as shown in Figure 10-4.

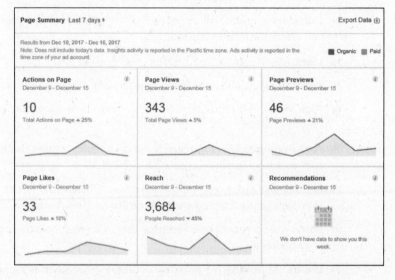

FIGURE 10-4:
The top of the Overview report.

The following list goes over the various parts of this report in detail:

>> **Actions on Page:** This section shows you the number of clicks you received from your contact info and call to action button.

>> **Page Views:** The Page Views section shows you how often people viewed your page when they were logged in and logged out.

>> **Page Previews:** This section shows you the number of times people previewed your Page content by hovering over your Page name or profile.

- » **Page Likes:** The Pages Likes section shows the total number of people who like your Facebook Page and the percentage increase or decrease of this number compared with the previous week. An increase is shown in green; a decrease is shown in red.

- » **Reach:** This section shows the number of people who saw any content associated with your Page (including any Ads or Sponsored Stories pointing to your Page) over the past seven days. The percentage to the right of this number is the increase (green) or decrease (red) over the past week.

- » **Recommendations:** The Recommendations section shows how many times your Page was recommended by others.

- » **Post Engagements:** This section details how people have interacted with your Posts, including likes and shares.

- » **Videos:** The videos section shows how many times that users viewed videos for more than three seconds.

- » **Page Followers:** This section details the actions of new followers.

- » **Recent Promotions:** The Recent Promotions section shows you how each of your current promotions has performed.

- » **Your 5 Most Recent Posts:** This section shows you statistics on your five most recently published updates. We discuss these stats in greater detail in the section titled "Evaluating Posts with the Posts Report," later in this chapter, but for now, just know that the data in this report covers reach and engagement for your five most recent posts.

- » **Pages to Watch:** This section shows you how the Pages you watch are performing. You can select any page to add to this list. Simply click the Add Pages button and search for the Facebook Page that you want to include in your "Pages to Watch."

Note: Each summary section within the Overview report allows you to click through to each full report to see more comprehensive data.

Although the Overview report lacks the data you need for a comprehensive analysis of your Facebook marketing, it provides a great deal of useful data. Checking it each day allows you to see quickly whether your audience and its level of engagement is growing or shrinking.

Promoting Your Message by Using the Promotions Report

The Promotions report shows you the performance of the ads you created. To view the Promotions report, click the Promotions tab within Facebook Insights (see Figure 10-5).

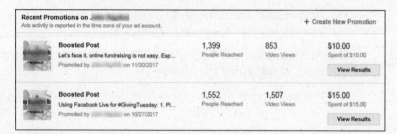

FIGURE 10-5: The Recent Promotions list.

The various parts of the Promotions report detailed in Figure 10-5 are as follows:

>> **People reached:** This part of the report shows the number of people who saw your ad.

>> **Videos viewed:** If you are using videos in your promotions, you see the number of people who watched them.

>> **Budget:** This shows you how much of the budget that you set was spent for this promotion.

If you click the View Results button to the right of each ad, a screen pops up, as shown in Figure 10-6.

On the View Results screen, in addition to the information you saw on the previous Promotions screen, you see the demographics that you targeted (gender, age, and location) and the length of the promotion. Also, you can choose to view your results when viewers looked at your promotion from their Desktop News Feed or Mobile News Feed.

Evaluating the performance of your ads helps you determine such things as

>> **Demographics:** How well you have targeted the specific audience who is interested in your content

FIGURE 10-6:
The View Results
pop-up screen for
a promotion.

>> **Desktop and Mobile Feed:** On which devices your audience is viewing your content

>> **Video:** Whether the videos you are displaying have content that resonates with your fans, and whether they like the video format

Understanding Your Followers with the Followers Report

The Followers report shows you the number of followers you obtained within a specific date range. You can select a custom range to analyze, or choose one of three predefined segments of time: one week, one month, or one quarter.

To view the Followers report, click the Followers tab within Facebook Insights (see Figure 10-7), which also shows you the Total Page Followers As of Today. This graph gives you a big-picture look at the followers you have gained over the most recent period. You can assess whether your current strategies are successful.

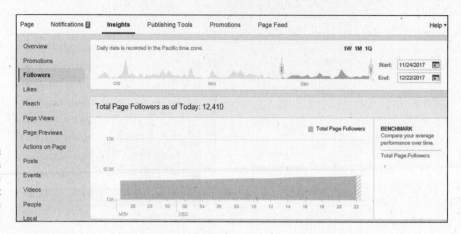

FIGURE 10-7:
The Followers report tells you specifics about the followers you are acquiring.

The Followers report also shows you:

TIP

>> **Net Followers:** Here you see a breakdown of the Unfollows, Organic followers, and Page followers so that you can evaluate such things as whether your paid advertising is effective and how may followers you are losing.

The term *Organic Follower* refers to someone who sees and likes your content whom you did not reach via an ad or other paid content.

Notice that for each of the measures for Followers, you can choose to compare your average stats over time using the Benchmark tool on the right side of the chart (refer to Figure 10-7). This tool helps you see how well you are growing your audience so that you can adjust your choices.

>> **Where Your Page Followers Happened:** This chart shows you how often your Page was followed and where it happened. The venues tracked are Uncategorized Desktop; On your Page; Page Suggestions; and Search.

Using the Likes Report for Smarter Fan Acquisition

The Likes report shows your fan growth, as well as the locations from which Facebook users have liked your Page (that is, from the News Feed or another source).

To view the Likes report (see Figure 10-8), click Insights on the navigation bar and then click the Likes tab.

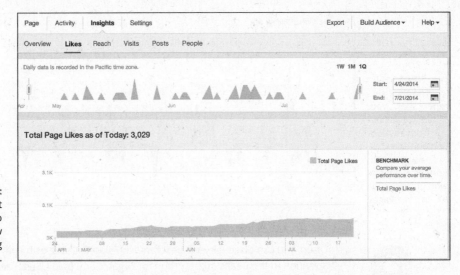

FIGURE 10-8:
The Likes report
allows you to
analyze how
you're acquiring
fans.

At the top of the Likes report, you can select the date range for the report. Select a custom range to analyze, or choose one of three predefined segments of time: one week, one month, or one quarter.

Make sure that you select a period before and after any changes you've made in your strategy. This way, you can see whether the strategy is working. If your campaign starts on July 1, for example, make sure that you include data from June in this report so that you can compare your fan-acquisition strategy in July with your fan-acquisition strategy in June.

TIP

The Followers, Page Views, Page Previews, Actions on Page, Shop tab, and Reach tab also include this feature for customizing the date range.

The following list gives you a deeper look at the various sections of the Likes report:

>> **Total Page Likes As of Today:** Immediately below the date-selection tool is the Total Page Likes As of Today section, which shows you the running total of accumulated likes over the periods you selected.

To the right, you can compare your average growth this period with your average growth in the previous period. You can see this benchmark data simply by clicking the Total Page Likes link below Benchmark.

>> **Net Likes: What Changed:** In addition to seeing fan growth, Facebook shows you how many people have unliked your Page, how many people have liked your Page from an ad, and the resulting net Likes, as shown in Figure 10-9.

You can also benchmark Unlikes, Organic Likes (acquired without ads), and Paid Likes (acquired with ads).

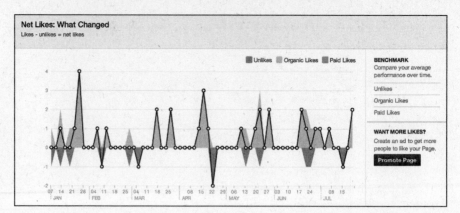

FIGURE 10-9:
The Net Likes report shows you fan acquisition from ads and organic Likes, as well as the number of people who unliked your Page.

TIP

Often, you can discover your best fan-acquisition strategies by paying attention to the peaks in this graph for organic and paid Likes. These spikes indicate successful strategies and tactics you've already employed to acquire Facebook fans. Repeat these strategies as long as they continue to work.

>> **Where Your Page Likes Came From:** The last section of the Likes report, Where Your Page Likes Came From, shows you the sources of your new fans. The graph shown in Figure 10-10 shows you the sources of the fans you acquired in the selected date range.

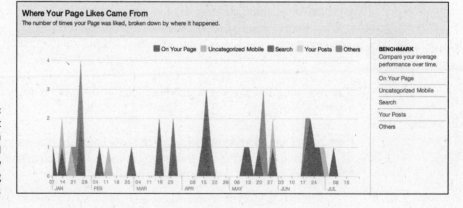

FIGURE 10-10:
The Likes report shows you fan acquisition (and attrition) and how people are liking your Page.

Reaching Fans with the Reach Report

Facebook defines *reach* as the number of people your post was displayed to. Facebook users see your Page posts in three ways:

>> **Organic reach:** When someone visits your Page or sees a post from your page in the News Feed, he's reaching your Page *organically*.

>> **Paid reach:** When someone sees your updates because you paid for her to see it, you're getting *paid* reach. Paid reach, of course, is generated with Facebook Ads and Boosted Posts.

>> **Viral reach:** When people like, comment, and share your Facebook Page updates, their friends see that activity in their News Feeds. This type of reach is called *viral* reach.

The Reach report within Facebook Insights shows you how many people you've reached with your Facebook marketing efforts.

To view the Reach report, click Insights and then click the Reach tab (see Figure 10-11). The Reach report shows the number of unique Facebook users who viewed your Page stories, Events related to your Page, and Ads promoting your Page or its posts.

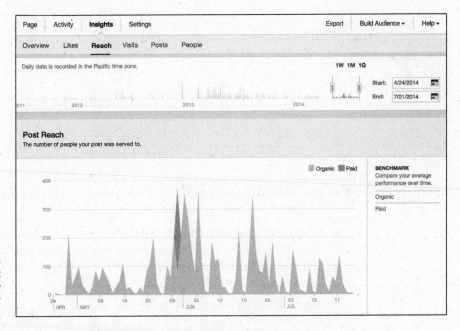

FIGURE 10-11:
The Reach report shows you how people see your Page updates.

As with the Likes report, you can adjust the date range at the top of the Reach report.

Again, *reach* means the number of individual people who saw your content. Four sections are available on the Reach tab:

>> **Post Reach:** This section shows you how many people saw your Page updates in News Feed, on your Page, or in a Facebook Ad. The graph shows two types of reach:

  ● **Organic:** Shows the number of unique Facebook users who saw content related to your Page in News Feeds, in the ticker, or on your Facebook Page.

  ● **Paid:** Shows the number of unique Facebook users who saw a Facebook Ad or Boosted Post for a Page Post.

  You can also view how your current reach compares with your reach during the previous period (see Figure 10-12), which is extremely valuable because it serves as an important alert to optimize or adjust your marketing strategy.

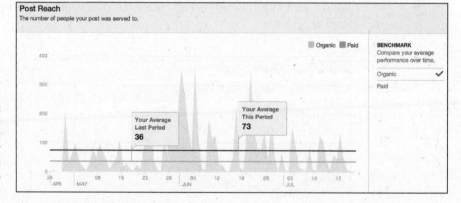

>> **Recommendations:** Displays the number of times your Page was recommended in posts and comments.

>> **Reactions, Comments, Shares, and More:** This section shows you the rate of reactions, comments, shares, and more over the selected period. As in the Post Reach section, you can compare your current performance with performance in the previous period.

  Benchmarking comments and shares can help you discover ways to create more viral reach through comments and shares.

>> **Reactions:** This section shows you how people reacted to your Page Posts.

>> **Hide, Report as Spam, and Unlikes:** All Facebook users can give Facebook feedback about the content they see in their News Feeds. This section shows you the rate of people hiding, reporting, marking your content as spam, and unliking your Page.

You can also *benchmark* (compare the current period with the previous period) Hides, Report as Spam, and Unlikes for your Page content.

>> **Total Reach:** This section is similar to the Post Reach section in that it compares paid and organic reach. But Total Reach includes any activity on your Page, including posts, posts by other people, mentions, check-ins, and any posts you promote with Facebook Ads.

TIP

Check-ins on Facebook are a way for users to tell their friends and the Page what their location is. When you check in on a Page, a list of nearby locations pops up, and you can choose the one that matches yours.

Delving into Engagement with the Page Views Report

The Page Views report shows you the total number of views your Page received broken out by your Page sections, demographics, and source within a specific date range. You can select a custom range to analyze, or choose one of three predefined segments of time: one week, one month, or one quarter.

To view the Page Views report, click the Page Views tab within Facebook Insights, as shown in Figure 10-13. In this figure, you see the total number of views your Page received and a By Section tab that contains additional data broken out by views of your Home page, Posts, Videos: Other, Jobs and Live Videos.

REMEMBER

Your categories may be different depending on the type of business you selected.

This report also shows the total number of people who viewed your Page and tabs, including by

>> **Section:** Which tab on your page they clicked

>> **Age and gender:** An aggregate of their age by gender

>> **Country:** Where they are located

>> **City:** What city they are in

>> **Device:** The device on which they viewed the page

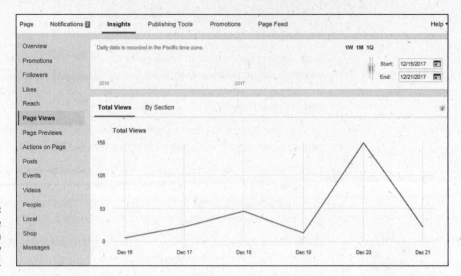

FIGURE 10-13:
The Total Page Views graph with the By Section tab.

This report also shows the Top Sources, which are the major platforms that sent traffic in the form of views. In this case, Facebook, Google.ca, and Google.com are the ones.

The Page Views information is extremely useful because you can not only see where your views occurred but also learn the demographic makeup of those fans and what venue they were sent from. This helps you determine whether your content is getting attention.

Using the Page Previews Report to Evaluate Interactions

The Page Previews report shows you the total number of Page Previews you received and the total number of people who previewed them within a specific date range. You can select a custom range to analyze, or choose one of three predefined segments of time: one week, one month, or one quarter.

To view the Page Previews report, click the Page Previews tab within Facebook Insights (see Figure 10-14). In this figure, you also see the total number of Page Previews.

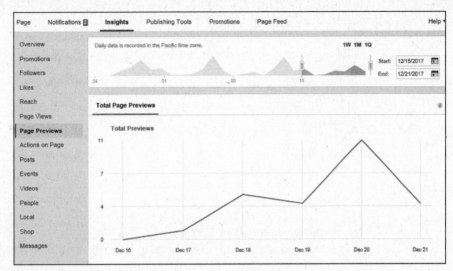

FIGURE 10-14:
The total number
of Page Previews
and the number
of people who
previewed them.

Next you see the total number of people who previewed the page and, using the By Age and Gender link next to it, you see the breakdown by age and gender.

Monitoring Actions on Page Report

The Actions on Page report is very robust and shows the total number of actions people take on your Page. You also see a breakdown of the kinds of actions people take on your Page within a specific date range. You can select a custom range to analyze, or choose one of three predefined segments of time: one week, one month, or one quarter.

To view the Actions on Page report, click the Actions on Page tab within Facebook Insights, as shown in Figure 10-15. In this figure, you also see the Total Actions on Page and tabs that contain additional data for people who clicked Get Directions, your website, your phone number, and the Action button.

>> **People Who Clicked Action Button:** This graph shows you what people did when they saw your call to action (CTA) button. This is important because it tells you whether the message on the Action button is compelling enough to click. These clicks are broken down by age and gender, by country, by city, and by devices. This helpful chart shows you the demographics of the people taking action to communicate with you. You also see whether they are using mobile or desktop devices.

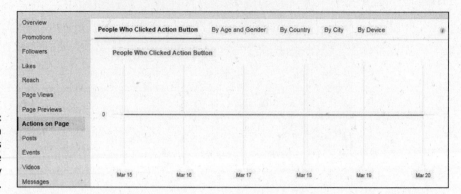

FIGURE 10-15:
The Actions on
Page report tells
you what people
did when they
visited your Page.

>> **People Who Clicked Get Directions:** These clicks (see Figure 10-16) tell you the number of people who wanted to get directions to your event or business. This indicates that they are very interested in learning more about you and possibly becoming a customer.

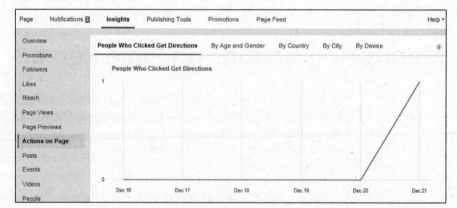

FIGURE 10-16:
The number of
people who
clicked Get
Directions.

>> **People Who Clicked Phone Number:** This shows you the number of people who wanted to know your phone number. Your assumption would be that if they wanted your phone number, they intended to communicate with you.

>> **People Who Clicked Website:** These click links tells you the number of people who were sufficiently interested in your content to visit your website.

Evaluating Posts with the Posts Report

The Posts report shows you the ways that Facebook users have engaged with each post, when your fans are online, and how each type of post (image, status update, and so on) performs.

To view the Posts report, click the Posts tab within Facebook Insights (see Figure 10-17).

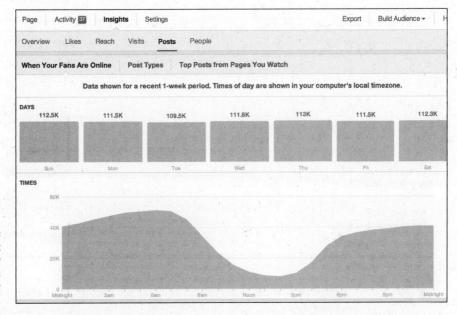

At the top of the Posts report are three tabs that contain additional data:

>> **When Your Fans Are Online:** This tab shows you how many Page fans are online for each day during the most recent week and for each hour of the day. You can view the hours for a specific day by mousing over that day of the week at the top of this tab. If you want to increase engagement with your fans, post your updates during the peak times shown on this tab.

>> **Post Types:** If you want to know how photos, videos, status updates, and links perform, you'll love this tab. It shows you average reach and engagement for photos, status updates, videos, and links (see Figure 10-18). Post types include link clicks, photo views, video plays, in addition to likes, comments, and shares.

TIP

If you want to increase engagement and reach for your Page updates, publish more types of posts that get the most likes, comments, and shares. Based on the data in Figure 10-18, for example, you should post more photos to get more likes, comments, and shares.

>> **Top Posts from Pages You Watch:** This tab shows you the top-performing posts on the Pages you watch. You can add Pages to your watch list simply by clicking the Add Pages button. If you want an easy way to source great content for your Facebook Page, add Pages from similar businesses that you admire.

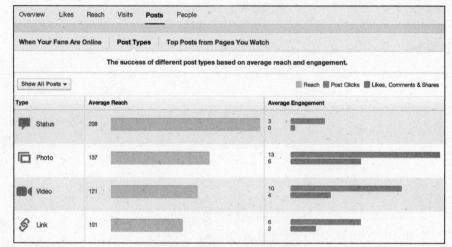

FIGURE 10-18:
The Post Types report shows you average reach and engagement for each type of post.

Scroll down in the Posts report and you see the All Posts Published section. This section contains a table that describes how Facebook users engaged with each of your Page updates published for a recent one–week period. You can sort the Reach and Engagement columns and select various data to be displayed in each column.

This report can help you understand what types of stories increase engagement. In other words, it shows you what your fans want to talk about, which is half the battle!

The columns in this report are as follows:

>> **Published:** The date that your post was published (your computer's local time zone).

>> **Post:** The content of the post. Clicking any of the links in this column allows you to see detailed analytics for the post in a small pop-up window.

>> **Type:** The type of post published (status update, video, photo, or link).

>> **Targeting:** How each post was targeted (location and language).

>> **Reach:** The number of people who saw your post. You can break this statistic into paid/organic reach and fans/nonfans by choosing the desired option from the Reach drop-down menu (refer to Figure 10-13).

>> **Engagement:** The ways Facebook users engaged with your content. You can view engagement in several ways including Post Clicks, Likes/Comments/Shares, Hide/Spam, and Engagement rate. *Engagement rate* is the percentage of people who commented on, liked, shared, or clicked a post. It's essentially a score for the quality of your post — the higher the percentage, the higher the quality.

>> **Promote:** You can choose to Boost a post from this column. A megaphone icon indicates that a post hasn't been promoted but can be. Read more about Boosted Posts in Chapter 11.

You can view more details for each post by clicking the link for the post in the Post column(see Figure 10-19). When you do so, you can see the number of Likes, comments, and shares for the post, and shares of the post.

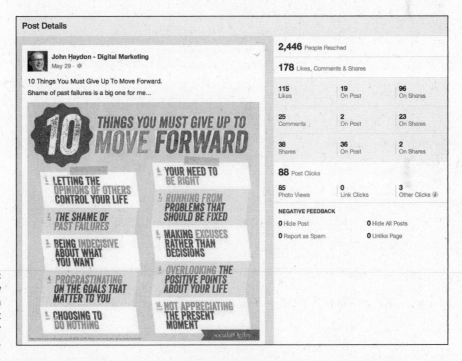

FIGURE 10-19: You can view details on engagement and reach for each post.

REMEMBER

By analyzing post-level data, you can understand what type of content your fans engage with most. You also begin to see what type of content gets the most comments, likes, and shares. In other words, the information in this report improves your ability to engage existing fans, attract new fans, and create more awareness of your business throughout Facebook.

Evaluating Events with the Events Report

The Events report shows you how well you drove people to get information about your events for the last 7 or 28 days.

To view the Events report, click the Events tab within Facebook Insights (see Figure 10-20). In this figure, you see both the number of people you reached and the number of views of your event page. There are tabs that contain additional data broken down by the following:

>> **Awareness:** The number of people who saw information about your event

>> **Engagement:** The number of people who responded in some way to your Event information

>> **Tickets:** How many people bought tickets to your event

>> **Audience:** The demographic makeup of the people who took some action — their age and gender

>> **Upcoming/Past:** A drop-down option (bottom of the page) that shows you information about your upcoming events and the ones you held in the past

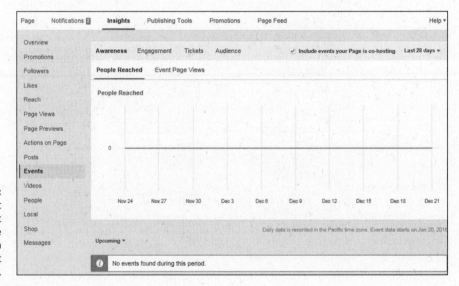

FIGURE 10-20: The Events report tells you about how people engaged with your event information.

Monitoring Engagement with the Video Insights Report

The Video Insights report shows you how well your videos are performing within certain date parameters. To view the Video Insights report, click the Videos tab within Facebook Insights (see Figure 10-21). The default date range for videos is 7 days. If you want to see a specific set of dates, you can click the pull-down to choose stats from Today, Yesterday, The Last 7 Days, the Last 14 Days, the Last 28 Days, This Month, This Quarter, or Custom.

For your video to count as a video view, Facebook requires that the user watches for three seconds or more.

Also in Figure 10-21, within Performance, you see the following:

>> **Minutes viewed:** This shows you the aggregate number of minutes viewed, which includes replays and views less than three minutes long. To count as a video view, Facebook requires that the user watches for three seconds or more. Under the number of minutes, you see the percent change from the previous seven days (or the date range you chose).

>> **Video Views:** Shows the number of times videos were watched for three seconds or more. Under the number of videos viewed, you see the percentage change from the previous seven days (or the date range you chose). From a drop-down menu that appears when you click Video Views, you can also view whether the video was organic or paid.

Top videos show you a list of your top-performing videos (see Figure 10-22). They are broken down by

>> **Video:** The video you choose from the displayed list

>> **Published:** The time and date that your video was published

>> **Minutes Viewed:** The total minutes viewed, including both the replays and the views that lasted less than three seconds

>> **Video Views:** The total number of views over three seconds

Click drop-down menu for date range options

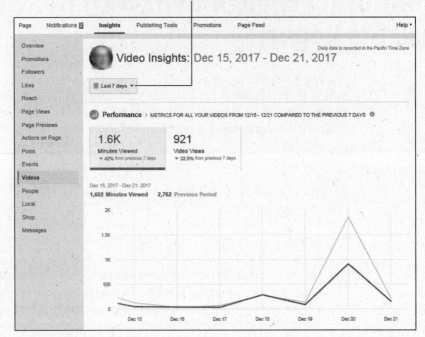

FIGURE 10-21:
The Video
Performance
report shows you
the aggregate
number of
minutes viewed
and the number
of videos viewed.

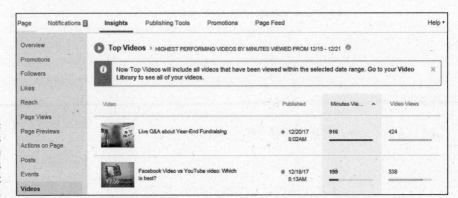

FIGURE 10-22:
The Top Videos
report shows you
which videos
received the most
engagement.

Viewing Demographics with the People Report

The People reports contains demographic, location, and language information for Facebook users who like your Page, see your content, engage with your posts, and check in to your business (see Figure 10-23).

To view demographic information, click one of the four tabs:

» **Your Fans:** Demographic information about people who like your Page

» **Your Followers:** Demographic details about those who follow your Page

» **People Reached:** Demographic information about people who see your Page updates

» **People Engaged:** Demographic information about people who like, comment, share, or click your updates

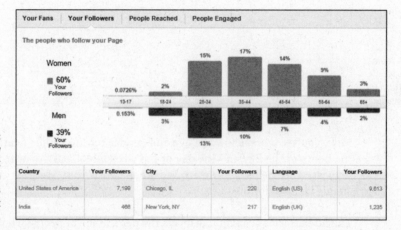

FIGURE 10-23:
You can view demographic information on Facebook users who talk about your Page.

Reviewing the Local Report to Learn about Activity Nearby

The Local report shows you the activity going on around your business location. You can see peak hours of action, demographic info, and Ad performance as it relates to people who are near your physical location.

To view the Local report, click the Local tab within Facebook Insights (see Figure 10-24). In this figure, you see a visual of your business location. You can choose to view data within a specific date range (One Week, One Month, and One Quarter) and Region. (All the data is anonymous, so you're not invading anyone's privacy.)

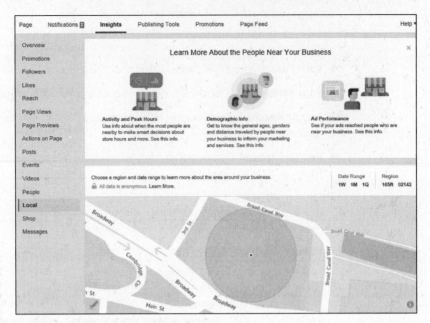

FIGURE 10-24:
The Local report shows you people around your business location.

Next, you see a breakdown of age and gender for the people nearby. You also see the hours of the day and the day of the week when activity near your location is highest. This helps you determine what hours your store or service business should be open for business.

The Ad performance graph displays the percentage of people who saw your ad on Facebook who were within 165 feet of your business in relation to your ad spending. This shows you which days were high-performing days.

The People Nearby graph (see Figure 10-25) shows you data concerning people within 165 feet of your location hourly (for a 24-hour period), weekly (days of the week for one week), overall (trend data that shows you people nearby in relation to people nearby who saw your ads) and by check-ins (the number of people who checked into your business).

The Demographics graph, shown in Figure 10-26, shows you people within 165 feet of your business within the last month. You can display this information in a bar graph or line graph format depending on which display button you choose. The data is broken out by

>> **Age:** Gives the percentage of each age range of people nearby

>> **Gender:** Gives the percentage of each gender of people nearby

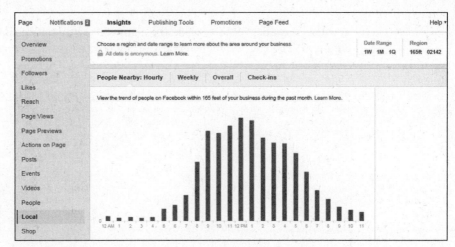

FIGURE 10-25: The People Nearby graph shows you trend data for several time and date ranges.

>> **Home Locations:** Shows people who live within 165 feet of your business, or people who travel from 165 feet to get to your business

>> **Age and Gender:** Shows the aggregate of age and gender of people nearby

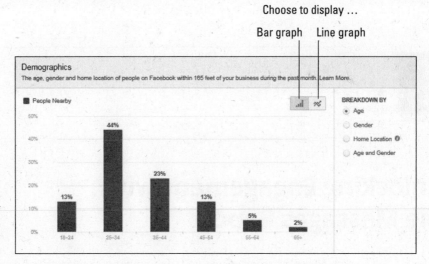

FIGURE 10-26: Demographics of people within 165 feet of your location.

Using the Shop Report to Evaluate Sales

The Shop report displays an overview of views, purchases, and sales within a specific date range. You can select a custom range to analyze, or choose one of three predefined segments of time: One Day, One Week, One Month, or One Quarter.

To view the Shop report, click the Shop tab within Facebook Insights (see Figure 10-27). You see the overview of Shop activity and change in percentage from the previous week.

Next you see the Shop activity broken down by views and purchases, followed by All Products in This Shop (see Figure 10-28.)

Unlocking Engagement with the Messages Report

The Messages report shows you the number of conversations your Page had with fans on Messenger for date ranges that include Today, Yesterday, the Last 7 Days, the Last 28 Days, or the Last 180 Days.

To view the Messages report, click the Messages tab within Facebook Insights (see Figure 10-29). The Messages report data is broken down by the following:

>> **Total conversations:** This shows you the number of times you had a conversation with a person on Messenger and the percentage change over the date range chosen.

>> **Your responsiveness:** This is an important metric. It shows you the percentage of messages you answered and the average response time. It also shows you the percentage change over the date range chosen. You can gauge your ability to serve customers with this data.

>> **Deleted conversations:** This shows you how many conversations people had with your Page that they deleted, as well as the percentage change over the date range chosen.

>> **Marked as spam:** This shows you both the number of conversations and percentage that was considered spam.

>> **Blocked conversation:** This shows you both the number of conversations and percentage that were blocked.

TIP

Obviously, if you don't have Messenger set up, the report will show zero conversations.

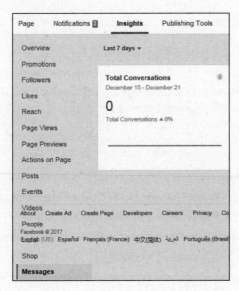

FIGURE 10-29:
The Messages
report.

Exporting Insights Data

Facebook displays a limited amount of data in the native Facebook Insights tool, which we cover in the section "Exploring Facebook Page Insights," earlier in this chapter. You can obtain additional data by exporting Insights data into a spreadsheet application, such as Microsoft Excel.

You can export either Page-level, post-level, or video data from Page Insights simply by choosing Insights ⇨ Overview and then clicking the Export button in the top-right corner of the Overview tab. After clicking Export, a pop-up window appears (see Figure 10-30).

FIGURE 10-30:
The Facebook Export Insights pop-up window.

From the Export pop-up window, select from the following:

>> **Data Type:** Page-level, post-level, or video. (You can export only 500 posts at one time.) For example, the types of information that you can get from exported Page-level data include the number of people each day who saw your Page content and the number of people each day who engaged with your Page.

>> **Date Range:** The amount of data you export has presets including yesterday, this month, and this quarter (see Figure 10-31). If you are doing comparisons, make sure to export enough data to make them meaningful.

>> **File Format:** The choice of either the native Excel format (.xls) or comma-separated value (.csv) will allow you to view the report in Excel.

>> **Layout:** Choose whether you want to create a custom report or export all the available data.

When you're ready, click the Export Data button, and the file will download to your device.

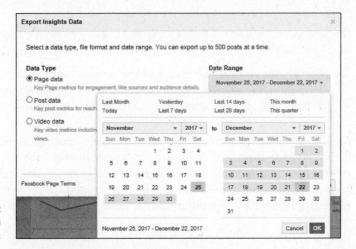

FIGURE 10-31:
Selecting a data range to export.

Using Third-Party Analytics

Although Facebook Insights is an invaluable tool for measuring your Page activity, sometimes you want to have additional information at your disposal, such as the keywords users entered to find your Page or the average amount of time people stay on your site.

Facebook made its Page Insights data available to third-party solutions through its Open API (Application Programming Interface). Several companies have already integrated this data into their existing services. Leading analytics companies such as Webtrends and IBM Digital Analytics have begun to roll out new offerings with Facebook data alongside their existing website analytics. The following list includes several such companies:

>> **Webtrends:** You can use this detailed analytics package via self-installation or the Webtrends services team. This service is paid, and you must contact Webtrends for package pricing based on your needs. You can find more info on this product at http://webtrends.com/solutions/campaign-optimization/facebook-campaign.

>> **Post Planner:** In addition to various Facebook Page publishing features, this tool includes a simple yet powerful analytics module that allows you to sort updates by comment, like, and engagement rate. For more information, see www.postplanner.com.

>> **Hootsuite:** This social media management tool allows users to schedule posts on a variety of social media platforms (Facebook, Twitter, LinkedIn, and so on). This tool also includes a reporting module that allows you to select what Facebook Page Insights data you want to track. These reports are perfect for

managers because the data is presented in a way that's easy to understand. You can find more info about this tool at https://hootsuite.com.

>> **AgoraPulse:** This suite of Facebook Page management tools allows you to export an easy-to-read Microsoft PowerPoint presentation about your Page Insights. Find out more at www.agorapulse.com.

REMEMBER

Keep in mind that these companies won't be able to give you more data about your Facebook Page than what you already access through the Facebook Insights reports and the data export. What they will give you are different ways of presenting that data (graphs, charts, and so on), as well as additional resources for analyzing the data (consulting, educational webinars, and so on).

4

Marketing beyond the Facebook Page

Chapter **11**

Using Facebook Advertising to Promote Your Business

With more than 2 billion Facebook users worldwide, Facebook Ads can reach an audience 18 times bigger than a Super Bowl's television audience. If you're not looking to go global (which is most likely the case), you can target Facebook Ads to specific demographics (location, gender, relationship status, education, brand preferences, musical tastes, and so on). You can even target specific segments within your customer base!

Facebook's ad platform makes it easy to create your ad, select your target audience, set your budget, set a start and end date, and measure results. Ads can be purchased based on cost per impression (CPM) or cost per click (CPC). And unlike Google Ads, Facebook Ads allow advertisers to leverage Facebook's *social graph* — a massive collection of every Page, group, app, and interest liked by Facebook fans.

Facebook also lets advertisers target customers, segments of email subscribers, and even people who visit specific pages on their websites.

In this chapter, we show you how to use Facebook Ads to drive traffic to your website, increase your Facebook Page fan base, and increase engagement on your Page posts. We introduce you to the available advertising options and how to use them. You can find tips on determining your advertising budget, targeting your audience, writing ad copy, uploading an effective image, and designing an ad. Finally, you get help creating your landing-page strategy and evaluate your ad's effectiveness in fulfilling your marketing goals.

Introducing Facebook Ads

According to Facebook, the social network giant had 1.74 billion mobile monthly active users as of February 2017. These consumers spend more time using Facebook than any other social network, Google, or Yahoo!. This makes sense when you remember that Facebook has become the most popular way for people to connect with their friends.

Facebook Ads also allows you to form a sustained relationship with potential customers. By linking the ads to your Facebook Page, you can keep the user engaged within the Facebook environment.

To help advertisers, Facebook provides an overview of how to use Facebook Ads, a Facebook Ad guide, and a series of case studies at https://www.facebook.com/business/products/ads (see Figure 11-1).

Consider AARP, which offers a great example of using Facebook Ads to build sustained relationships. AARP's goal with Facebook Ads was to increase awareness of its brand and offerings. The organization wanted to change how people perceive AARP as a brand. Its core audience is people between 45 and 64 years old with interests including travel, finance, and sports. AARP used Facebook Ads to deliver compelling photo and video ads to 11.2 million Americans ages 45 to 64, leading to a double-digit increase in brand relevance among its core audience.

The content highlighted people doing inspirational things.

According to Nielsen, 14 percent of 45- to 64-year-old Americans saw AARP's ads in their News Feeds. Nielsen also reported a 29 percent increase in this group's desire to find out more about AARP and a 24 percent increase in willingness to recommend AARP to a friend. Pretty amazing results! (See Figure 11-2.)

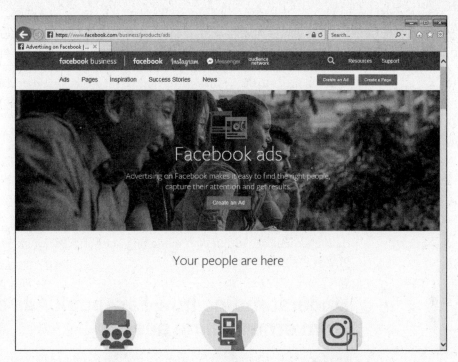

FIGURE 11-1:
Facebook Advertising's home page with resources for advertisers.

FIGURE 11-2:
AARP used Facebook Ads to increase awareness and brand loyalty among people ages 45 to 64.

Using Facebook Ads as part of your overall marketing mix

The worst possible way to use Facebook Ads is to use them as the sole tactic within your marketing strategy. It may be tempting to think that because you're paying for ads, you'll automatically get a good return. But lacking a plan that incorporates all of your marketing channels usually creates less-than-satisfactory results.

In other words, you have to include other channels — such as email marketing, in-store promotions, and radio ads — in your marketing strategy. The more you combine all channels in a cohesive ad strategy, the more results you'll get from each channel. All this ties back to having a clear objective and a clear understanding of your audience, which we talk about in Chapter 3. An email marketing campaign to promote your Facebook Page, for example, will be more effective if it's combined with a Facebook Ad for your Page that's geographically targeted to where most of your email subscribers are located. A Facebook user who isn't a Page connection (fan) but is on your email list will be more likely (pun intended) than someone who isn't a newsletter subscriber to like your Page because she gets twice the exposure to your campaign.

You've heard the phrase "A rising tide lifts all boats"? Well, integration is the tide that lifts each boat within your marketing arsenal. A Facebook Ad is just one type of boat in the harbor.

Understanding how Facebook Ads differ from other online ads

Facebook Ads leverage relationships and connections between friends, which makes Facebook Ads different from almost every other type of Internet ads. Banner ads target the assumed audience of a specific website. SportsIllustrated.com has banner ads that target mostly men who like sports, for example, and Google Ads target people based on what people search for online. The great thing about Google Ads is that they target people who are looking for something they need. But those ads can't target people before they express that desire by searching for it on Google.

Facebook Ads, however, target people based on their precise interests and also on people's connections to your business. A hair salon, for example, can target an ad to the Facebook friends who liked that salon's Facebook Page. This second feature — connections — is what sets Facebook Ads apart from any other kind of ad. Facebook calls this extremely complex network of connections the *social graph*.

Understanding Facebook's targeting options

Targeting your audience is as important as the ad itself, and Facebook allows you to specifically target only the audience you desire. To understand exactly whom you should target, start developing personas, or personality characteristics, to represent your target audience. *Personas* are simply imaginary prospects or clients with entire back stories, quirks, challenges, and needs for what you offer. The real value of personas is in how you imagine each of them reacting to your products or services. Well-developed personas can make it easier to target your ads on Facebook effectively. Take Jane as an example. She's a 30-year-old professional who works in downtown Boston. She doesn't have a car because she wants to lower her carbon footprint, but she loves meeting up with friends on Cape Cod to go surfboarding. She's smart and very selective about what she shares online. Jane would be a persona for Zipcar, Zappos, and REI because these companies cater to customers who are environmentally conscious. For more on personas, see Chapter 2.

You can also use Facebook Graph search to research the interests and Pages liked by your Facebook fans. Entering the phrase *Pages liked by women who like [name of your page]* in Facebook's search box gives you a list of the most popular Pages with your female Facebook fans (see Figure 11-3).

FIGURE 11-3:
Facebook Graph allows you to research interests and Pages liked by your Facebook fans.

Here are some ways that you can target ads in Facebook:

>> **Targeting by location:** Facebook allows for precise location targeting based in part on your profile data and the IP address of the computer that users log in with or their precise country, state/province, city, or postal code. Most cities in the United States, Canada, and the United Kingdom allow you to expand the targeting to surrounding areas of 10, 25, and 50 miles if you target specific cities.

>> **Targeting by interests:** Facebook lets you define your target audience by using terms people include in their Facebook profiles. These terms may be drawn from people's interests, activities, education, and job titles; Pages they like; or groups to which they belong.

>> **Targeting by connections:** You can target people who are already connected to your Facebook Page or people who aren't already connected to your Page so that your existing fans aren't shown your ad. You can also target the friends of people who are already connected to your Page, which is a powerful feature because friends of fans are more likely to become fans themselves. (Birds of a feather flock together.)

>> **Targeting by email:** You can target specific people within an email list — for example, customers who made a purchase in the past year. People on your email list are interested in you by definition. Being on your email list is a very conspicuous expression of their interest in your product or service.

>> **Targeting by website visits:** You can target people who visited a specific page on your website, such as a page promoting a product or service. As you can imagine, this feature can be highly effective. Many visitors won't purchase a product right away, but a Facebook Ad reminding them to return to your page often encourages them to complete the purchase.

TIP

To maximize the total reach of your campaign, start by casting a wide net (broad, general targeting). Then finely tune the targeting specifications until you reach an optimum balance between targeting specifics and the number of people targeted.

Setting your budget

Facebook employs a bidding structure for its advertising inventory based on supply and demand. If there's greater demand to reach a specific demographic, the ad typically has higher bids.

For most ads, you pay for *impressions* — that is, the number of people who see your ad. Facebook optimizes your ad so that it's shown to the people who are most likely to help you reach your goal. If you want more people to like your Page, for example, your ad will be shown to the people who are most likely to become fans of your Page.

Facebook has advanced options that provide a suggested bid for you based on what other ads that reach this demographic historically cost. For these options, Facebook offers two types of pricing:

>> **Cost per click (CPC):** With CPC, you pay each time a user clicks your ad. If your goal is to drive traffic to a specific Page, paying based on CPC is probably the best performer for you. Ask yourself how much you're willing to pay per click.

>> **Cost per impression (CPM):** With CPM, you pay based on how many users see your ad. If your objective is to get as many people within your target demographic to see the ad but not necessarily click through, ads based on a CPM basis may be your best option. Ask yourself how much you're willing to pay per 1,000 impressions.

Facebook also provides two specific payment choices under the following conditions:

>> **Cost per action (CPA):** With CPA, you pay only if a specific action is taken if someone sees your ad. You can employ this method only if you define your ad result at the time of purchase.

>> **Cost per like (CPL):** With CPL, you pay only if someone likes your page after clicking your ad. You have to choose Page Likes as your ad result. You can monitor your campaign to see whether the ad performs at your given bid. You can also set a daily maximum budget. (For details, see "Managing and Measuring Your Ad Campaigns with Ads Manager," later in this chapter.)

TIP

Having clear goals for your ad allows you to more effectively select targeting criteria and whether to pay for CPM, CPC, CPA, or CPL.

Creating Winning Ads

Before we go into detail about how to create an ad on Facebook, we want to tell you how to create compelling ads that drive clicks. In the following sections, we discuss ways to write effective ad copy and choose the optimal image. We also discuss the importance of knowing your audience and delivering incentives that are right for them. Finally, it's important to know the restrictions that govern Facebook Ads so that you create ads that are more likely to get approved.

Writing effective copy

Each Facebook format has its own limits and specs, but be assured that you can't waste a whole lot of words. Be direct, straightforward, and honest about your objective. Keep in mind that Facebook is also about building trust, and your copy must show openness and willingness to share and connect with your audience. Also note that when you use Sponsored Stories, your ad copy is provided by the update.

TIP

Facebook Ads with specific calls to action deliver higher rates of user engagement. The Facebook Ad in Figure 11-4 tells the user exactly what she's expected to do.

Following are four guidelines on Facebook Ad copy:

>> **Pose a question in your headline or in the body of the ad.** Don't be afraid to use a question mark where appropriate.

>> **Reference your target audience.** By relating to your audience, you're more likely to grab their attention. Consider giving shout-outs such as "Hey, housewives . . ."

>> **Be direct.** Tell your target audience explicitly what you want them to do, such as "Click here to receive your free T-shirt."

>> **Use influencers' testimonials.** To establish credibility, consider highlighting an endorsement, such as "Voted South Jersey's best pizza."

TIP

When you use keywords of interest to target an ad campaign, it's always a good idea to include those keywords in the ad copy.

FIGURE 11-4:
This ad uses a specific call to action to increase click-through rates.

Choosing the right visuals

A picture is worth a thousand words. This is why ads accompanied by images or videos overwhelmingly perform better than text-only ads. Facebook provides five different visual formats for you to choose from when creating your ads. We discuss them in the section "Creating a Facebook Ad," later in this chapter.

However, a good rule is to use images that are easily recognizable, aren't too intricate in detail, and feature bright colors without the use of the blue that's so strongly identified with the Facebook logo and navigational color scheme.

Here are four tips for selecting the right visuals to get your Facebook Ad noticed:

>> **If your visual includes people, they need to reflect the demographic you're targeting.** People like to see people who look like them.

>> **Test different images with the same copy.** When you test a single factor, such as the ad's image, you can easily identify the stronger-performing image.

>> **An amateur video or photo style sometimes works better than stock photography.** A more personalized approach can help you stand out in the crowd. (See Figure 11-5.)

FIGURE 11-5:
The image is one of the most important elements in your ad.

>> **Make your image stand out with a decorative border.** Consider adding a branding element around the image or making the ad current. (During the holiday season, for example, add a decorative holiday border.)

Simplifying your offer

Because you have only a small amount of space to communicate your offer via your Facebook Ad, don't waste words or overcomplicate things. Your call to action needs to be direct, clear, and easy to follow. Cleverness and wit aren't as effective as the simplest words possible.

Devising a Landing-Page Strategy for Your Ads

If you're familiar with online marketing, you understand the importance of making a good first impression with your ad link. Your *landing page* (as it's known in advertising) is the page that opens when users click your ad. It can be an internal Facebook Page or an external website. All engagement begins on the landing page.

Successful landing pages provide an easy path to *conversion,* or realizing your goal. A conversion can include capturing user data via an input form, driving membership for your Page, getting people to sign a petition, or simply making a sale. Regardless of your objective, if your landing page doesn't deliver the desired result, your campaign is worthless.

Facebook allows you to create ads that link to an internal Facebook location or an external website (URL). The following sections explain how to choose a URL destination for your ad.

Landing on a Facebook location

As a best practice when running a Facebook Ad campaign, link your ads to an internal Facebook location as opposed to an external website. For internal Facebook Ads, you can link to a Facebook Page, a Facebook Page update, an app Page, or an event Page.

If you're advertising a Facebook Page, you can send users to a customized landing tab within your Page. Figure 11-6 shows the Post Planner landing page, which features a live training session.

FIGURE 11-6:
The landing page
for Post Planner.

TIP

The bottom line is to bring visitors to your Facebook Page, where they're just one click away from becoming fans. Because you have access to your fans' profiling data, your fan base can become an extremely valuable marketing asset.

Chapter 6 goes into more detail about creating custom tabs. For now, keep these three things in mind to increase conversions on your custom tab:

>> **Include only one call to action.** Present users too many options, and they're less likely to take the action you want them to take. If you want them to join an email list, don't also ask them to follow you on Twitter.

>> **Use as few words as possible.** Most of the time, you should be able to cut your copy by 50 percent, which is easy to do when you think about what users need to know versus information that's peripheral to that action. If users are entering their email addresses as a way to join a contest, for example, email them later with the less-important details about that contest.

>> **Measure conversions.** If you're focusing on acquiring emails on your custom tab, make sure that you create a unique web form for the tab. Most quality email marketing services allow you to track how many people are joining a list via each web form (see Figure 11-7).

Name	Type	Displays	Submissions	S/D	Unique Displays	S/UD
Capture on Blog	inline	1343	227	16.9%	1242	18.3%
Facebook Pages	inline	643	315	49.0%	613	51.4%

Landing on a website

Facebook allows you to refer your ad visitors to an external web address (URL), provided that it adheres to the company's advertising policies and guidelines at https://www.facebook.com/policies/ads/.

Linking to an outside website offers you greater control of your landing page's content, technology, and design. You may already have a finely tuned landing page that you prefer to drive ad traffic to, regardless of where the traffic originated, and you can employ much more sophisticated web analytics on your site that are presently available on Facebook.

Because ads can be purchased on a CPC basis, you can opt to pay only when a user clicks through to your Page, regardless of whether it's an internal Facebook Page or a page on an outside website.

Making sure that your website is responsive

On a *responsive* website, the content (pages, text, videos, and photos) automatically resizes in response to the particular device that a viewer is using. Any website that you can easily view on both a mobile device and a web browser is responsive.

These days, having a responsive design is more important than ever, and it will continue to be important as an increasing percentage of Facebook users access the site on their mobile devices. As of February 2017, 1.74 billion Facebook users were accessing the site from a mobile device each month according to Facebook (https://s21.q4cdn.com/399680738/files/doc_presentations/FB-Q316-Earnings-Slides.pdf). If a user clicks over to your website and it isn't responsive, he will be more likely to leave your website instead of buying your product or service or joining your email list.

Creating a Facebook Ad

The process of creating Facebook Ads can seem daunting, but Facebook walks you through a process of steps that we detail in turn.

Take the following first steps to begin creating a Facebook Ad:

1. **Go to the Facebook Ads home page at** https://www.facebook.com/advertising.

2. **Click the blue Create an Ad button in the top-right corner.**

   The Ads Manager page appears, displaying the steps required to create an ad, as shown in Figure 11-8.

TIP

   You can click a step in the list to move to that section if you're not following the steps in order.

Here's an overview of the sections:

>> **Campaign:** In this section, you choose your objective from 11 different choices.

>> **Ad Set:** Here, you set up the parameters of your ad, which includes:

   ● Naming your ad set

   ● Determining where you want your traffic to go

- Creating your offer

- Targeting your audience

- Selecting your placement

- Setting your budget and schedule

>> **Ad:** In this section, you design and finalize your ad by doing the following:

- Choosing your identity (Page) to display

- Determining your format

- Selecting your media

- Adding your links

Step 1: Developing your campaign

The first step in creating a Facebook Ad is to select your objective. Facebook provides 11 objectives to choose from (see Figure 11-8).

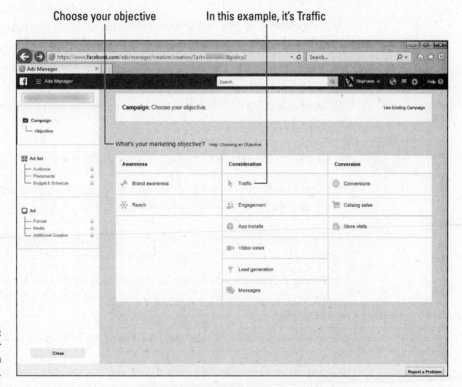

FIGURE 11-8: Choosing your campaign objective.

TIP

The objectives line up with three of the categories we discuss in Chapter 2, in the section about the marketing funnel. They are Awareness, Consideration, and Conversion.

If you want to promote awareness, you have the following choices for objectives:

>> **Brand awareness:** Helps people recognize your brand

>> **Reach:** Shows your ad to the greatest amount of prospective fans

If you want people to put your business under consideration as their choice to buy or support, you can choose one of these:

>> **Traffic:** Drives people to visit a venue of your choice; for example, it can send them to your website.

>> **Engagement:** Helps more people to become aware of you and engage with your Page. For example, this could encourage people to comment or like your Page.

>> **App Installs:** Helps you get more people to install your app on their mobile devices.

>> **Video views:** Helps you get more views for a video that you post on your Page.

>> **Lead generation:** Helps you get information about people who want to know more about what you do.

>> **Messages:** Prompts people to engage in Messenger with your business to get more information or answer questions.

TIP

See Chapter 16 for details about how to use Facebook Messenger.

If you want to effect a conversion that causes people to buy your product or service, you can choose the following objectives:

>> **Conversions:** Helps encourage specific actions on your website, such as making a purchase or joining your email newsletter.

>> **Product catalog sales:** Applicable if you have created a catalog from which people can view products. The catalog will display these products to encourage sales.

>> **Store visits:** Encourages people who are nearby to visit your location.

To select an objective, simply click one of the 11 objectives. For this example, we chose Traffic.

When you click the Traffic objective, Facebook displays content at the bottom of the page, as shown in Figure 11-9.

To set up the Traffic objective, follow these steps:

TIP

1. **Select Create a Split Test to create a split test.**

A split test allows you to create different versions of your ad variables, such as images or target audience, and test them against each other to see which is more effective.

2. **Input the name of the campaign.**

3. **Click the Continue button.**

If you're setting up a new account, the Continue button may say Set Up Ad Account.

FIGURE 11-9:
Creating and naming your Traffic campaign.

Step 2: Creating your ad set

An ad set is a Facebook Ad feature that allows you to organize your ads more easily. After you have named your campaign, you need to input information to create an ad set. Campaigns and ad sets are like folders, and the largest folder is a *campaign*, which contains ad sets. Each ad set contains several Facebook Ads.

To the right of the Facebook Ad Set, you see an Audience Size estimator that represents the approximate number of people who will be exposed to your ad (see Figure 11-10.)

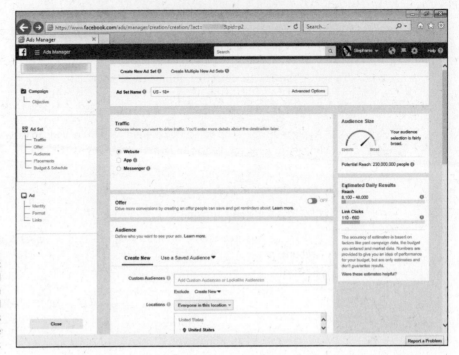

FIGURE 11-10:
The estimated reach in Facebook's Ad tool provides real-time numbers.

The audience size shown changes as you add or remove targeting factors in the following steps as you create your ad set.

To create an ad set, follow these steps:

TIP

1. **Input your name in the Ad Set Name field.**

   Name your ad set so that it describes the audience, campaign, or type of ads contained within the ad set. You could name an ad set Moms in Boston, for example, to differentiate it from an ad set targeting moms in New York City.

2. **Choose where you want your traffic to go in the Traffic section.**

   Decide where to send the traffic generated from this ad. Your choices are your website, an app, or Messenger. Click one of these options. You can define this destination more fully later in the process, but you should be clear about your intention now. Each choice has its own distinct characteristics.

3. **Set up the details for your offer in the Offer section.**

   You are prompted to create an offer only if you have chosen one of three objectives: Traffic, Conversions, or Store Visits. If you want to create an offer, click the Off button to On. When you click it to On, a screen pops up that displays your profile name. To proceed, click the Create the Offer button. A screen pops up that displays what your offer will look like and walks you through the process.

Next, you need to target your audience by selecting the targeting criteria (see Figure 11-11).

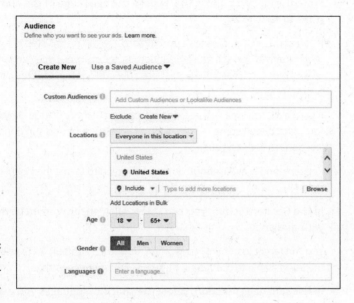

FIGURE 11-11: Targeting your audience for your ad campaign.

TIP

Think of targeting in terms of a bull's-eye: The closer you get to the center, the narrower the circles are; the farther out you go, the wider the circles are. (For more information on targeting your ad, see "Understanding Facebook's targeting options," earlier in this chapter.)

4. **In the Audiences field, choose Create New.**

You are presented with two options.

5. **Select Custom Audiences or Use a Saved Audience.**

If you choose Create New to create a new audience, you can choose one of the two default options, Target Ads to People Who Know Your Business or Reach New People on Facebook Who Are Similar to Your Most Valuable Audiences, by clicking the drop-down link under the Create New text box. If you want to create a saved audience, click that link and choose one of the options offered. To learn more about custom audiences, see Chapter 2.

6. **In the Locations field, choose an option from the drop-down menu.**

The menu options are Everyone in This Location; People Who Live in This Location; People Recently in This Location; and People Traveling in This Location. If you have a physical location, choosing a Location option lets you hone in on those who live near your location. Next, you can choose among nearly 100 countries to target, and each ad can reach up to 25 countries. You can also drill down to the state or province, or to the city level. For many cities, you can even specify up to 10, 25, or 50 miles surrounding the city.

7. **From the Age drop-down list, choose the age range of the audience you want to see the ad.**

   If you know your audience's approximate age range, this step is a great way to target them. If you sell retirement homes, for example, you can target people 55 and older. To reach the widest possible audience, accept the default setting: Any.

REMEMBER

   If you reach too small an audience, your ad may not generate any click-throughs. Widen some factors, such as age range, or add surrounding locations to your targeting.

   Keep in mind that Facebook doesn't allow you to target members younger than 13.

8. **In the Gender section, you can select All, Men, or Women as the gender of your audience.**

   You can target just men, just women, or both. By default, All is selected, making the ad available to the widest number of members possible.

9. **In the Languages section, select the specific languages you want to target.**

10. **In the Detailed Targeting section, you see Include People Who Match at Least One of the Following. Click Browse to see several options, as shown in Figure 11-12.**

FIGURE 11-12: Facebook allows you to target your ad to various broad categories and then drill down to specific options.

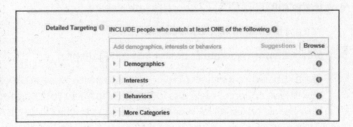

To see the choices within each category, click the left arrow next to the name. From there, you can click again to drill down to choose specific options. They include the following:

- **Demographics:** This category includes general demographics such as Education, Income, Home, and more.

- **Interests:** Refers to Pages people have liked hobbies, activities, and so on.

- **Behaviors:** You can target people based on their consumer behavior, the mobile devices they use, and other behavior collected by companies that Facebook partners with.

- **More Categories:** These categories include your Facebook Partners and others with whom you do business.

- **Exclude People Who Match at Least One of the Following Categories:** Click the Exclude People link and choose the Browse button if you want to see categories of people whom you do not want to see your ad.

- **Expand Interests When It May Increase Link Clicks at Lower Cost Per Link Click:** Select this check box if you want Facebook's algorithm to determine whether expanding chosen interests will result in reducing the cost of your clicks.

11. In the Connections section, shown in Figure 11-13, select one of the following options from the drop-down menu to add a connection type:

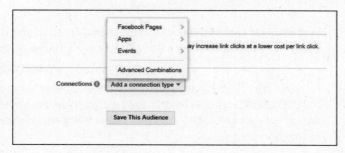

FIGURE 11-13: Choosing to connect to people who like your Page, Apps, Events, or a combination of those.

- **Facebook Pages:** This option allows you to target people and friends of those people who like your Facebook Page, or to exclude people who like your Page.

- **Apps:** This connection type gives you the option to target people and friends of those people who used your app, or to exclude people who used your app.

- **Events:** This option allows you to target people who responded to your event, or to exclude people who already responded to your event.

- **Advanced Combinations:** Select this option if you want to create a mix of the preceding options.

When you have completed your Connections choices, click the Save This Audience Button.

TIP

Pay close attention to what options you select to see whether they align with your advertising goals. Targeting users who aren't fans of your Page, event, group, or app makes sense, for example, if your goal is to acquire new fans.

12. **In the Placements section, select the radio button for Automatic Placements or Edit Placements (see Figure 11-14).**

Unless you have specific devices or platforms that you want to remove, we recommend that you select Automatic Placements to let Facebook determine placement.

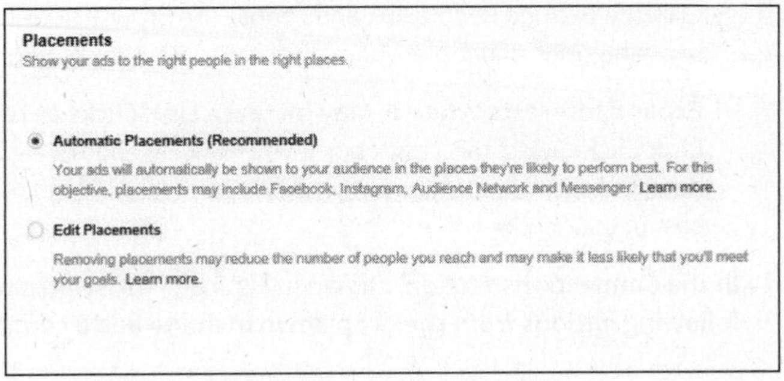

FIGURE 11-14:
You can choose to let Facebook determine where to show your ads or choose specific places yourself.

13. **In the Budget area of the Budget and Schedule section, use the drop-down menu to select either a Daily Budget or a Lifetime Budget.**

Your budget is the maximum amount of money you want to spend. You can set your maximum budget for a daily expense or for the lifetime of the campaign. Selecting a daily amount to spend gives you the most control throughout your campaign because it ensures that your ad will run every day during your ad schedule.

14. **Set your Ad Schedule.**

You have two options:

- **If you want the campaign to start today and run indefinitely:** Select the Run My Ad Set Continuously Starting Today radio button. This option is not recommended, especially for new advertisers.

- **If you want to choose a specific date range:** Deselect the Run My Campaign Continuously Starting Today check box and enter the starting and ending date and time.

TIP

If you are a Facebook Ad novice, select start and end dates for your ads that are no further apart than five days. Keeping the duration short prevents you from wasting money while allowing you to maintain tight control of your Facebook Ad. You would rarely select Run My Ad Set Continuously Starting Today.

15. **Click the Show Advanced Options link if you want to set additional options for bidding optimization.**

If you click Show Advanced Options, you see options described in the following Steps 16–21.

16. **Click Optimization for Ad Delivery for ways to optimize how you deliver your ad.**

You see a drop-down menu with the following choices (shown in Figure 11-15):

● **Link Clicks:** If you choose to optimize your ads for clicks, your ad is served to the Facebook users who are likely to click the ad. You're still charged each time your ad is served, but Facebook serves that ad to people who are most likely to click the ad.

● **Landing Page Views:** If you choose to optimize your ad for Landing Page Views, your ad is served to the Facebook users who are likely to click the ad and load the Landing Page. For this option, you need to install the Facebook Pixel so that you can track views.

● **Impressions:** If you choose to optimize your ad to receive the most impressions, you're charged each time your ad is served, based on your bid.

● **Daily Unique Reach:** If you choose to optimize your ad for reach, people see the ad once a day.

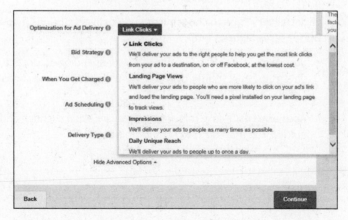

FIGURE 11-15:
Picking the metric you want to optimize.

17. **Click Bid Strategy to choose one of two bidding strategies:**

● **Lowest Cost:** If you use the default, Lowest Cost, you will get as many clicks as come with the budget you set.

- **Target Cost:** If you select the Set a Bid Cap check box, you're asking Facebook to optimize clicks based on your target (bid cap) budget. This choice is available only to those who choose the Ad Objectives — App installs (Consideration), Conversions, or Catalog Sales (Conversions).

18. **Click When You Get Charged to determine when you will be charged for ads.**

Your choice will depend on the objective you have chosen. You have two options:

- **Impression:** This is the default option. You are charged based on impressions (CPM), which means that your bid represents every 1,000 impressions, or ad views.

REMEMBER

Facebook requires that if you are creating a new ad account, you must spend $10 for impressions before switching to Link Clicks.

- **Link Clicks:** Click the link More Options and you'll be given the ability to select Link Clicks (CPC), which means that you're charged on a cost per click (CPC) basis.

19. **Click Ad Scheduling** to choose the schedule on which your ads run. You have two choices:

- **Run Adds All the Time:** Facebook chooses when to serve your ads.

- **Run Ads on a Schedule:** If you set a lifetime budget, you can pick the days and times when your ad will be seen.

20. **Click Delivery Type to choose from two delivery options if you click More Options (see Figure 11-16):**

- **Standard:** This choice ensures that your spending occurs at a pace that doesn't exhaust your budget too soon. We recommend choosing this option.

- **Accelerated:** Choose this option if you are experimenting and want results quickly. You must set a bid cap for this option.

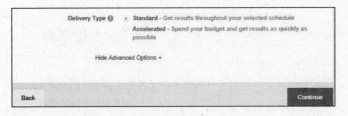

FIGURE 11-16:
Deciding the pace
at which your ad
will be served.

21. **After you have completed all your ad set choices, click the Continue button to move to the next step, creating your ad.**

Step 3: Creating your ad

You're now at the third and final step in the ad process. In this section, you select your content, finalize your ad design, and confirm your order.

1. **In the Ad Name text box, type the name of your campaign or keep the default name that appears in that text box.**

    If you want to rename the Ad, click the Advanced Options link and enter a new name.

2. **Keep the default link, Create New Ad, to create a new ad from scratch.**

    (We devote a separate section, "Using an Existing Post to Create Your Ad," later in this chapter, to the other option that appears here.)

    For the Create New Ad link, you see the Identity and Format choices (see Figure 11-17).

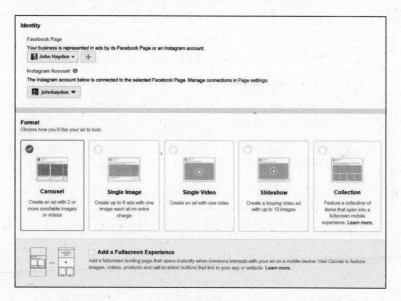

FIGURE 11-17: Choosing the link Create New Ad.

3. **In the Identity section, select the business Page (or other account, such as Instagram) that the ad is for.**

    If you have more than one business Page, use the drop-down menu to select the one associated with this ad. If you have an Instagram account, you see it listed also.

4. **In the Format section, select the format for your ad:**

- **Carousel:** Scrolls two or more selected videos or images in your ad.

- **Single Image:** Presents one image in your ad.

- **Single Video:** Presents one video in your ad.

- **Slideshow:** Presents up to ten images on a loop in your ad.

- **Collection:** The most robust option, this format presents both images and video in your ad. On a mobile device, it opens to a full-screen display.

TIP

Collections may not be available for all Objectives.

5. **Select the Add a Fullscreen Experience check box (below the Format section) if you want to create a landing page that will open to a full screen on a mobile device.**

Facebook provides you with prebuilt templates to choose your design, as shown in Figure 11-18. You can also click the link for Use the Advance Canvas Builder if you want additional design options.

Carousel format

Selected box

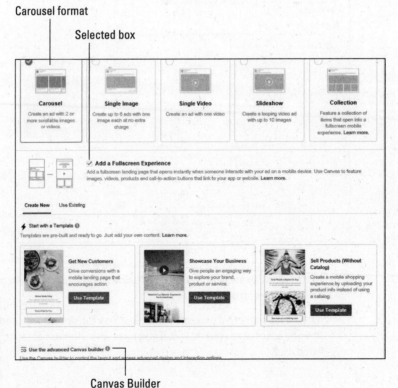

FIGURE 11-18:
Selecting the
Fullscreen
Experience check
box with the
example of the
Carousel choice.

Canvas Builder

The options you are given to select images or video will be different depending on which format you choose and whether you add the Fullscreen Experience. Follow the individual instructions for selecting your images or video based on the format you have chosen.

In the Ad Preview section, you see a preview of your ad layout (see Figure 11-19). As you move through the Links section on the left of your screen, you see your ad change.

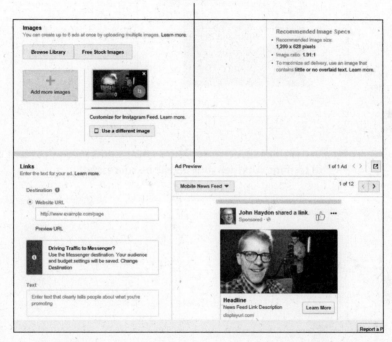

FIGURE 11-19: A preview of how your ad will look.

The drop-down menu (the default is Mobile News Feed) gives you 12 choices for where you want your ad to appear, as shown in Figure 11-20. Not all choices are visible in this figure.

Obviously, you want to determine where your ad will appear when you are making your plan and considering your objectives. If you wait until you're creating your ad, you may make the wrong choice and waste your money.

pixels
1.91:1
ad delivery, use an image that
e or no overlaid text. Learn more.
Mobile News Feed
Feature Phone
Desktop News Feed
Instant Articles
Desktop Right Column
1 of 1 Ad
1 of 12
John Haydon shared a link.
Sponsored
Headline
News Feed Link Description
displayurl.com
Learn More

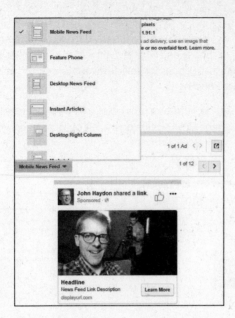

FIGURE 11-20: Selecting where you want your ad to appear.

6. **In the Links section (see Figure 11-21), enter the key content that will determine whether your ad will be successful:**

Adding content

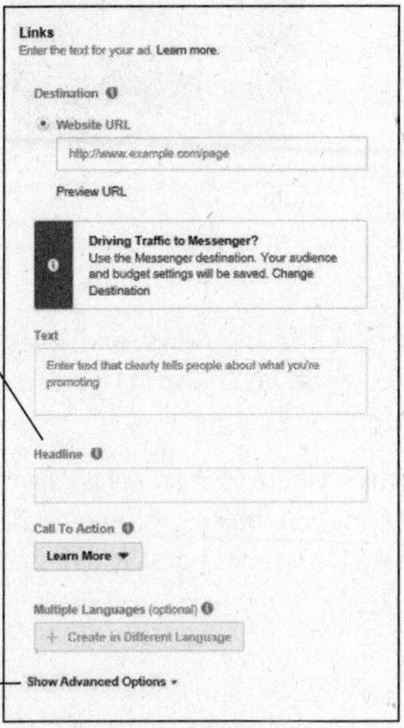

Links
Enter the text for your ad. Learn more.
Destination
Website URL
http://www.example.com/page
Preview URL
Driving Traffic to Messenger?
Use the Messenger destination. Your audience and budget settings will be saved. Change Destination
Text
Enter text that clearly tells people about what you're promoting
Headline
Call To Action
Learn More
Multiple Languages (optional)
Create in Different Language
Show Advanced Options

Show Advanced Options link

FIGURE 11-21: Setting up your content including your headline and call to action.

- **Destination:** Where your viewers will go when they view your ad.

- **Text:** Explain your promotion and make it sound enticing.

- **Headline:** The headline is all-important. If you don't grab readers with your headline, they may not read further.

- **Call to Action:** Facebook provides you with a drop-down menu of suggested calls to action that have been successful.

- **Multiple Languages:** You have the choice of creating an ad in a language different from your own.

7. **If you click the Advanced Options link (refer to Figure 11-21), a screen pops up with additional items. You can add an optional link and a News Feed description, as well as review and confirm your ad, as shown in Figure 11-22.**

In the next section, Advanced Options, you can also set up conversion tracking and view performance data (covered in the next section) which is very valuable.

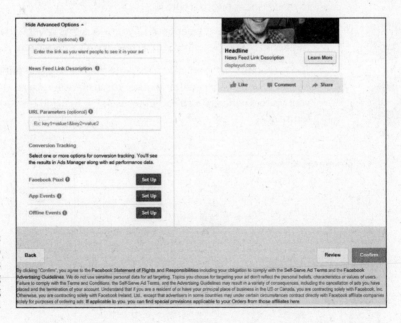

FIGURE 11-22: Setting up advanced options and reviewing and confirming your ad.

If you click the Advanced Options link, you can add your URL Parameters (optional) and choose to set up Conversion Tracking (see Figure 11-23).

TIP

URL Parameters gives you additional information about the performance of your ad. Check with your webmaster if you want to configure it.

FIGURE 11-23:
Setting up
Conversion
Tracking.

In the next section, you see three tracking options:

- **Facebook Pixel:** To set up the Facebook Pixel (see Figure 11-24), click the Confirm button. A check mark appears on the screen. Another screen then appears that says, "Let's make it work by creating some code" and asks you to read instructions to create it.

TIP

Adding this pixel to the back end of your website is beyond the scope of this book. To complete this setup, contact your webmaster.

TIP

The Facebook Pixel is an important piece of code that you put in the header of your website. After that code is in place, it records the actions of your visitors (who are also Facebook users) so that you can target them in future ads.

FIGURE 11-24:
Setting up your
Facebook Pixel.

- **App Events:** This setting lets you add events to your analytics tracking. When you click Set Up, you receive the following link to learn more: `https://developers.facebook.com/docs/app-ads#register-your-app`.

- **Offline Events:** This setting lets you add offline events to your analytics tracking. When you click Set Up, you receive the following link to learn more: `https://business.facebook.com/offline_events/`.

To learn more about Events, see Chapter 13.

TIP

8. **Click the Review button after you finish creating your ad to see the completed ad.**

   The Order page appears, recapping your ad's creative elements, targeting, type of bid (CPC or CPM), bid price, daily budget, and duration of ad *flight* (the time period that an ad runs).

   If this is your first time creating an ad, you will be asked to complete your payment.

REMEMBER

   You may see a message saying "Your Ad May Not Run" if the ad is not fully in compliance. For example, your ad may contain too much text, preventing it from reaching a larger audience. Make the changes requested. If you are unsure about what to do, click the Request Manual Review button.

WARNING

9. **Click the Confirm button if everything looks correct.**

   When you click the Confirm button, you are agreeing to comply with Facebook's Rights and Responsibilities.

   On the following page, a message from Facebook appears, confirming the creation of your ad and providing some other information about its approval status and more.

   After your ad is approved, you receive an email from Facebook, notifying you of the approval and including a link to the Ads Manager.

Using an existing post to create your ad

A great way to increase your visibility with your existing audience and possibly reach new audience members is to create an ad from an already published post. It's easy and can be set up quickly.

To create an ad from an existing post, follow these steps:

1. **Click the Use Existing Post link to create an ad from a post you have already published (see Figure 11-25).**

2. **In the Identity section, select the business Page (or other account, such as Instagram) that the ad is for.**

If you have more than one business Page, use the drop-down menu to select the one associated with this ad.

Use Existing Post

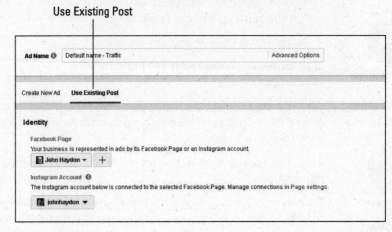

FIGURE 11-25:
Selecting the Use
Existing Post link
to create your Ad.

3. **In the Creative section, select the post you want to use from the drop-down menu.**

If you also want to set up Advanced Options, click the Show Advanced Options link (see Figure 11-26).

Click the drop-down menu

FIGURE 11-26:
Selecting the post
you want to use
for your ad.

After you select your post, Facebook shows you an ad preview and asks you to select where you want the ad to run from the drop-down menu (see Figure 11-27).

Drop-down menu

FIGURE 11-27:
Previewing your
ad and choosing
where it will run
from the
drop-down menu.

4. **Click the Review button after you finish creating your ad to see the completed ad.**

A screen pops up, asking you to review the campaign name, the ad set parameters, including placement, budget, and schedule, and the ad name.

5. **Click the Confirm button if everything looks correct.**

When you click the Confirm button, you are agreeing to comply with Facebook's Rights and Responsibilities.

Creating Boosted Posts

A Boosted Post is a type of Facebook Ad that creates exposure for specific posts on your Facebook Page. The types of posts that can be promoted include status updates, photos, videos, events, and milestones.

Promoted posts are labeled Sponsored and show up only in the News Feeds of people who like your Page (and those people's friends). Promoted posts aren't shown in the right column of Facebook. Promoted posts also show up in mobile News Feeds, which is huge considering that nearly 2 billion mobile users are on Facebook.

Creating a Boosted Post from your Facebook Page

Unlike other Facebook Ads, Boosted Posts are easy to create directly from your Page. To create a Boosted Post, follow these steps:

1. **Click the Boost Post button in the bottom-right corner of any Facebook Page post.**

   This button appears as long as you have admin status.

   A Boost Post window with several choices pops open (see Figure 11-28).

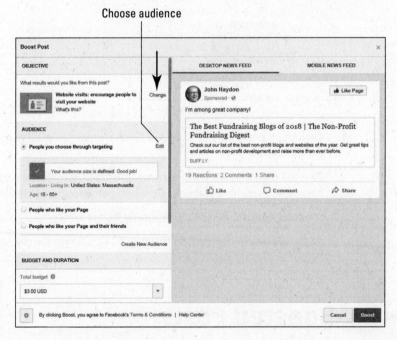

2. **In the Objective section, click the Change link on the right and choose one of the following options:**

   - **Website visits:** Encourage people to visit your website.
   - **Engagement:** Ask for reactions, comments, and shares.

   Click Save when you're finished.

3. **In the Audience section, choose among these options:**

- People You Choose Through Targeting

- People Who Like Your Page

- People Who Like Your Page and Their Friends

The last two of these are pretty self-explanatory. When you select the first choice, People You Choose Through Targeting, and click the Edit button, the People You Choose through Targeting Audience dialog box appears. Here, you can enter any of four different criteria for targeting your audience:

- **Gender:** Male or female.

- **Age:** You can specify any range of people as young as 13 and as old as 65+.

- **Locations:** You can be as specific as cities or as broad as countries, and you can choose to add more than one location.

- **Detailed Targeting:** You see an option called Include People Who Match at Least One of the Following. Click the browse link to see suggestions for Demographics, Interests, and Behaviors. You can also click the Exclude People link to see the same options.

4. **Finally, before you leave the Create Audience dialog box, consider giving your target audience a name.**

This saves your selections for use in a future post. To name your target audience, enter a name for your audience in the Name field; then click Save.

5. **In the Budget and Duration section, decide what your budget will be, as well as the number of days you want your ad to run (see Figure 11-29):**

- **Budget:** Set your desired budget for the promotion. The drop-down menu options vary depending on where you are running the ad and the size of the ad.

- **Duration:** Select the run dates for your Boosted Post. Your choices are 1 to 14 days. Depending on your selection, you are shown the date your ad will cease running and the amount you will spend per day. You also see the estimated number of people you will reach.

REMEMBER

The budget you set to use this option is a lifetime budget, not a daily budget.

6. **In the Tracking Conversions section, move the Facebook Pixel button to On to use the code you created previously.**

7. **In the Payment section, when you see the account to which your payment will be charged (see Figure 11-30), enter your credit card information at the prompt.**

FIGURE 11-29:
Setting your
budget and the
number of days
you want to
run it.

People you will reach

Pixel to track analytics

FIGURE 11-30:
Using the
Facebook Pixel
for tracking and
setting the
account to which
your payment is
charged.

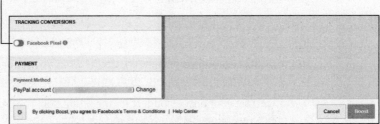

TIP

You have to enter your credit card information if you haven't purchased a
Facebook Ad before. This information will be saved as a payment option in
your Facebook Ads account.

8. **Click Boost.**

   When you click Boost, you are agreeing to Facebook's Terms and Conditions.
   A pop-up window appears, informing you that Facebook has to review the ad.
   (The review period usually takes 15 minutes.)

Viewing real-time analytics for Boosted Posts

You can see real-time stats on how your ad is performing. To do so, click the See Results (dollar amount) button below the post that you boosted. The resulting data (see Figure 11-31) is explained in more detail later in this chapter.

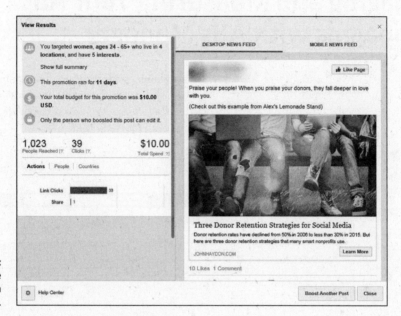

Creating Multiple Campaigns

Facebook makes it easy for you to duplicate an existing ad, change variables, and launch multiple multifaceted ad campaigns. An advertiser has several reasons for duplicating ads, including the following:

>> **Reach multilingual audiences:** You can use Facebook's language targeting on an ad-by-ad basis.

>> **Test which variables in ads perform best:** By changing variables, you can optimize the campaign to the better-performing ads.

>> **Test different bids and models (CPC versus CPM):** This setting enables you to determine which model is most economically efficient.

You can easily pattern a new ad from an existing one. When designing your new ad (as we describe in the section, "Step 3: Creating your ad," earlier in the chapter), you can copy an existing ad by selecting that ad in the Ads Manager and clicking the Create a Similar Ad link, which opens a new window.

Managing and Measuring Your Ad Campaigns with Ads Manager

After you create an ad with Facebook, you want to keep tabs on that ad's performance. Facebook's Ads Manager is your personalized hub where you can view all your ad activities and edit ad campaigns. To access Ads Manager, visit www.facebook.com/ads/manager (see Figure 11-32).

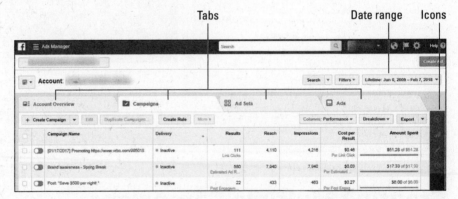

FIGURE 11-32: The Ads Manager screen.

On this screen, you see how Ads Manager is organized. It has four tabs:

» **Account Overview:** This tab gives you a big-picture look at how all your ads are doing.

» **Campaigns:** At the campaign level, you can see how a particular campaign is performing.

» **Ad sets:** The ad sets level shows you a summary of the performance of your ad sets (the ads you grouped together).

» **Ads:** This tab shows you how a specific ad is performing.

In the top-right corner of this page, you can select the date range for which you'd like to view data. You can also pause the ad, edit the budget, or change the dates for the ad in the top-left corner of this page using the icons on the right.

Looking at your account overview

Click the Account Overview tab, shown in Figure 11-33. (You have to scroll down to see all the screens in this view.)

In the upper-right corner, this screen shows you the overall ad performance based on the time frame you chose.

Here you see charts for four measures. In this case, the measures are Link Clicks, Reach, Amount Spent, and Impressions. If you click each section, you see a drop-down menu that lets you choose other options related to that measure. In this way, you can choose exactly what metrics you want to see, giving you an easy way to customize your data.

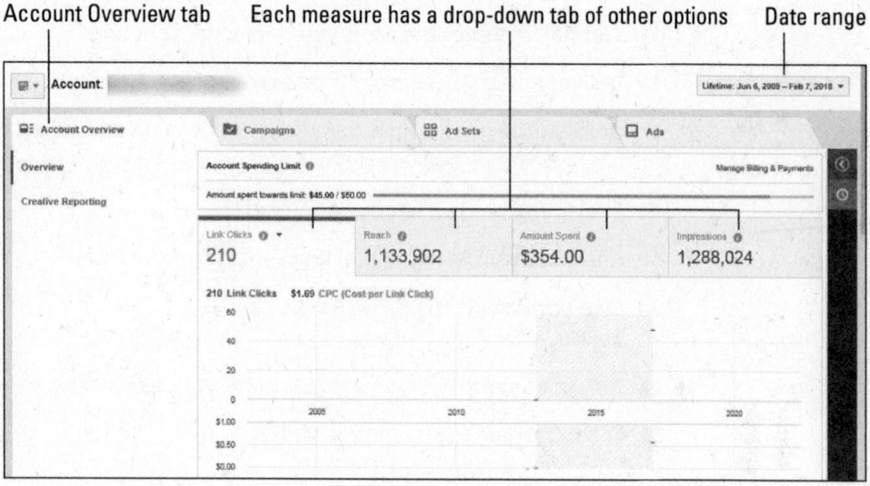

Account Overview tab   Each measure has a drop-down tab of other options   Date range

FIGURE 11-33:
Account Overview
screen with
drop-down
menus to select
data you want to
view.

As you scroll down to the next screen, you see an accounting of your ads by objective. As you may recall, when you set up your ads, you had to select an objective. This screen gives you a good idea as to how well you reached your objective based on the money you spent.

To see more data about each objective, click the link under each objective.

Next, you see how your ads performed with regard to age and gender. You can also see age and gender separately broken out. Notice that the drop-down menus allow you to change the measures by which you analyze this data.

To the right of the age and gender charts, you see a time analysis that tells you what time your metric occurred. Note that you can click the two drop-down menus to select other measures to track on a timeline.

Next, you see data broken out by location. You can use the radio buttons to select data by the categories of Country, Region, or DMA Region (Designated Market Area regions, which are used by Nielsen to map U.S. regions based on television viewing). This data gives you a very clear idea of where in the world your ads are viewed.

Viewing performance data

You can view your data for each campaign. Facebook does a good job of balancing the Ads Manager's ease of use with powerful sorting features.

The Campaigns tab (shown in Figure 11-34) features the most important data on your ad's performance. You can view the following information:

>> **Campaign name:** The name you created for your ad(s).

>> **Delivery:** Tells you whether the ad is running.

>> **Results:** The number of actions as a result of your ad. The action will be based on the objective that you choose.

>> **Reach:** The number of people you can reach.

>> **Impressions:** The number of times your ads were shown.

>> **Cost per Result:** The average price paid for each action based on your objective.

>> **Amount Spent:** The estimated total amount you spent on an ad.

>> **Ends:** The date your campaign ends.

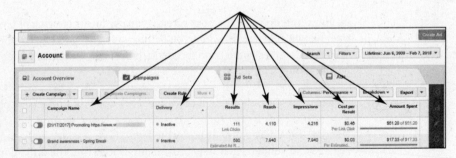

FIGURE 11-34:
The Facebook Ads Manager shows your latest ad campaigns.

Viewing campaign details

To view campaign details, simply click the chart icon under the campaign name. On the resulting screen, you see graphs and other details about that campaign.

TIP

You have to hover your mouse over the campaign name to see the chart icon appear.

REMEMBER

What you see on your screen will vary depending on the ad sets you have created.

On the left side of the page, you see the Performance data in the following categories: Link Clicks, People Reached, and Amount Spent. Clicking the Demographics link shows you your audience with regard to age and gender. Note that you can click the drop-down menus to view other metrics categorized by age and gender.

If you click the Placement link, you see what platform the ad was shown on. In this case, the ad was shown on Facebook. To the right of the screen is a drop-down menu that shows you the device type your ad appeared on.

Understanding Other Facebook Ads Manager Features

The Facebook Ads Manager also includes several features and resources that help you save time and get more out of your Facebook Ads. This section provides a summary of these features and resources for marketers.

Accessing your Facebook Page from Ads Manager

To access a single page listing of all your Facebook Pages, go to (https://www.facebook.com/ads/manage/pages.php). There, you can view Insights for your Page, view Page notifications, and log in as your Page.

Creating and scheduling Facebook Ad reports

You can create reports and get them delivered by email from the following Ads Manager tabs: Campaigns, Ad Sets, and Ads. To create and schedule a report, follow these steps:

1. **Choose the measures you'd like to track from within one of the three tabs.**

   After you have the report the way you'd like to see it, you can set up a report to be sent to you on a regular basis.

2. **Click the Reports icon to see a drop-down menu on the upper-left side of the screen (see Figure 11-35).**

   A text box opens.

3. **Click the Save New Report link and input the name of your report.**

4. **Select the Schedule Email box if you want to schedule an email to be sent to you.**

   A new screen opens.

5. **Choose your preferred schedule and click Save.**

Click report icon

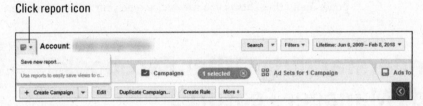

FIGURE 11-35:
Create and schedule reports in Facebook's Ads Manager.

Adding other users to your Facebook Ad account

You can give other Facebook users access to your Facebook Ad account. Additional users can have general access to the account or only view reports. Added users won't have access to your personal Facebook profile or to any other ad account.

TIP

If you have more than one person in charge of marketing at your business, or if you work with a marketing consultant, consider adding that person as a user on your Facebook Ad. To add another user to your ad account:

1. **Go to** https://www.facebook.com/ads/manager/account_settings/.

   You may have to log in again. On the right side of the page, see Add Account Roles.

2. **Click the Add People button.**

   Enter any additional user's name and choose the person's role from the drop-down menu on the right side.

3. **Click the Confirm button.**

Tracking payment transactions

Click the Billing & Payments link at the upper right of the Account Overview tab in Ads Manager to view details about your payment transactions for each of your campaigns (see Figure 11-36). On that page, you can also click the Payment Settings button to change the way you pay for your ads.

Finding out about your business resources

The Learn More icon takes you to an overview of all of Facebook's resources available to businesses: Pages, Ads, Sponsored Stories, and Developer Platform at `https://www.facebook.com/business/resource`.

Chapter **12**

Using Facebook Offers to Sell Products and Services

Is Facebook just for building a fan base and getting people engaged? Or can you actually use Facebook to sell products and services? With various e-commerce applications and email acquisition apps, the answer is: *both.* Facebook Pages allow you to engage customers, and Facebook Offers get your customers buying your wares and talking to their friends about your business.

How does this feature work? Suppose that Threadless (John's favorite T-shirt company) posts a limited offer for $10, and you choose to redeem that offer. As soon as you click Get Offer, John's friends see *"John just claimed an offer from Threadless."* John's action of claiming the offer may not make all his friends buy T-shirts, but it will certainly be attractive to all the Threadless customers in his network!

In this chapter, you see how to use Facebook Offers to promote your business. We show you how to create an offer and then promote the offer with Facebook Ads, your Facebook Page, and your email list. You also see how offers can enhance your current sales process.

Understanding Facebook Offers

Facebook Offers encourages people to share your business with their friends when they claim your offer. When people claim your offer, they make a commitment to buy your product or service as well as share that commitment with their friends. Facebook Offers lets you make any offer to increase sales, repeat business, or leads. You can offer a discount with a purchase, for example, as shown in Figure 12-1. Then Facebook users can claim your offer in your store, on Facebook, or in both places.

FIGURE 12-1:
Facebook Offers
increases sales
and gets
customers to tell
their friends.

Here's how Facebook Offers works:

TIP

>> **Offer Post:** You create an offer on your Page by using the Publisher, where you typically upload photos and post text updates. You don't pay a fee to create an offer post. Your offer is shown on your Page with other posts.

You can choose to boost the offer post at the time you create it. *Boosting* a post is an advertising method that allows you to choose an extended audience beyond your own. You can either choose to target friends of friends or choose a specific audience. You do pay a fee to do this because it is advertising.

>> **Offer Ad:** When you buy a Facebook Ad to promote the offer, your offer can show up with other ads on the right side of the Page or in the News Feed. Boosting Facebook Offers isn't free, but it's a very powerful way to grow your business. You can also track the usage data in Insights to help you improve your offer.

Three types of offers are available for you to use to promote sales and build word-of-mouth advertising:

>> **In Store Only:** People who claim the offer can print the offer email or show it on their smartphones to your sales staff. If your goal is to increase foot traffic in your store, this option is your best choice.

>> **In Store & Online:** People can redeem the offer in your store or on your website.

>> **Online Only:** People can redeem your offer only by clicking or tapping a link in the offer email and visiting your website. If your goal is to increase website traffic, this option is your best choice.

Creating an Offer for Your Page

You can create an offer from your Page Publisher by following these steps:

1. **Go to your Page, and underneath the Write Something, box, you see a graphic button that says Create an Offer (see Figure 12-2). Click it.**

Create an Offer

FIGURE 12-2:
Beginning to
create an offer.

2. **Write a title and description in the Tell People about Your Offer box.**

    Make the value of your offer simple to understand, such as "Limited space for one-on-one meetings." Several details must be included (see Figure 12-3), as follows:

    ● Date the offer expires

    ● A photo(s)

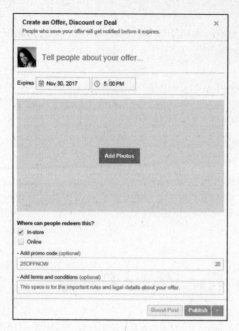

FIGURE 12-3:
A view of the
offer details.

- Where people can redeem the offer (optional)

- Add terms and conditions (optional)

3. **Choose an expiration date by clicking a day in the future.**

TIP

Limit your offer to a week or less because after a week, you reach the point of diminishing returns.

4. **Upload a thumbnail photo for your offer.**

Select one of your most recent photos posted to your Page or upload a new photo(s).

5. **Put a check mark in the box to let the customer redeem it in-store, online (you'll need to add a URL), or both.**

6. **Add a promo code (optional).**

7. **Add terms and conditions (optional).**

8. **Go to the Publish button drop-down menu.**

The drop-down menu lets you choose either Schedule, Back Date, or Save Draft. If you choose Schedule, a window pops up, asking you to schedule an offer.

TIP

You are also given the option to click the Boost Post button from this screen.

9. **Click Schedule Offer and choose the date you want your offer to go live.**

Your offer is published on your Page at that date.

TIP

When customers view the offer from the Offer link on the left side of your page, they can save it for later or view past offers, making it more accessible.

Getting the Most from Your Offer

Using Facebook Offers as an effective part of your marketing strategy requires more than simply knowing how to create one (which is pretty easy, as you've just seen).

As with any other promotional strategy, the message and the offer are what really determine success. Do your customers need what you're offering? Is the free offer or discount something they'd truly get excited about? The more clearly you can answer these questions, the more successful your offer will be.

TIP

Here are nine tips for getting the most from Facebook Offers:

» **Offer something remarkable.** Offering real value makes customers happy, but offering remarkable value inspires those happy customers to tell their friends. If your favorite restaurant offered a free bottle of wine with reservations booked online, no doubt you'd claim that offer. Give people something they'll make remarks about (something *remark*able).

» **Keep the offer simple.** Write a headline and summary that inspire people to claim your offer. Use simple language that's concise and easy to understand, such as "Get a free coffee with a full breakfast" or "Ten percent off gym membership."

» **Be clear about restrictions.** Mention any time limits or other restrictions. Otherwise, you'll end up spending too much time explaining the offer to confused and disappointed customers.

» **Be clear about how to claim the offer.** Don't leave people guessing about what to do after they claim the offer. Clearly state what they need to do next, such as "Show your phone to the salesperson." Fortunately, Facebook sends an email with instructions to anyone who claims the offer.

» **Keep the offer fresh.** If you run an offer too long, people lose interest. You want to make them happy, and you want them to tell their friends.

» **Don't run too many concurrent offers.** Doing so only causes confusion among your customers and your employees.

>> **Prepare your employees.** Make sure that all your employees understand the terms of the offer, how people will redeem it, and what customers get when they claim the offer. Be clear about how to handle customers who ask about the offer after it expires.

>> **Stock the warehouse.** Make sure that you have enough of what you're offering to honor all offers during the run.

>> **Be cheerful.** Make sure that your customers are treated in a cheerful manner when they claim a deal. The last thing you want is for a customer to feel that the sales staff was reluctant about honoring the deal. Be cheerful. We could say this three times, and that wouldn't be too many times.

Promoting Your Offer

After you create your offer you need to make people aware of it by promoting it. An ad alone won't make the offer a success, however. Promote your offer as much as possible. When people claim it, a story is created in their News Feed so that all their friends are exposed to your business. Also, the total number of claims is displayed (see Figure 12-4), which adds a social-proof element and strengthens the offer.

TIP

Social proof is a psychological concept that says that people look at the actions of other people to determine what the correct thing to do is in a given situation. In this instance, the number of claims indicates that others have accepted the offer, so it must be good.

FIGURE 12-4:
When people claim your offer, stories are generated in their friends' News Feeds and the total number of claims is displayed.

and 6 other friends claimed an offer from Macy's.

Get 25% off your purchase of $100 or more. Save BIG on the latest trends!

Get Offer
15,359 claimed this offer for free.

Like · Comment · Share Offer · 30 minutes ago

Promoting your offer on your Facebook Page

Many of your potential customers are exposed to your business through their friends who use Facebook. When one of your fans comments on or likes a post on your Page, Facebook distributes that action in their friends' News Feeds. In the same way, you can create awareness about your deal by posting stories about it on your Page. This leverages the word-of-mouth feature that's inherent on Facebook.

Here are effective ways to use your Page to promote your offer:

>> **Announce the offer a couple of times.** If a product is associated with the offer, upload a photo and post a link to the offer in the photo description. In this update, ask an engaging question like "Who's hungry for a free appetizer?"

>> **Use your Facebook cover to promote your offer.** Hire a graphic designer to create a Facebook cover promoting your offer. If you don't have the budget to hire a graphic designer, try using Canva.com (http://canva.com), a visual-content-creation tool.

>> **Create conversations about your offer when appropriate.** When someone claims the offer, mention it on your Page ("Jane just claimed the shrimp cocktail! Who likes shrimp?"). This technique invites fans and their friends to comment on your Page, creating more awareness of your deal.

These are just examples to get you started. Using your Facebook Page as a marketing tool is limited only by your creativity.

WARNING

Some promotional activities are prohibited on Facebook. Make sure that before promoting your deal, you review the Facebook Pages Terms at https://www.facebook.com/terms_pages.php.

Promoting your offer with Facebook Ads

Another way to promote your deal is to use highly targeted Facebook Ads. You can select specific geographic criteria as well as demographic information when you create your ad. Your criteria should be based on your knowledge of your target market and your ideal customer located in the vicinity of your business. With Facebook Ads, you can target a city, for example, or parents with children younger than age 5. (Read more about Facebook Ads in Chapter 11.)

REMEMBER

Don't forget to create mobile ads for your offers. The most updated information Facebook gives as of this writing is that mobile ads are up 4 percent between the last quarter of 2016 and the first quarter 2017.

Promoting your offer through other marketing channels

In addition to using your Facebook Page, you want to use other marketing channels to promote your offer. Many of your customers may not be active Facebook users but would still be interested in connecting with your business to take advantage of your offer. Consider the following options:

» **Email marketing:** Many businesses have an email list. Send out an email announcement of your deal with these tips in mind:

- **Write a compelling headline that gets the reader's attention.** This headline could simply be your offer summary.

- **Keep the body of the email short and concise.** You have only a few seconds after someone opens your email to grab her attention. Communicate the essence of your offer in as few words as possible.

- **Include an image.** Keeping the preceding point in mind, remember that a picture is worth a thousand words. Use a picture of the product or service you're offering.

- **Ask the reader to click.** In the middle of your email and at the end, clearly state what you want the reader to do, such as "Click here to become a fan of our Facebook Page." This way, you can continue to remind readers of the offer.

» **In-store promotion:** In addition to using email and your Facebook Page, you want to promote your deal in the store with posters, mentions at the cash register, and other traditional in-store promotional methods.

Why promote an offer that's intended to encourage in-store traffic to people in your store? The critical thing to remember about using Facebook Offers is that in addition to encouraging foot traffic, you create awareness about your business as people claim offers.

Earlier in this chapter, we mention an example offer of a free coffee with a full breakfast. When customers claim that offer, many of their Facebook friends are exposed to the coffee shop because their friends will see that they claimed the offer. Some of them will become new Facebook fans, and some of them will claim an offer and show up at the coffee shop as well!

» **Creating your own group**

» **Creating and using events**

» **Boosting your events**

Chapter **13**

Using Facebook Groups and Events for Your Business

Facebook Pages keep Facebook users interested in your business, and Facebook Ads help spread awareness about your products and services. But to successfully market your business on Facebook, you should go further — to Facebook Groups and to promotions and events.

This chapter discusses how you can use groups, promotions, and events to grow your audience by promoting brand awareness and building community. You see how to create your own group on a topic that engages potential business clients, as well as how to promote that group to attract members and prospective customers. We also show you how to create events, and how to promote those events to your fans.

Discovering Facebook Groups

Facebook Groups allow people to connect with one another and collaborate around shared interests. As you can imagine, people share countless interests.

One example is this Facebook Group focused on knitting, as shown in Figure 13-1.

Groups are different from Pages or profiles because groups are less about promoting a business and more about people connecting around a shared interest or cause. And because groups focus on shared interests, using groups to promote your business as a primary objective usually isn't a good idea.

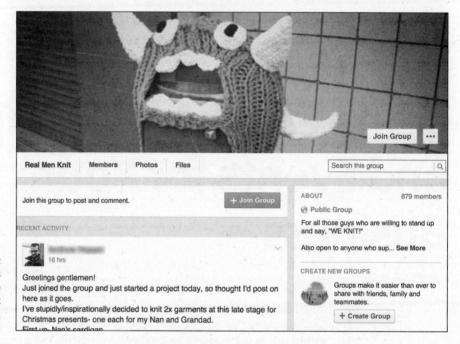

FIGURE 13-1:
Facebook Groups allow people to connect about shared interests, such as knitting.

Promoting your business in a Facebook Group isn't recommended, for two main reasons:

>> People join groups to connect with other people. Marketing messages tend to be received as uninvited annoyances.

>> Groups lack the viral potential that Facebook Pages have. When a group member posts an update to the group, the only people who see it are other members of the group.

Facebook Groups aren't good for promoting your business, but they are great for networking with potential customers in a way that focuses on the group's interest and on creating value for the group as a whole.

Understanding How Facebook Groups Fit in with Your Business

The best way to use Facebook Groups for your business ultimately depends on what kind of business you have.

If the nature of your business is networking, you could use groups as a central part of how you interact with customers. Businesses such as these can use groups to network with people:

>> Chambers of commerce

>> Membership networks

>> Alumni associations

These organizations could create private groups as an additional way to publish exclusive news or content for customers or to alert customers about special sales or events. They could also use groups to share PDF files and Microsoft Word, Excel, and PowerPoint documents.

A Facebook Group can even be used as an additional customer support channel where customers can learn from one another and even answer questions for other customers. Best Friends Animal Society (www.facebook.com/bestfriend sanimalsociety) once used email to communicate with its nonprofit partners. Although this approach had some success, many partners weren't receiving emails or reading them.

Eventually, the organization switched to using a secret Facebook Group as a connection point, which has been extremely effective for partner communications.

Another common way that business owners use Facebook Groups is to network and collaborate with people who share an interest related to their business. Post Planner, for example, has a Facebook Group for social media marketers to find out about changes in social platforms, best practices, and other news (see Figure 13-2).

If you have a local business, such as a barbershop or a restaurant, you can use Facebook Groups to create a peer network of local business owners as a way to learn from one another and share best practices and promotions. In this case, it may be smart to create a secret group so that no customers can see these conversations.

Make sure to establish a set of agreed-upon rules for the group so that everyone is on board with the purpose of the group. You wouldn't want a group member to show up only to share his own promotion. Make it clear that the purpose of the group is support so that all the participating local businesses become successful. Clearly state that if members post only news about their promotions, they'll be removed from the group.

FIGURE 13-2:
The Post Planner
Social Stars group
is interested in
social media.

Using Facebook Groups

The following sections go into more detail about the differences between Facebook Groups and Pages. They also discuss how to find, join, and participate in groups to help market your business. (For the lowdown on starting a group, check out the section "Creating Your Own Facebook Group," later in this chapter.)

Distinguishing Facebook Groups from Pages

Only an official representative of a business, public figure, nonprofit organization, artist, or public personality can create a Facebook Page and serve as its administrator (admin). Pages are designed to provide basic information about a business, feature community-building blocks (such as discussions and comments), upload user-generated content, and post reviews.

By contrast, any Facebook member can create a Facebook Group about any topic. Groups serve as a hub for members to share opinions and discussions about a topic.

When an admin updates a group's Page, the News Feed story includes the name of the group's admin. Pages, however, attribute updates to the Page and never reveal the admin's name. Groups even allow you to post updates via the status update box. And just as with Pages, you can post links, videos, and photos, and even set up an event directly from the status update box.

The following are some key differences between Facebook Pages and Facebook Groups:

>> **As the admin of a Facebook Group, you can dictate how open you want your group's membership to be.** Group admins can restrict membership access by requiring a member-approval process, whereas Pages can restrict members from becoming fans based only on age and location. You can make your group:

- **Open (public)** to all Facebook members
- **Closed** so that only members of the group can see the content, but anyone can see who is a member of the group
- **Secret** so that it's invitation only, and content or members aren't visible in a Facebook search

By contrast, all Facebook Pages are public.

>> **You can't add apps to a group, as you can to a Page.** Whereas Pages allow for a high degree of interaction and rich media with the addition of applications (apps), Facebook Groups don't allow the addition of apps.

>> **Groups lack the viral capacity that Pages offer.** When a group member posts an update or comments on an update, the only people who see those actions are other group members.

>> **You can't sponsor posts from the group.** Whereas Pages allow you to use published posts in an ad campaign, posts published in Facebook Groups aren't eligible for use in a Facebook Ad.

REMEMBER

Consider a Facebook Group if you want to have a serious discussion about a cause. You may choose to start a group if you have strong feelings and opinions regarding Facebook privacy issues and any changes, for example, and you want to have an ongoing discussion with fellow marketers on the topic.

The key is to keep the discussion flowing with the group members. Join a few groups to see how it's done before jumping in to create your own.

In the next section, we discuss how to find groups that may be relevant to your business.

Finding a group

Joining an existing community is much easier than creating one from scratch.

Finding a group isn't difficult. Just follow these steps to use the search box:

1. **In the search box at the top of your screen, type a topic that interests you and then click See More Results For at the bottom of the list.**

   If your business designs custom T-shirts, you can search for a group related to fashion. Use the search terms *fashion, designer clothes,* or *trends* to yield some groups that you may want to join.

2. **Click the Groups icon at the top of the search results page so that you look only at groups.**

   A Facebook search for *Facebook marketing groups* displays the results shown in Figure 13-3.

FIGURE 13-3: Results of a search for Facebook marketing groups.

3. **Search the results until you find a group you want to visit and then click the image or the group's name.**

   In the search results, be sure to note the number of members and the type of group, as well as any recent activity so that you have some indication of how active the group is.

   On the group page, note the recent activity (updates, photos, or videos). Some groups provide a description on their About tabs.

   The most important part of groups is the News Feed; that's really where the action is.

REMEMBER

   Join a group to get a sense of how active that group is and whether you want to contribute. See the following section, "Joining a group."

Joining a group

After you identify a group that matches your interest and has an activity level that matches your objectives, join the group and interact with the other members.

REMEMBER

Make sure that your intent is to learn from others and be helpful to the group. You want to establish yourself as a valuable member of the group, and not as someone who's simply interested in promoting his wares.

To join a group, navigate to the page of the group you want to join and click the Join Group link in the top-left corner, as shown in Figure 13-4. (See the "Finding a group" section, earlier in this chapter, for the lowdown on finding a group.)

FIGURE 13-4:
Joining a Facebook Group is as easy as clicking Join Group.

Accessing groups you joined

Your most recently visited groups are always listed in the left sidebar, below Shortcuts.

To access groups that don't immediately appear on your News Feed page, follow these steps:

1. **Click the Edit link next to *Shortcuts* in the left sidebar.**

   This link takes you to the Groups page, shown in Figure 13-5, where you have access to all the groups you've joined.

2. **Click the drop-down menu next to the group's name and choose Pin to Top.**

3. **Click Save.**

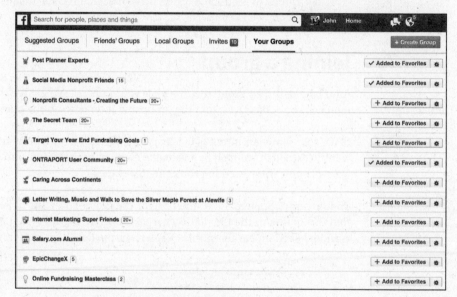

FIGURE 13-5: Access the groups you've joined.

Participating in a group

One of the Golden Rules of social networks and other forms of social media is to spend some time observing and listening to the conversation. Get a feeling for the rhythm of the group's conversations before you barge in and change things.

You'll find that only a portion of group members actively participate; many members just lurk. That's okay, and don't let that discourage you from participating. If you truly want to know more about groups, take the first step and jump into the conversation. That really is the best (and only) way to figure out how social networks operate.

A good place to start is to find a topic that you know a lot about and offer answers to any questions. This method is not only an easy, casual way to get started in group participation, but also goes a long way toward establishing yourself as a helpful member of the group and an expert on particular subjects.

WARNING

Don't try to sell your goods and services directly. Nobody appreciates a hard sell in this arena, and you may even be labeled a spammer. In the long run, being useful and helpful to group members positions your business in the best possible light.

You may find that in some of the larger groups, people try to hijack the conversation by posting links to their own groups or related websites. Don't try this tactic. Technically, these links are spam, and Facebook members have very low tolerance for spammers. Any member who's considered to be a spammer can have his profile shut down by Facebook. Facebook has strict terms for selling products with a Facebook profile.

Creating Your Own Facebook Group

If you've found an existing group that seems to be fruitful, focus on being useful in that group instead of starting your own group. If you can't find a group related to your business, you may want to start your own.

Creating a group is quite simple, requiring just a few simple steps, which the next few sections describe.

Securing your group's name

Before jumping in and creating your group, search for the name you want to use for your group so that you can see whether any existing groups or Pages have that same name. (See the earlier section "Finding a group" for details.)

Selecting a name that's never been used on Facebook isn't required, but a unique name does help you distinguish yourself. Select a name that's easy to understand but also stands out and differentiates your group from others like it.

Setting up your group

After you choose a group name, create your group by following these steps:

1. **On the Groups page (**www.facebook.com/bookmarks/groups**), click the Create Group button in the top-right corner.**

    The Create New Group dialog box appears, as shown in Figure 13-6.

FIGURE 13-6:
The Create New
Group dialog box.

2. **Provide basic information about your group.**

This information is as follows:

- **Group Name:** If you've already done the research (see the earlier section "Securing your group's name"), plug in the name you chose.

- **People:** This section allows you to invite your friends to become members of your group. Just start typing a name in the box, and Facebook brings up a list of friends' names that match.

- **Privacy:** Your group can be public, closed, or secret.

Here are some notes about your privacy settings:

- **Public groups** can be found by anyone on Facebook when doing a search. Anyone can join the group, and anyone can see group content.

- Anyone can see the group description and members of *closed groups,* but only members can see group content.

- **Secret groups** can't be found in a search or even in member profiles; they truly are secret. Membership is by invitation only; therefore, only members of the group see the group's content.

TIP

When you are creating your group, you can also select a box that adds the group name to your Shortcuts list.

All members can post comments, photos, videos, links, events, and documents, which is essentially a group's version of creating a note. Keep this in mind when setting your privacy levels.

WARNING

Depending on your needs for the development of your group, you may want to keep the group secret until you're ready to launch.

3. **Click the Create button.**

4. **(Optional) Select a group icon.**

   You have a variety of options, as shown in Figure 13-7.

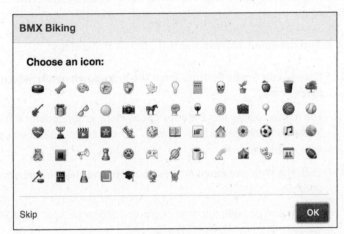

FIGURE 13-7:
All groups offer
an optional icon.

5. **Click OK.**

   Congratulations! You've created your first group!

6. **Fill out the group description on the About tab and add a cover image, as shown in Figure 13-8.**

FIGURE 13-8:
Creating a group
description helps
set expectations
for the group.

Setting up a group URL and email address

Groups have an amazing feature that allows members to send emails that automatically post as updates to the News Feed. You can also create a unique URL for the group.

To set up the email address and URL, follow these steps:

1. **Choose Edit Group Settings from the drop-down menu (which looks like three dots).**

   You may recognize that the information in the group settings is the basic information that you provided earlier, but this time, you can set up a group email address.

2. **Click the Web and Email Address button, and choose a personalized email address.**

   All group email addresses end in groups.facebook.com. Select what you like for both your email prefix and your URL.

   You have only 50 characters to work with, so choose wisely!

TIP

3. **Click the Customize Address button.**

   You return to the Basic Information page.

4. **Click the Save button to finish.**

Configuring other group settings

In the basic settings area of your group, you can also decide who can post in the group (all members or just admins). You can also decide whether you want admins to approve posts by members before they're published, as shown in Figure 13-9.

Deleting a group

Facebook won't allow admins to delete groups, but Facebook automatically deletes groups that have no members. If you created the group, you can delete the group by removing all members and then yourself. To remove members, click the gear icon below a member's name, and select the option to delete him or her.

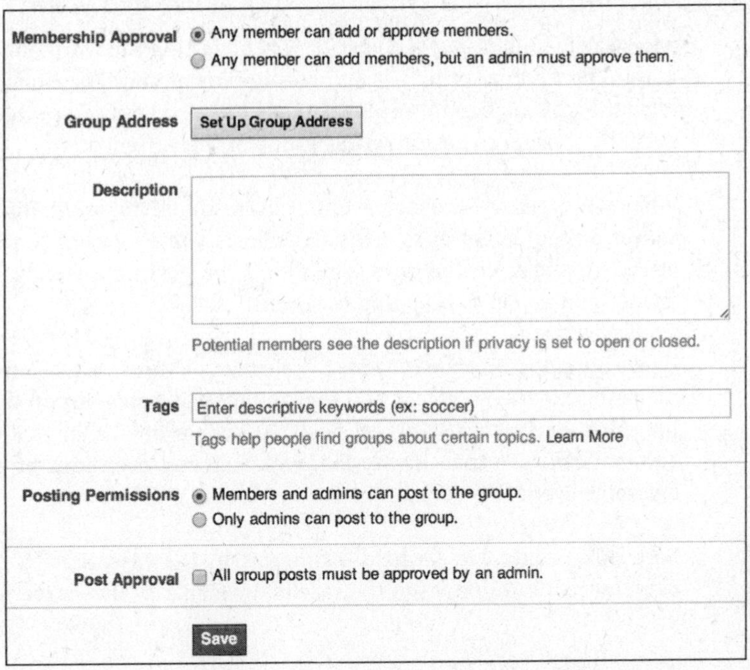

Membership Approval	⦿ Any member can add or approve members.
	○ Any member can add members, but an admin must approve them.
Group Address	**Set Up Group Address**
Description	
	Potential members see the description if privacy is set to open or closed.
Tags	Enter descriptive keywords (ex: soccer)
	Tags help people find groups about certain topics. Learn More
Posting Permissions	⦿ Members and admins can post to the group.
	○ Only admins can post to the group.
Post Approval	☐ All group posts must be approved by an admin.
	Save

FIGURE 13-9:
Group admins can decide who can post in the group and whether content needs approval.

Using Insights with Facebook Groups

Facebook responded to the need that group admins had to be able to analyze what was happening in their groups. Previously, Insights did not allow activity tracking in groups. Facebook added Insights for groups so that admins can determine how fast their group is growing and which members are the most active, among other things. Such tracking helps you understand what your members care about.

TIP

At the time of this writing, Facebook lets admins use Insights only for groups with a minimum of 250 members.

Using Facebook Events to Promote Your Business

On Facebook, an *event* is a way for members to spread the word about upcoming social gatherings, such as parties, fund-raisers, and conventions.

Facebook Events is also a powerful way of getting the word out beyond your normal in-house marketing list by inviting fans of your Facebook Page or members of your Facebook Group. Facebook users can also help you promote your Facebook event by sharing the event with a group of their friends.

When you create a Facebook event, it lives on forever, long after the actual physical (or online) event ends. This fact allows you to stay in touch with those who attended, and even the ones who didn't, by posting a steady stream of photos, videos, and updates recapping the event.

By encouraging attendees to post their own pictures, videos, and comments, you make the experience richer and much more interactive for all those on your guest list. Also, each time someone posts to your event Page, many of their friends automatically see that interaction, which creates even greater awareness of your awesome event and your business.

REMEMBER

Facebook Events can be held offline, as in the case of a fund-raising walk or conference, or online, as in the case of a webinar or live-streaming event.

Creating an event

To create an event, you first must decide what the purpose of your event should be. Generally speaking, the purpose of most events is to get people introduced and interacting. Obviously, these interactions will be among the people who care about your business and the interests related to your business. These connections are valuable; they help promote your business because they're associated with your brand. You should also decide whether to make the group private or public.

Next, develop a strategy that makes your event so compelling that people can't help but talk about it with their friends. The Austin Weird Homes Tour, which helps fight poverty, is one example (see Figure 13-10).

To create an event, log in to Facebook, go to your Page, and then follow these steps:

1. **Click the Events, Products, Job+ link in the Publisher or the Events link on the left menu.**

2. **Click Create an Event from the list of options.**

FIGURE 13-10:
Make sure that
your event is so
interesting and
remarkable that
people talk
about it.

3. **Fill in the following details about your event (see Figure 13-11):**

- **Basic Info:** Briefly describe your event in a way that makes it attractive to your audience.

- **Event Photo or Video:** Add or change the photo or video that represents your event.

- **Event Name:** Type the name of your event.

- **Location:** Enter the place where the event will be held. If the event will be held at your business location, enter your Facebook Page.

- **Frequency:** From the drop-down menu, choose how often the event takes place — Once, Daily, Weekly, or Custom.

  To customize the Frequency of your Event, use the drop-down menu. Choose the Custom link and set the event dates; then click Done.

TIP

- **Starts and Ends:** Enter the date and time of the event.

- **Details:** Let people know specific information about the event.

- **Category:** Select a category from the drop-down menu for your event. This category helps people find your event.

- **Description:** Enter more details about the event.

- **Keywords:** Start typing and choose from the list that appears. Think of the words that people will type in to find you.

FIGURE 13-11:
Giving as much
information
about your event
as you can helps
your audience
find you.

- **Kid Friendly:** Select the check mark box if the event is Kid Friendly.

- **Tickets:** Tell people where they can obtain tickets.

- **Ticket URL:** Enter the URL of the web page where people can buy tickets to the event.

- **Options:** This designates those who can post or edit in this event.

- **Co-hosts:** Add any pages or friends who are cohosting this event with you.

- **Posting Capability:** You can choose to let anyone or only admins post to the event Timeline.

- **Guest list:** Choose whether to display the guest list.

Use as many rich keywords as possible in the Name and Details fields, because Facebook Events are indexed by search engines, which could mean extra traffic for your event.

4. **Click Publish or click Save Draft if you are not ready to publish and want to save your work.**

    If you click Publish, your event is created, and an update is published in the News Feed for your fans to see. If you want to schedule your event and not publish it immediately, click the drop-down menu from the Publish button and click Schedule. Select your dates and click Schedule.

Changing the cover image of your event

The next thing you want to do is make the event even more attractive with a cover image.

You can add a cover image by clicking the Change Photo or Video button in the center of your event Page. You have a choice of uploading a new photo or video or using one that you've already published on your Page (refer to Figure 13-11).

TIP

The main image for your event is 1,200 pixels wide and 628 pixels tall. Facebook recommends that you create an image with these dimensions to promote the event.

Inviting friends to your event

Inviting friends to the event isn't mandatory; you can simply publish your event and hope for the best. Facebook makes inviting friends to your event so easy, however, that it's hard not to. Also, it's a good idea to get the ball rolling because you're holding an event to promote your business in some way. So why wouldn't you invite people to get the word out about your event?

You can invite friends to your event in several ways:

>> **Invite button:** Click the Invite button below the cover photo of your event Page and select either Choose Friends or Invite by Text or Email. Choose the people you want to invite and when you have made your choices click the Send button.

WARNING

Inviting non-Facebook members to an event means that they need to register with Facebook before responding to your request, so be judicious about using this option. If you think that some non-Facebook users you've invited will be hesitant to sign up for an account just for this purpose, make sure to include an alternative way for them to contact you to RSVP.

>> **Invite button for the list of attendees: Click the Invite button under the list of attendees who have responded to add more people to your event after you have published it.** A list of your contacts pops up. You can either type in names or click them and then click the Send button.

>> **Share in Messenger:** Type names in the Share in Messenger box to add people to whom you want to send a personal message.

In the Add a Message box, provide something compelling for the reader, and make sure that the value that invitees receive by coming to your event is front and center in your message. You can invite your first 100 people with this method. Click the Send button.

Facebook allows each event host to invite a total of only 500 attendees per event.

REMEMBER

Boosting your event

If you want to ensure that more people see your event, you can Boost it. When you Boost an event, you create an ad and select a targeted audience to receive it.

Click the Boost Event button to the right of your event on your Event page and then follow these steps:

1. **In the Ad Creative box, describe the event you are promoting.**

   You can add an image or video.

2. **In the Audience box, click the Edit link next to People You Choose through Targeting (see Figure 13-12).**

3. **Choose your budget and time frame from the drop-down menu in the Budget box.**

   You see an estimate of the people you will reach based on the amount of your budget.

4. **Choose how long to run the ad from the calendar box.**

5. **Approve or change the payment method.**

6. **Click the Boost button.**

   When you click the Boost button, you agree to Facebook's terms and conditions.

REMEMBER

Editing your event

Making changes in your event's page is easy. Simply choose the Event link in the left menu. Click the Edit button (see Figure 13-13). In the resulting page, you can change nearly everything about the event, including the location and time. You can also choose to cancel the event.

Edit link

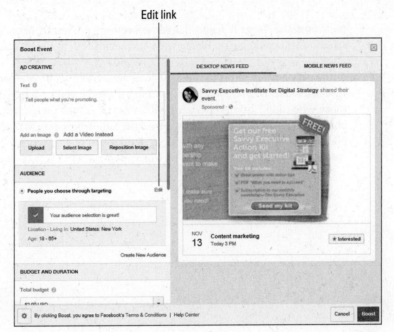

FIGURE 13-12:
Selecting your
target audience.

Click Edit Event

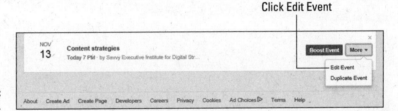

FIGURE 13-13:
Edit your event.

Exporting your event

Choose Export Event from the drop-down menu (three dots), and Facebook allows you to export your event to a calendar on your desktop or to a web-based calendar.

Following up after an event

Smart marketers follow up after a Facebook Event to build a post-event community and extend the value of that event. If you had a very healthy debate with lots of questions, you could post a transcript in your Notes section for attendees or even nonattendees. If some questions weren't answered because of time constraints, you could write the answers and send them to the attendees, too.

At the very least, a short thank-you note, sent via email or Facebook mail to those who attended, is just good form. Sending a "Sorry you couldn't make it" note to those who didn't attend, perhaps with a recap, is also good form. Taking several photos of the event and posting them is the single best way to reach out. By taking photos, tagging them with attendees' name, and posting them, you can leverage the viral power of the Facebook platform.

Chapter **14**

Integrating Facebook into Your Other Marketing Channels

The best kind of Facebook promotion takes advantage of existing marketing activities to cross-promote your Facebook presence. Driving users to your Facebook Page from other marketing channels allows you to take advantage of the hard work you've invested in all your other marketing efforts, in addition to all the great work you're doing with Facebook. Social media marketer Kim Garst promotes workshops, training, and feeds from Instagram and Pinterest with custom tabs (see Figure 14-1).

In this chapter, we cover how best to integrate your Facebook presence into your existing marketing programs. Also, we show you simple strategies that you can use to promote your Facebook Page outside Facebook. We explain the ways in which companies add Facebook to their email marketing campaigns, websites, and blogs, and show you how to integrate Facebook into your own social media marketing campaigns. We also show you search engine marketing tricks and tips.

FIGURE 14-1:
Kim Garst integrates her many social channels on her Facebook Page.

Making Facebook Part of Your Marketing Mix

After you set up your Facebook Page, you can start promoting it to your existing customers to build an engaged Facebook community. But first, you must prepare your Facebook Page for those new visitors!

Begin by publishing informative, relevant content that keeps your fans engaged, which can eventually lead to increased sales, subscriptions, or other business objectives. But remember to choose quality over quantity!

REMEMBER

The more fans who interact with your Page, the more stories that are generated to their friends' News Feeds, resulting in a viral effect. These word-of-mouth features — friends telling friends about the brands they interact with — represent the real marketing power of Facebook.

The following sections give you the lowdown on getting started on cross-promoting your Page.

Posting content new fans can engage with

When potential fans visit your Page for the first time, they'll likely ask "What's in it for me?" Make sure that recent posts are useful, interesting, and relevant to the communities you're promoting your page to.

Start by assessing the interests and personalities of your existing communities. If you're promoting your Facebook Page to your Pinterest community, for example, make sure that your recent posts on your Facebook Page reflect the topics of your most popular boards and pins. This way, when your Pinterest followers visit your Facebook Page, they'll be more likely to engage with your Page posts and like your Page.

An easy way to accomplish this goal is to repost the most popular Pinterest pins, Instagram photos, and so on. Again, just make sure that the content is relevant to the audience to whom you're promoting your Page.

To understand what your email subscribers want, research your most popular email messages based on open rates and click-throughs. Most email marketing solutions, such as MailChimp and Constant Contact, allow you to analyze how subscribers interact with your email messages.

Choosing a custom Facebook username

Before you start promoting the very long and abstract URL that Facebook has assigned to your Page, consider creating a custom username for your Page. A *username,* or short URL, lets you easily promote your business or organization in a variety of other channels, including TV, radio, and print. If you don't have a username, the frustration of having to remember a long URL means that you could lose a lot of potential customers. Your username appears after `facebook.com` when someone views your Page. The username for the Airbnb Page, for example, is simply airbnb:

```
facebook.com/airbnb
```

Also, Facebook allows Page admins to use `fb.com` as a domain, so the iTunes Facebook Page URL could also be `fb.com/itunes`. This makes it even easier for your fans to remember and find your Page faster:

```
fb.com/airbnb
```

REMEMBER

You must register to have a username for your profile before getting one for your business Page. You also have to be an admin of the Page for which you'd like to create a custom username.

If you don't already have a username, you can create a custom username easily by following these steps:

1. **Log in to Facebook and click the down arrow at the top right (the Page Name drop-down menu).**

2. **From the Page Name drop-down menu, choose the Page (if you're an admin for multiple Pages) for which you want to create a username.**

3. **Click the About tab on the left side of that Page.**

   You see information about your Page.

4. **Click the Create Page @username link next to Username in the General section, as shown in Figure 14-2.**

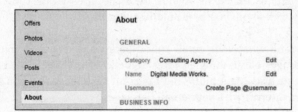

FIGURE 14-2:
Creating a username.

A screen pops open, as shown in Figure 14-3.

FIGURE 14-3:
Entering a username for your Page.

TIP

The best option for your username is the name of your business, but if that's not available, consider trying an industry-related keyword.

5. **In the text box, enter a username that makes sense for your brand and to your fans.**

   Facebook immediately lets you know whether the name is available.

6. **If you see a message that your name is available, click the Create User button to claim that name.**

   If you get a notification that your Page isn't eligible, maybe you still need to create a username for your profile, or someone else has already taken your selected username.

   If you did everything right, you see pop-up screen that says, "You're all set!" To close the screen, click the OK button.

Now you can let the world know about your Facebook Page URL, as described in the next section.

Cross-promoting your Page

Your Facebook URL, or web address, is a new touchpoint for your customers. But unless you let people know about your Page, your Facebook marketing efforts won't help your business.

That's why you need to plaster your Facebook URL everywhere: on your printed marketing materials, in your store, in your radio ads, on your business cards, and so on. In short, you should promote your Facebook address wherever you market your business offline.

Social media can really boost your company's visibility and brand awareness, but it does have a downside: Many businesses end up with fragmented media, as when a business has a Facebook Page but doesn't mention it in its email newsletter, or when it posts a sign that says "Find us on Facebook" but fails to promote in-store activities on the business Page.

Therefore, you need to establish a strong policy of cross-promotion that gives customers and prospects a cohesive experience across all channels. This integrated approach increases the overall effectiveness of all channels.

Here are some ways you can integrate your various marketing channels:

>> In your email signature, list all the ways that the reader can connect with you (Facebook, Twitter, Instagram, and so on).

>> On your website, list your social media channels (including Facebook) on a separate Page. Encourage website visitors to join these communities by briefly describing what they can expect after following or liking.

The preceding options are ideas on how to cross-promote your Facebook Page by getting users to discover your various sites, which then drives them back to your Facebook Page. A variety of third-party applications can display your latest blog posts, Twitter feed, Instagram feed, and other social platforms, all within your Facebook Page.

Facebook also allows you to use Facebook Social Plugins on your website, adding many of the same capabilities that have made Facebook so popular, such as commenting, the Like button (discussed in detail in Chapter 15), and the capability for visitors to share your website content with their Facebook friends or groups. Read Chapter 15 for more information on Facebook plug-ins.

Leveraging your Facebook presence via email, website, and blog

Most likely, more than half the people you email for your business have Facebook accounts. Because all Facebook Pages have their own URLs, you can copy and paste your Page's URL into your corporate email, inviting customers and prospects in your database to sign up as fans.

Better yet, you can add a Facebook Like button to an email, as well as on your website or blog, as described in the following sections.

TIP

Several third-party apps, such as WiseStamp, help you inject a little Facebook into your email signature by automatically adding your latest Facebook Page status update to the bottom of your email messages. This creates an opportunity to automatically engage email recipients who might find your latest Facebook Page update interesting. Find instructions on how to do this at

```
http://apps.wisestamp.com/emailapps/facebook-page
```

REMEMBER

The more ways you allow your fans to share and consume content, the more content they consume and share. Integrating Facebook into your email and website marketing offers you a viral distribution channel like no other.

TIP

Another way to promote your Page is to use the Page Plugin, which lets you embed a content feed from a Facebook Page to your website. See Chapter 15 for details on how to use it.

Promoting Your Facebook Presence Offline

Companies invest a lot of their marketing budget in offline activities such as events, direct marketing, and outdoor advertising. Increasingly, offline efforts are driving online results. Do all that you can to promote your Facebook Page in the real world, such as by including your Facebook Page URL in your offline communications.

Everyone from politicians to celebrities to the owners of small businesses to the heads of Fortune 500 companies is leveraging the offline world to promote a Facebook presence for a simple reason: Facebook's social features make Facebook a great place to interact and build relationships with consumers in unprecedented ways. The viral aspects of the Facebook platform are also ideal for spreading a message beyond the original point of contact.

Although this chapter discusses many great online strategies to enhance your Facebook presence, you can also promote your Page in offline ways that may be more in line with your traditional marketing efforts, not to mention more effective for many of the small businesses, stores, restaurants, and community groups that market on Facebook. Closing the loop between marketing online and offline can be as simple as hanging a sign in your store window saying that you're on Facebook and giving your Page name.

Networking offline

Grow your network in the real world as well as online: Join business networking groups, attend conferences and trade shows for your industry, and get involved in local organizations that hold frequent events. By joining professional organizations and attending industry events, you can establish your credibility in your particular niche. You can also connect with the other influencers and industry movers and shakers. Always network, whether through professional events or casual get-togethers. After all, what better opportunity is there to be able to hand out business cards that include your Facebook Page URL?

If people want to find out more about your business, direct them to your Facebook Page. Let them know about all your business's social media outposts — not just Facebook, but also Twitter, LinkedIn, YouTube, Flickr, SlideShare, and so on. Invite your real-world social network to connect with you online.

Placing the Facebook logo on signs and in store windows

If you own a restaurant, retail store, or professional office, put up a decal in your window or a sandwich board on the checkout counter that asks your customers to visit your Facebook Page. Make sure that anyone who visits your establishment can see the sign. Let your customers know that you offer them something of value on your Page. Encourage them to like your Page and become fans.

Tell your customers that you plan to reward them for visiting your Page. Give them a discount, a coupon, or special content (such as recipes if you own a restaurant). Often, the people with whom you engage offline every day are your best potential Facebook supporters. Invite your real-world customers to connect with you on Facebook, and don't forget to reach out and connect to them by rewarding them for their continued support.

Referencing your Page in ads and product literature

Spread the love and your Facebook Page URL wherever you can. Put your Facebook Page address on all printed materials. Use the Facebook logo and your Page link on your business cards; letterhead; direct-marketing campaigns; print, radio, and TV ads; catalogs; product one-sheets; customer case studies; press releases; newsletters; and coffee mugs, umbrellas, T-shirts, mouse pads, and holiday gifts. Basically, you want to place your Facebook URL wherever eyes might look.

Don't forget to get employees involved in spreading the word about your Facebook presence. Make sure to inform the people who work for your business about your Facebook Page, because they can become your biggest brand ambassadors.

Optimizing Your Page for Search Results

Optimize your Page so that it shows up at the top of Facebook's internal search results, as well as your favorite search engine. A poorly indexed Page can result in a lot of missed opportunities because visitors just can't find your Page.

Facebook users can also leverage the trillions of connections (that is, the so-called *social graph*) in their search queries of content that's been shared with them to produce a narrow spectrum of results. For example, users can search for *Rock Music listened to by teachers* or *Books liked by people who like Led Zeppelin* (see Figure 14-4).

If other users have chosen to make their content available to everyone, members also can search for their status updates, links, and notes, regardless of whether they're friends. Search results continue to include people's profiles as well as pertinent Facebook Pages, groups, and apps. Users can also filter the results so that they see only posts by friends or public posts.

FIGURE 14-4:
Facebook's graph search displays books liked by Led Zeppelin fans.

Using search engine optimization to drive traffic

Pages hosted by Facebook tend to rank well in search engines, including Yahoo! and Google, particularly when users search for businesses or people. In addition to making your content easy to find on Facebook, consider making your content easy for Google and other search engines to find and index.

Here are some practices to help you optimize your Facebook Page for search engines:

>> **Play the name game.** Choose your Page name and username wisely. A pizza shop named Pete's Pizza will get buried far down in search results, but naming your Page something like Pete's Pizza-Minneapolis will bump you to the top of the search results for people who are looking for pizza in Minneapolis. (For details on how to acquire your username, see "Choosing a custom Facebook username" earlier in this chapter.)

>> **Anticipate keywords in text.** When you write your description and the overview section of your Page's About tab, use descriptive keywords that people are likely to search for. To go along with the preceding pizza example, make sure to mention what your restaurant is known for, so go with something like this:

> *We have the best New York–style pizza, the hottest wings, and the coolest staff in all the Twin Cities! Stop by one of our three metro locations: St. Paul, Minneapolis, or our newest shop near the Mall of America in Bloomington.*

>> **Use custom content.** Use iframes or HTML. Include relevant keywords that complement your description and Info sections. Include relevant links in the code.

>> **Anticipate keywords in titles.** When adding content such as photos, discussion topics, and status updates, use appropriate keywords in the titles. If your pizza shop recently donated food to a local school, post pictures of the kids enjoying the special treat with a caption like this:

> *Pete's Pizza staff enjoying some pizza with the kids at Main Street Elementary School.*

>> **Exploit plug-ins.** Add one or more of Facebook's Social Plugins (see Chapter 15) to your website or blog. Integrate Facebook buttons, Share buttons, and Like buttons to increase the number of links to your Facebook Page. (See "Leveraging your Facebook presence via email, website, and blog," earlier in this chapter, for details on creating these buttons.)

>> **Get topical.** Whenever you create an update on Facebook, such as a discussion topic on a Page, choose topics that your intended audience is likely to search for. If you want to know whether your fans would be interested in a whole-wheat pizza crust option, post that question on the discussion board and point out some of the health benefits of using whole-wheat crust (think fiber).

REMEMBER

If you take the time to optimize your content, you see the benefits in your Page traffic and fan engagement. If people can find you in search results quickly and easily because you've posted interesting, engaging information, they're more likely to return to your Page in the future. Future visits mean interested fans and fun interaction!

TIP

Stories posted in the early morning or in the evening have higher engagement rates, because people typically check their Facebook feeds when they get up, get to work, or wind down for the night.

Driving more Likes to your Page

Are you doing all you can to encourage people to like your Facebook Page? Okay, you're not Apple or Taylor Swift, but you can think like a marketer and increase your number of fans, level of engagement, and interaction by employing some best practices in fan building.

Here are four ways to attract more fans to your Facebook Page:

>> **Email your fans.** John has a client who received more than 3,000 fans in one week simply by sending an email to its rather huge email list. Do this; it's very easy, and you may be surprised by how many new Facebook Page connections you receive. When you write this email, be very clear about what people can find on your Page that they won't find elsewhere. Give them a compelling reason to like your Page.

>> **Promote your Page during a webinar.** If your organization does webinars on a regular basis, make your Facebook Page the place where you answer follow-up questions.

>> **Run promotions on your Page by using a customized tab.** If you own a photography studio, use a third-party app like ShortStack to run a contest in which people submit and vote on photos.

>> **Review your Page's Insights on a regular basis.** Insights helps you understand how your visitors are engaging with your content and keep track of what's resonating and what's not. (See Chapter 10 for more on Insights.)

Integrating Instagram into Your Other Marketing Channels

Instagram is one of the social platforms of choice to tell a visual story about your company. Even if you haven't presented your company in a visual way until now, you need to make the transition. Including Instagram in your social media strategy adds a personal touch. Your customers are expecting it, and it will drive discussion. According to a report by eMarketer in 2017, more than one in five people in the United States logged on to Instagram in 2016.

Making a plan for Instagram

Instagram was launched in 2010 and purchased by Facebook for $1 billion in cash and stock in April of 2012. (The point being that Facebook paid that much for a reason.) It's a platform that you can't ignore, and its relationship to Facebook makes it a natural feature to incorporate into your overall Facebook plan. So how do you get the most synergy from integrating Instagram with your Facebook Page?

In Chapter 3, in the section about what to include in your marketing plan, we detail six steps to follow to create a Facebook marketing plan. You should consider some of the same points when making your Instagram plan to make sure that you create a strong alliance between them.

Here are four aspects to consider for your Instagram plan:

>> **How your Instagram audience differs (if at all) from your Facebook audience:** According to Smart Insights, 59 percent of Instagram users are 18 to 29 years old. Thirty-eight percent are women and 26 percent are men. This audience is young but is known to be active buyers. To begin planning your integration, look at how Instagram users compare to your current audience on Facebook. Start by looking at the audience engaging with your company on Instagram. Search your corporate names (also products, Chief Officer's names, and so on) and see whether you're using related hashtags or photos. Look at your Facebook personas (covered in Chapter 2) and use what you know about them as your baseline. You want to listen to what's being said on Instagram and the types of fans that already exist, and build from there.

>> **Which marketing objectives complement your objectives on Facebook:** You're likely targeting such objectives as brand awareness and increasing conversions. See how you can extend these with the use of Instagram. Looking at all your business goals is critical so that you don't exclude anything important.

>> **What your Instagram content strategy will be:** People who come to Instagram want to see a steady stream of content. Worry less about what time of day you publish if you are consistently posting with a cohesive voice and recognizable branding. User-Generated Content (UGC) is also popular, so plan to encourage fans to post their own pictures and videos.

>> **What content you will create specifically for Instagram:** Your Instagram bio has 150 characters and one link. You also have a branded profile picture. Make these elements count! Don't forget to use hashtags with all your Instagram content; that's how people find you. Also crucial is to include captions with your pictures. Everyone reads them, and they set the tone for your fan engagement. Experiment with different content formats, too, to determine which ones your fans respond to. If you're wondering about using filters, or which filter to use, look at other business users in your genre and see they're choosing. As a business, you want to consider the image that you want to project.

Instagram provides several effects called filters that allow you to change the way your photo looks. Users of each genre on Instagram (such as fashion or food) have filters that they favor. Also, Instagram introduced *face filters,* which allow you to put whimsical items on the nearest face in the photo.

Utilizing Instagram Stories

One great way to encourage social interaction is to post on Instagram Stories. Instagram Stories lets you post photos or videos to appear on Instagram for 24 hours, after which they disappear. According to Facebook, Instagram Stories had 300 million daily users by September 30, 2017. Using the Instagram Stories app makes it easy to attract viewers. Stories show up at the top of the feed (on mobile devices) when people log in. The top of the feed is prime real estate (see Figure 14-5).

FIGURE 14-5: Instagram stories display at the top of the screen.

You have to convert your Instagram account to a Business Profile account to be able to have people shop directly from your account and track Insights data. To make this conversion, go to your Instagram profile on your mobile device, tap the gear icon, and follow the instructions.

When you create Instagram Stories there are two questions you should ask yourself to get the maximum value from each story:

>> **How can you maximize shopping opportunities?** You can now create ads directly in Instagram, so consider doing so as a viable option. You can also work with influencers, which are people who talk about your products to their large audiences. In addition, consider third-party tools such as Have2Have.it (https://have2have.it/; see Figure 14-6) and Inselly (https://inselly.com/), among many others, that provide links to Instagram marketplaces, where you can sell the goods that you tag in your feed.

FIGURE 14-6:
Have2Have.it lets you link your account to an Instagram marketplace.

TIP

According to eMarketer, 71 percent of U.S. brands used Instagram as a marketing channel in 2017. They predict that this number will rise to 82 percent in 2018. As of this writing, Instagram is rolling out shopping capabilities. Watch for these capabilities as they develop to explore additional revenue streams.

>> **Which Instagram measurements will you look at to determine your success?** From your Instagram account, you can track several measurements on Insights, including Impressions, Reach, profile visits, and website clicks. You can also track data on several other metrics based on where they came from, including Posts, Action on Page, and Stories. Checking these frequently is a good idea so that you can adjust and reach your overall goals.

TIP

To learn more about using Instagram for business, see *Instagram For Business For Dummies,* by Jennifer Herman, Eric Butow, and Corey Walker (Wiley).

Getting Inside Your Customers' Heads

One last word on cross-promotion: To promote your Facebook presence in a way that truly makes sense, you need to identify the places where your customers and prospects hang out, as well as the websites they visit when they're buying from your competitors.

You can develop a deeper understanding of these behaviors in at least three ways:

>> **Analyze the behavior of your current customers.** Analyze the customers on your website, in your CRM (customer relationship management) system, in your email list, and on your Facebook Page. Ask yourself where customers start and finish and where they are during each phase of the buying cycle (investigating, deciding, comparing, and purchasing).

>> **Spy on your competition.** Find out what they're doing by joining their email lists, following their activity on Facebook, and even buying their products or services.

>> **Test new approaches.** Test and measure new ways to integrate your marketing channels with some of the ideas in this chapter.

The more you can focus on your fans and customers, the more successful you'll be!

Chapter **15**

Integrating Facebook Features into Your Website with Social Plugins

Facebook offers 11 ways of integrating users' social activities with your website. These ways — called *Facebook Social Plugins* — allow you to set up your website so that whenever a reader interacts with your site, such as by leaving a comment on a blog post, a story about that action appears on that person's Timeline.

Facebook's Social Plugins can personalize the content that your visitors see, display the names of Facebook friends who have visited the site, or allow visitors to engage with their Facebook friends without having to log in to your website. By integrating these plug-ins with your website, you essentially give your website the capability to engage Facebook users, increase website traffic, increase brand awareness, and even build your Facebook fan base.

In this chapter, you find out about the different Social Plugins available and which ones you can implement to meet your marketing objectives. We show you how to turn your site into a more personalized experience for your users by adding the Like Button plug-in. We also introduce the Share and Comments plug-ins, which let Facebook users share their opinions about your content with their friends. Finally, you find out how to use the Like Embedded Post plug-in to increase engagement with your Facebook Page, and how to use the Send button to allow visitors to send messages to Facebook friends about content from your website.

Extending the Facebook Experience with Social Plugins

Social Plugins allow visitors to your website to view content that their Facebook friends have liked, commented on, or shared. If visitors to your site are logged in to their Facebook accounts (most users are always logged in), they can help your website content spread throughout Facebook without ever leaving your site.

Facebook has created a special section within its developer site (at `https://developers.facebook.com/docs/plugins`; see Figure 15-1) that explains the Social Plugins, provides tools for generating the code needed to embed each Social Plugin in your site, and showcases superior implementations on real-world websites. The plug-ins are free to use and allow you to add an interactive layer to your site that complements your Facebook marketing strategy. You can use these plug-ins individually or in tandem, extending to your site many of the same features that people have become familiar with inside Facebook.

Deciding which plug-in (or combination of plug-ins) to integrate into your site can be a bit daunting because some of the capabilities overlap. To help you decide which plug-in is right for your needs, here are brief descriptions and examples of each:

TIP

>> **Comments:** This plug-in gives users the option to add a comment to your website from their Facebook account. They can also share it with their friends on Facebook. The added exposure through the News Feed can provide you a good source of additional traffic (see Figure 15-2).

You do have options to delete or report negative comments, but you have to manage the process manually.

>> **Embedded Comments:** The Embedded Comments plug-in allows comments from your Facebook Page to be displayed on your website or other web pages.

FIGURE 15-1:
Facebook's
Social Plugins
developer page.

FIGURE 15-2:
The Comments
plug-in allows
visitors to add a
comment to your
website.

>> **Embedded Posts:** The Embedded Posts feature allows you to embed public posts from your Facebook Page or profile in the content on your website. You can embed a Facebook Page update in a blog post that elaborates on the topic of that Page update, for example. This method lets your website visitors engage with your Facebook Page updates from your website. If they want to like, comment on, or share that update, they're redirected to that post on Facebook.

>> **Embedded Videos:** This plug-in allows you to display any videos in your Facebook Video Library or Facebook Live on your website. You can also display any other video that is public.

>> **Like Button:** This simple one-button design allows anyone who's signed in to Facebook to show approval of your content. The Like count increases as more people click it. When a user clicks the Like button, a news story publishes to his News Feed, and this story includes a link back to the content on your site. If your site offers a lot of content that users can like individually (such as in a catalog, blog, media site, or product description), the Like button is a good way to establish more opportunities to connect with users.

>> **Page Plugin:** This plug-in permits you to display any Page that is on Facebook on your website. As long it is public, you can add it.

>> **Quote Plugin:** This feature allows people on Facebook to highlight specific text on your Page and share it in their own post, adding to your credibility and helping to promote your business.

>> **Save Button:** This helpful plug-in allows Facebook users to save your products or services to their own private list and be updated when you add deals.

>> **Send Button:** Similar to the Like Button plug-in, the Send Button plug-in allows Facebook users to send your website's content to specific friends (using Facebook messages) or Facebook Groups. This plug-in also gives website visitors the option to email your website content.

>> **Share Button:** This button plug-in allows people to share your website content on Facebook. Website visitors can share with particular friends or a specific group. They can also share in a private message to their friends.

REMEMBER

Although these Social Plugins may allow your site to display visitors' personal Facebook data, they won't actually pass that data to your site — that is, you can't track that data, manipulate it, or store it in a database — and visitors' profile pictures and comments are visible only if they're logged in to Facebook.

Adding Plug-In Code to Your Website

Adding a Social Plugin to your site is as simple as embedding a single line of code in your website's HTML code, in much the same manner that you add a YouTube video. Most of the sections in the rest of this chapter explain how to generate the code needed to embed most of these plug-ins within your site. After you have the code, follow these general steps to incorporate it into your website:

1. **Open the HTML file for your web page, using whatever editor you typically use to make changes in your files.**

2. **Go to the spot in the HTML file where you want the Social Plugin to appear.**

3. **Input the lines of code generated on the Facebook Developers site into the HTML file.**

4. **Save the HTML file and, if necessary, upload the new HTML file to your website.**

5. **Using a web browser, go to that web page (refresh your browser, if necessary) and make sure that the plug-in appears in the correct location.**

Note: You must have access to your website's source files. If you don't know where these files are located, get your website developer to point you in the right direction.

In most cases, installing another plug-in is just a matter of using a different line (or lines) of code in Step 3. Refer to the Facebook Developers page for each plug-in for the specific code you need.

Integrating Facebook Insights into Your Social Plugins

One great thing about using Social Plugins is that they let you measure how those plug-ins are being used and determine who's using them. As you can imagine, this data is critical information that can help you with marketing and even product development.

Facebook allows you to use Facebook Insights to see how visitors to your website interact with the Facebook Social Plugins you've installed on your website. When a user shares a link to your site on Facebook by using the Like button, for example, that action can be tracked in a Facebook Insights report about your website.

The next few sections show you how to do this.

Setting up your website as a Facebook application

To access Insights data for your website, you must create a Facebook application. Creating a Facebook application allows you to associate an application ID with each Social Plugin on your site, which enables Facebook to track the ways Facebook users interact with the plug-in. Creating an app gives you the capability to access Insights for each of your plug-ins.

TIP

We recommend that you work with a professional web developer on this section if you're a novice.

To create an application, follow these steps:

1. **Visit** https://developers.facebook.com/apps **and click the Create a New App button on the right side of the page.**

2. **Enter the requested information, as shown in Figure 15-3:**

TIP

   If you're creating an application for the first time, you must grant Facebook permission to access your basic information.

   - **Display Name:** This name is a unique name for the application you're creating. Because only you will see this info, you can simply use the name of your website or the Social Plugin you're creating the app for.

   - **Contact Email:** Use the email you use for Facebook communications.

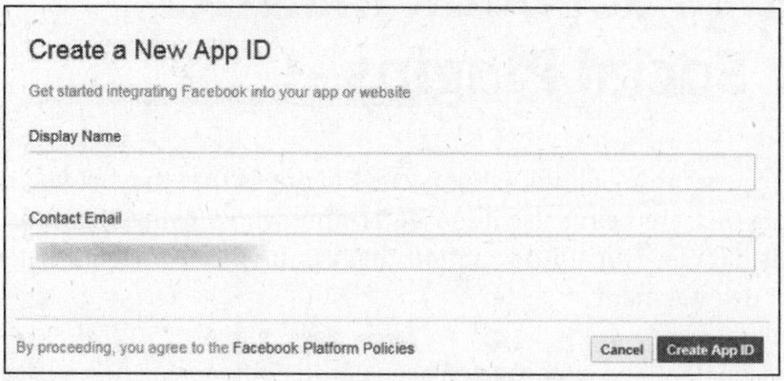

Create a New App ID

Get started integrating Facebook into your app or website

Display Name

Contact Email

By proceeding, you agree to the Facebook Platform Policies.   Cancel   Create App ID

FIGURE 15-3: The first window you see when creating a new app.

3. **Note that by creating an app, you're agreeing to the Facebook Platform Policy.**

   Read more about the policy at https://developers.facebook.com/policy.

4. **Click Create App ID.**

5. **On the next screen, enter the captcha as you see it and then click Submit.**

   A screen opens asking you to select a product.

6. **Click the Set Up button for the Analytics option.**

   A screen opens, asking you to select a platform (see Figure 15-4).

FIGURE 15-4: Choosing the web platform for your app.

7. **Click the Web option to add the platform.**

Next, to allow Facebook to integrate with your app, you follow a four-step process:

1. **Set up the Facebook software developer kit (SDK) for JavaScript.**

   To do this, you need to include the JavaScript SDK for the app on your web page, right after the opening `<body>` tag. The JavaScript code appears in the window after you configure the desired app (see Figure 15-5). Click Next when done.

   REMEMBER

   The goal is to allow Facebook's platform to collect information about the way people interact with the Social Plugins on your website. Your application ID, then, allows Facebook and your website to talk to each other.

2. **For Tell Us About Your Website, enter the URL of your website and click Save and then the Continue button.**

3. **For Log App Events, copy the code you see on the screen to log the events (actions people take). Then click Next.**

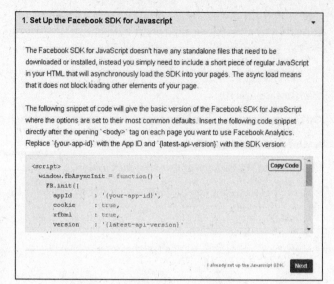

FIGURE 15-5:
The code window for each app includes the JavaScript SDK for your website.

4. **For Logging Web Activity, copy the code you see onscreen to a button click handler (it tells you whether the button is clicked) in the app.**

   Facebook then asks you launch the app. Click the button where you added the code, thereby logging your first event. Then click Next.

   You can now view your Facebook Analytics Dashboard to debug your app by going to https://www.facebook.com/analytics. Click the name of your app to view your dashboard. Facebook sends you to Activity ⇨ Event Debugging to ensure that your activities are being logged.

Adding Comments to Your Website

The Comments plug-in enables you to add a comments thread to any page on your website that allows visitors who are logged in to Facebook to add comments (see Figure 15-6). Users can choose to have their comments also posted to their Facebook profiles; those comments show up in those users' News Feeds, viewable by all their friends. By installing this plug-in, you allow users to leave comments and interact with you, and because their friends see that activity, you can drive more traffic back to your website.

A mobile version of this plug-in automatically shows up when a mobile-device user agent is detected.

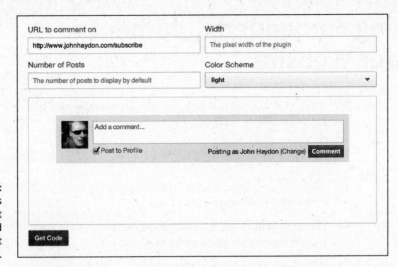

FIGURE 15-6:
Add a Comments
plug-in to get
users engaged
with the content
on your website.

To add the Comments plug-in to a page on your site, follow these steps:

1. **Visit** `https://developers.facebook.com/docs/plugins` **and click the Web button.**

2. **Fill in the requested information to customize your Comments feature (refer to Figure 15-6), as follows:**

   • **URL to Comment On:** Enter the specific URL of the web page for the comment box.

   • **Width:** Select the desired width of the plug-in in pixels.

   • **Number of Posts:** Select the desired number of posts to display by default.

3. **Click Get Code and add to your website.**

TIP

You can add a Comments plug-in to any piece of content on which you want to solicit user feedback. Consider integrating it into product review pages or your blog, or use it to gauge user interest on website-related topics such as a new layout.

REMEMBER

If you integrate the Comments plug-in into your site, you need to monitor the comments closely and delete spam and malicious or overtly negative remarks.

Sharing Embedded Comments to Your Website

The Embedded Comments plug-in lets you display comments on your website that come from your Facebook Page.

To add the Embedded Comments plug-in to your web page, follow these steps:

1. **Visit** `https://developers.facebook.com/docs/plugins` **and click the Embedded Comments link.**

2. **Fill in the requested information to customize your Embedded Comments plug-in (see Figure 15-7), as follows:**

   - **URL of comment:** Enter the specific URL of the web page on which the comment appears.

   - **Width:** Select the desired width of the plug-in in pixels.

   - **Include Parent C (If URL Is a Reply):** Select this box if you want to display the original comment to which you are replying.

3. **Click Get Code to add that code to your website.**

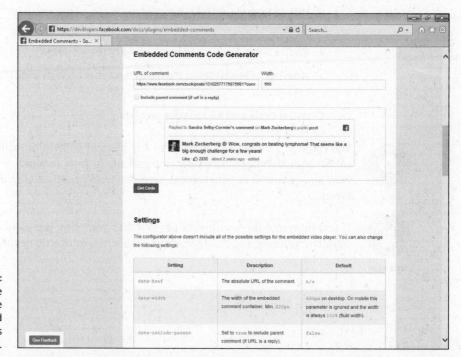

FIGURE 15-7: Creating the code for the Embedded Comments plug-in.

Creating More Reach with the Embedded Posts Plug-In

The Embedded Posts plug-in lets you add specific Facebook posts from your Page or profile to your website.

To generate code for the Embedded Posts plug-in, follow these steps:

1. **Visit** `https://developers.facebook.com/plugins` **and click the Embedded Posts link.**

2. **Fill in the requested information to customize your plug-in (see Figure 15-8):**

   - **URL of Post:** Enter the Facebook URL for the post. Clicking the date associated with this post redirects visitors to this URL.

   - **Width:** Select the width you'd like to use for the plug-in. It's best to select the width of the page or the post you want to place the embedded post in.

   TIP

   You have the option to select the check box if you want to include the parent comment (the entire post).

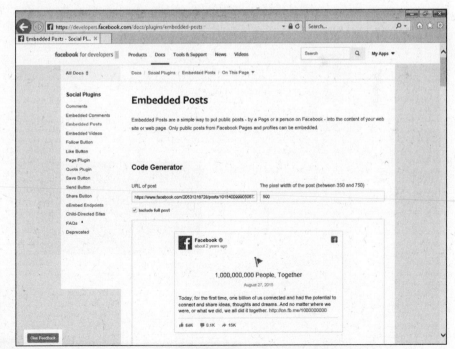

FIGURE 15-8: Generating code for the Facebook Embedded Posts plug-in.

3. **Click Get Code.**

4. **Copy the code and place it where you want it to show up on your page.**

Displaying Embedded Videos from Facebook

The Embedded Videos plug-in lets you share your own videos and other public videos from Facebook on your website.

To add the Embedded Videos plug-in to your web page, follow these steps:

1. **Visit** `https://developers.facebook.com/docs/plugins` **and click the Embedded Videos link.**

2. **Fill in the requested information to customize your Embedded Videos (see Figure 15-9), as follows:**

   - **URL of Video:** Enter the specific URL of the video you want to embed.

     Width: Enter the pixel width of the chosen video.

   - **Include Full Post:** Select this box if you want to display the post that accompanies the video.

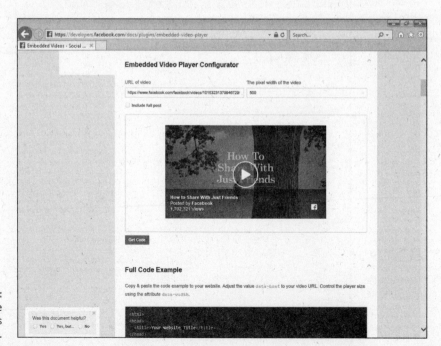

FIGURE 15-9:
Customizing the Embedded Videos plug-in.

3. **Click Get Code to add the code to your website.**

4. **Copy the code and place it where you want it to show up on your page.**

Getting More Visibility with the Like Button

The Like button lets visitors share your website content with their Facebook friends. When the user clicks a Like button on your site, a story appears in his friends' News Feeds with a link back to your website. This plug-in is a must if you publish regular content on your website.

To integrate Facebook's Like Button plug-in with your site, follow these steps:

1. **Visit** `https://developers.facebook.com/docs/plugins` **and click the Like Button link.**

2. **Fill in the requested information to customize your button (see Figure 15-10), as follows:**

   - **URL to Like:** Enter the exact URL you want visitors to like. Leaving this field blank defaults to the URL of the page on which the Like button is located.

   - **Layout:** Choose one of three options: Standard, Button Count, and Box Count. You can view each in the preview pane on the right.

   - **Show Friends' Faces:** Selecting this check box sets the Like button to Show Friends Faces of users who clicked the Like button.

   - **Width:** Enter the desired width of the Like button in pixels.

   - **Action Type:** Choose either Like or Recommend.

   - **Button size:** Choose a small or large button.

3. **Click Get Code.**

   If you chose the capability to measure how people are using this plug-in, select your app to the right of the This Script Uses the App ID of Your App text. See the "Integrating Facebook Insights into Your Social Plugins" section, earlier in this chapter, for instructions on creating an app.

   Copy the code and paste it into your website at the location where you want the plug-in to appear. If you're not familiar with how your website works, please get a professional to help you.

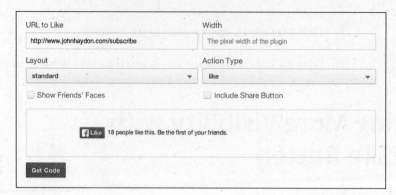

FIGURE 15-10:
Customizing a
Like button.

Sharing Pages Using the Page Plugin

The Page Plugin allows you to display on your website any page that appears on Facebook, which can facilitate promotions with other businesses on Facebook.

To add the Page Plugin to your web page, follow these steps:

1. **Visit** `https://developers.facebook.com/docs/plugins` **and click the Page Plugin link.**

2. **Fill in the requested information to customize your Page Plugin (see Figure 15-11), as follows:**

   - **Facebook Page URL:** Enter the specific URL of the Facebook Page you want to share on your website.

   - **Tabs:** Choose the tab you want users to click to share the Page.

   - **Width:** Enter the pixel width for the embed.

   - **Height:** Enter the pixel height for the embed.

   Use the following check boxes to customize the look of the Page to share:

   - **Use Small Header:** Select this box if you want to keep the original header of the Page small.

   - **Adapt to Plugin Container Width:** Select this box if you want to adapt the plug-in to the container width.

   - **Hide Cover Photo:** Select this box if you want to hide the cover photo of the original Facebook Page that you intend to share.

   - **Show Friends' Faces:** Select this box if you want to display the faces of friends who liked the page.

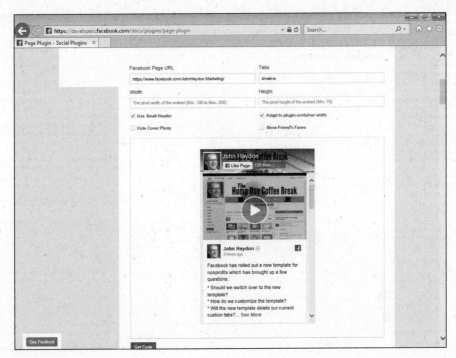

FIGURE 15-11:
Creating the code for the Page Plugin.

Quote Plugin

The Quote Plugin lets website visitors highlight any text on your Page and share it with their friends. Users don't need any special permissions to use a quote from your Page.

To add the Quote Plugin to your web page, follow these steps:

1. Visit https://developers.facebook.com/docs/plugins **and click the Quote Plugin link.**

2. **To see how the Quote Plugin works, click the Try the Plugin button (see Figure 15-12) and highlight any part of the sentence displayed (select part of this sentence to see the plug-in in action).**

When you highlight some of the text, you see a pop-up that says Share Quote.

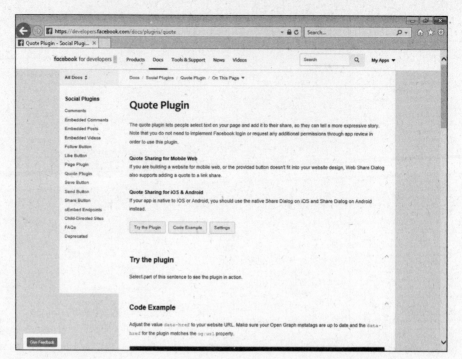

FIGURE 15-12:
Creating code for
the Quote Plugin.

3. **Click the Share Quote pop-up, and you get the screen shown in Figure 15-13 with a drop-down menu (near the top-left corner) that gives you the following choices:**

   • Share on Your Timeline

   • Share on a Friend's Timeline

   • Share in a Group

   • Share in an Event

   • Share on a Page You Manage

4. **After you make your choice, enter a comment under your profile picture that you want to make about the quote.**

5. **Click the Friends drop-down menu to choose who will see the share.**

6. **Click Post to Facebook.**

FIGURE 15-13:
Completing the
Share Quote
screen.

Save Button

The Save button lets website visitors save your products or services to a private list that they can view later and see any updated promotions.

To add the Save button to your web page, follow these steps:

1. **Visit** https://developers.facebook.com/docs/plugins **and click the Save Button link.**

2. **Fill in the requested information to customize your Save button (see Figure 15-14), as follows:**

   - **Link of a Service or Product to Save:** Make sure to link anything you're selling so that users can be reminded of them when you promote them.

   - **Button Size:** Choose Large or Small.

3. **Click Get Code.**

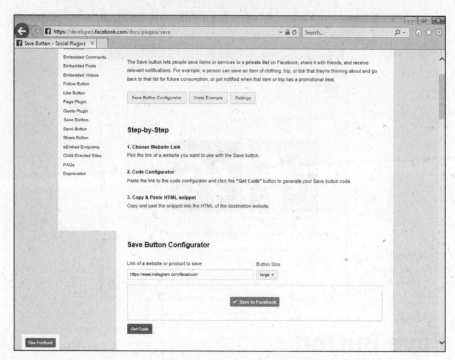

FIGURE 15-14:
Customizing a
Save Button.

Allowing for Private Sharing with the Send Button

The Send button lets visitors to your website send your content to friends. They can send a link and a short note as a Facebook message, Facebook Group post, or email message. The Share button is different from the Like button, which allows users to share content with their friends by publishing that content to their Timeline.

To add the Send button to your web page, follow these steps:

1. **Visit** https://developers.facebook.com/docs/plugins **and click the Send Button link.**

2. **Fill in the requested information to customize your Send button by entering the exact URL you want visitors to send under URL to Send (see Figure 15-15).**

3. **Click Get Code to add to your website.**

4. **Copy the code and place it where you want it to show up on your page.**

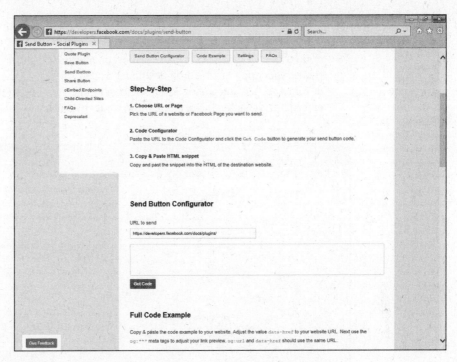

FIGURE 15-15:
Customizing a
Send button.

Allowing for Public Sharing with the Share Button

The Share button lets website visitors add a message to your website content before sharing it on their Timelines, with groups, or with friends in a Facebook message.

To integrate Facebook's Share Button plug-in into your site, follow these steps:

1. **Visit** https://developers.facebook.com/docs/plugins **and click the Share Button link.**

2. **Fill in the requested information to customize your button (see Figure 15-16), as follows:**

   - **URL to Share:** Enter the exact URL you want visitors to like. Leaving this field blank defaults to the URL of the page where the Like button is located.

   - **Layout:** Choose how the text and number should be displayed.

   - **Size:** Choose either small or large.

   - **Mobile iframe:** Click the box if you want to have the Share dialog displayed in an iframe on a mobile screen.

3. Click Get Code.

If you chose the capability to measure how people are using this plug-in, choose your app from the drop-down menu titled This Script Uses the App ID of Your App. See "Integrating Facebook Insights into Your Social Plugins," earlier in this chapter, for instructions on creating an app.

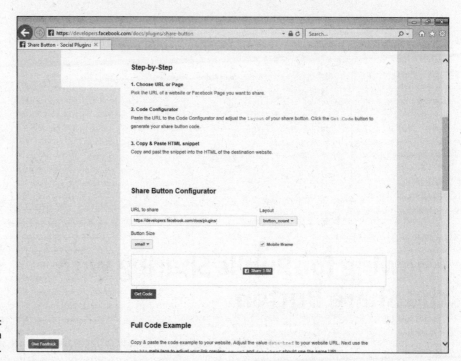

FIGURE 15-16: Customizing a Share button.

CHECKING YOUR PLUG-INS WITH DEBUGGER

Facebook provides the Debugger tool for you to check your plug-ins after you add them to your website. Use this tool to make sure that your plug-ins are installed properly. Visit https://developers.facebook.com/tools/debug, enter the URL of the web page you want to review, and click the Debug button. If you have a plug-in that isn't working, a warning message displays, letting you know where the issue is so that you can return to your HTML code and fix the problem.

online customers

» **Utilizing chatbots to provide responsive customer service**

» **Creating engaging streaming broadcasts with Facebook Live**

Chapter **16**

Stepping Up Your Customer Engagement

Mark Zuckerberg's announcement of News Feed changes in January of 2018 puts customer engagement at the center of your marketing efforts. (See more about News Feed changes in Chapter 3). To engage prospects and customers, online marketers need to focus on the advances in technology that make communicating with customers easier and with less friction than ever before. Enter Facebook Messenger and Facebook Live. Using these apps, both small and large companies can provide excellent customer service and develop stronger relationships with their customers. As the technology develops, marketers find new ways to monetize them.

In this chapter, you look at two technologies that add direct interactivity to Facebook Pages and help businesses more effectively engage their customers, develop leads, and sell products.

Using Facebook Messenger to Communicate with Customers

Did you know that as of this writing, more than 1.3 billion people use Messenger each month? Also, according to *Business Insider,* in 2015 the "combined user base of the top four chat apps (WhatsApp, Facebook Messenger, WeChat, and Viber) was larger than the combined user base of the top four social networks (Instagram, Facebook, Twitter, and LinkedIn)." This trend toward using chat apps shows no signs of abating.

Facebook added Messenger to its business Pages in 2017 in recognition of the fact that real-time and two-way communication help businesses more effectively find and convert customers. Messenger, with its near instant gratification and self-serve features, provides a more satisfying customer experience than calling tech support or emailing with questions. We all know from first-hand experience that calling customer support and sitting on hold is deadly. In fact, according to a survey done by Nielsen in 2016, 56 percent of people would rather message than call customer service. We're sure that you agree.

Benefitting from Messenger

So how can your business benefit from using Messenger? Here are several ways for both you and your customers to benefit:

>> **Offers a better customer experience:** Direct messaging gets customers quick answers that make the customer experience more satisfying.

>> **Differentiates your company:** You stand out when your customer responses are top notch. Competitors with lackluster performance will fall behind.

>> **Provides a one-stop shop for purchases:** Customer can place orders and you can accept payment right from your Facebook Page, which is great for impulse buys.

>> **Supplies better information for customers:** Customers can engage with Messenger to get product information when they need it.

Understanding guidelines for Messenger

To protect customer privacy, Facebook set down some guidelines for using Messenger to communicate with fans. Here are some things you can't do with Messenger:

>> **Initiate a messenger conversation:** You may communicate only with someone who makes a comment, either privately or publicly.

>> **Download customer email addresses:** When someone communicates through Messenger, you won't be able to download the person's email address.

>> **Send messages if your Page is blocked:** If someone has chosen to block you or your Page, you can't communicate using Messenger.

Enabling Messenger

To use Messenger, you need to enable it from your Facebook Page, as shown in Figure 16-1. Enabling Messenger is straightforward and takes only five steps:

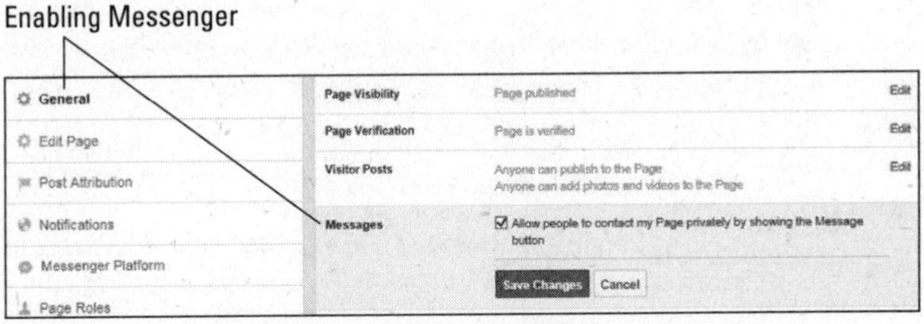

Enabling Messenger

FIGURE 16-1:
Enabling
Messenger.

1. **Click Settings at the top of your Facebook Page.**

2. **Choose General from the list of links on the left.**

3. **Click the edit link next to the word *Messages*.**

4. **Select the Allow People to Contact My Page Privately by Showing the Message Button box.**

5. **Click Save Changes.**

In the following sections, you see how using chatbots creates a great customer experience, and how to set chatbots up.

Developing a Better Customer Experience

As many online marketers look at their newly available customer data from a variety of sources, they realize that their customer experience is sorely lacking. Becoming more customer-centric is the mantra of savvy executives who understand that the companies who make it easy to find and use their products will prevail.

Providing customer service with chatbots

One of the best ways to differentiate yourself from your competitors is to provide outstanding customer support. Stellar customer service encourages people to become repeat buyers and sales advocates. Messenger excels in its capability to provide you with easy tools to wow your customers. What can it do for your business?

Here are five ways it can enhance your customer service. Messenger is

>> **Two-way and real-time:** Customers can get immediate answers instead of putting in a support ticket or waiting for an email reply.

>> **Private:** Customers who are dealing with sensitive matters can opt to make their communications private.

>> **An aid to solving problems:** Customers can immediately communicate their concerns and get answers. This helps keep the emotional temperature down when things go awry.

>> **Self-serve:** Customers can place orders or get critical logistics questions answered.

>> **Expands channel communication:** The website Messenger plug-in allows people to contact you privately from your FB Page. For more information about this plug-in, go to `https://developers.facebook.com/docs/messenger-platform/discovery/customer-chat-plugin`.

Using Messenger chatbots

You may have heard the term *chatbot* and wondered what it is. A *chatbot* is a piece of interactive software that uses artificial intelligence (AI) to respond to chat in a conversational way. If you have created a chatbot for your Facebook Page, your customers will be able to type questions into a chat window and receive preprepared content that answers their questions. The content can include text, video, links, and images.

One good example of a chatbot used to educate and entertain a company's users appears on the Food Network Facebook Page. If you click the Send Message button (shown in Figure 16-2), you see preset text saying that a company representative will instantly respond. It asks you to click the Get Started button. When you click that button, you are asked whether you want fun food facts sent to you; you can also ask for a recipe. This entire exchange is done by the chatbot.

Send Message

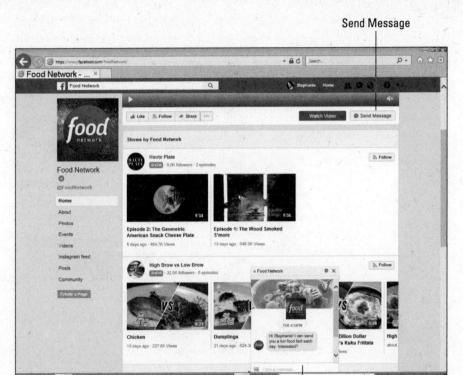

FIGURE 16-2:
Food Network's
Messenger
chatbot provides
recipes and
fun facts.

Messenger chatbot

Another great example is the chatbot used by 1-800 Flowers (shown in Figure 16-3). Its chatbot lets customers order right from the Messenger app on their Facebook Page. You can see how this encourages people to make a simple order.

Facebook has built-in settings that you can use to provide two-way customer service to your users. There are two Settings links that you need use to configure Messenger:

>> **Messenger Platform:** Select this radio button to go to the page where you set up how your chatbot will look (see Figure 16-4).

>> **Subscribed Apps:** The Apps that are connected to your Page will be automatically displayed here.

>> **Link Your App to Your Page:** You need to enter an Apple ID to connect native apps.

>> **Whitelisted Domains:** These are third-party domains that you say can be used with Messenger.

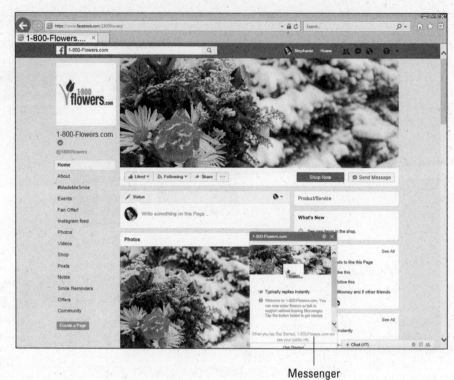

FIGURE 16-3:
Ordering with
Messenger on
1-800 Flowers.

Messenger

Messenger Platform setup

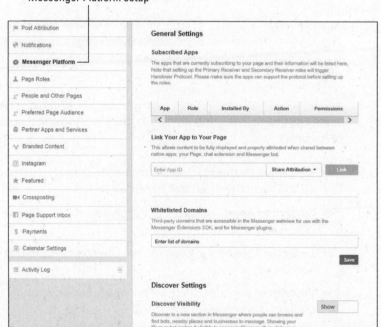

FIGURE 16-4:
Messenger
Platform settings.

TIP

Discover Settings — Discover Visibility: This setting allows your bot to be searched along with other bots. The default is Show. Unless you have a reason to make your bot harder to find, leave the default setting.

We recommend that you consult your webmaster or developer to ensure that your Messenger app performs correctly. You can find documentation here: `https://developers.facebook.com/docs/messenger-platform`.

>> **Messaging:** This section lets you set up how people can message your business Page and what messages they will receive in return.

To set up Messaging, go to Settings at the top of your Facebook Page and follow these steps:

1. Click the Messaging link, shown in Figure 16-5.

Messaging

☼ General	**Messaging Settings**
💬 **Messaging**	Set up how people can message your page
☼ Edit Page	
🖼 Post Attribution	**Sections**
🔔 Notifications	General Settings — Jump to Section
⚙ Messenger Platform	Response Assistant — Jump to Section
👤 Page Roles	
👥 People and Other Pages	**General Settings**
👥 Preferred Page Audience	**Use the Return key to send messages** — Yes
📱 Partner Apps and Services	When you have written a message, you can tap the Return/Enter key to send it.
✿ Branded Content	
📷 Instagram	**Prompt visitors to send messages** — No
★ Featured	Page visitors may see prominent ways to start a message with you if you're online or if your Page is very responsive to messages.
🎬 Crossposting	

FIGURE 16-5: The Messaging link.

2. Go to General Settings and click Yes or No to the following choices:

- **Use the Return Key to Send Messages:** The default is Yes. Leave the default choice if you're used to hitting the Return key after typing a line and want to do this when using the chatbot.

- **Prompt Visitors to Send Messages:** The default is No. If you click Yes, Page visitors will see indications that you are responsive to their messages.

3. Go to Response Assistant and click Yes or No to the five choices shown in Figure 16-6.

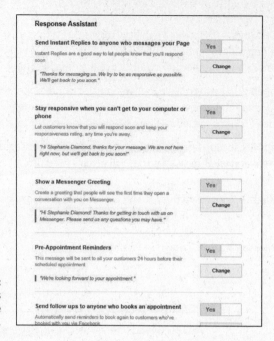

FIGURE 16-6:
Creating settings
for the Response
Assistant.

- **Send Instant Replies to Anyone Who Messages Your Page:** The default is No. If you click Yes, you see a prewritten message that says, "Thanks for messaging us. We try to be as responsive as possible. We'll get back to you soon." You can choose to edit this message by clicking the Change button.

  When you click the Change button, a window pops open (see Figure 16-7), showing you how your message will look on a mobile device. You can refine the message and click the Add Personalization link, which gives you the option to insert the person's first name, last name, or full name, as well as your Facebook URL into your reply. When you're done editing, click the Save button.

TIP

4. **(Optional) Personalize the name for each of the following settings.**

   The name is pulled from the person's profile. Displaying people's real names may make them feel more welcome. Decide what you think your target audience would prefer:

   - **Stay Responsive When You Can't Get to Your Computer or Phone:** The default is No. If you click Yes, you see a message that says, "Hi [*customer name*], thanks for your message. We are not here right now, but we'll get back to you soon!" You can choose to edit this message by clicking the Change button. If you do, a window pops open, showing you how your message will look on a mobile device. You also see a Schedule link (see Figure 16-8) that lets you set up the days and times on which the message will show when you are Away or Available. When you're done editing, click the Save button.

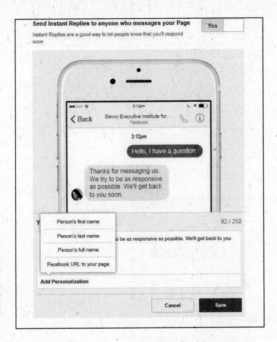

Choose Away or Available

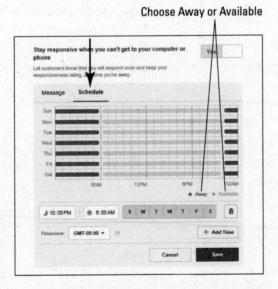

- **Show a Messenger Greeting:** The default is No. If you click Yes, you see a message that says, "Hi [*customer name*]! Thanks for getting in touch with us on Messenger. Please send us any questions you may have." You can choose to edit this message by clicking the Change button. If you click Change, a window pops open, showing you how your message will look on a mobile device. The greeting message is displayed and then the visitor's question appears (see Figure 16-9). When you're done editing, click the Save button.

FIGURE 16-9:
Your greeting message pops up when the visitor comes in.

- **Pre-Appointment Reminders:** The default is No. If you click Yes, you will see a message that says, "We're looking forward to your next appointment." You can choose to edit this message by clicking the Change button. If you do, a window pops open, as shown in Figure 16-10, showing you how your message will look on a mobile device. When you're done editing, click the Save button.

- **Send Follow Up to Anyone Who Books an Appointment:** The default is No. If you click Yes, you see a message that says, "Hi [*customer name*]! It's been a while since we last saw you. We'd love to have you back!" You can choose to edit this message by clicking the Change button. If you do, a window pops open, showing you how your message will look on a mobile device. If you click the Schedule link, shown in Figure 16-11, you can choose the number of times and the hour, day, week, month, or year that the follow-up message is shown after the previous appointment is booked. For example, if you're a dentist, you may choose to have the message pop up 3–4 months after a person's last appointment. When you're done editing, click the Save button.

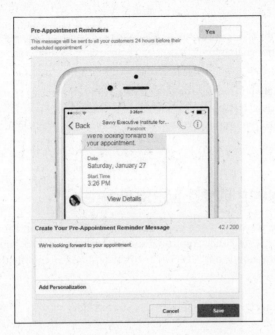

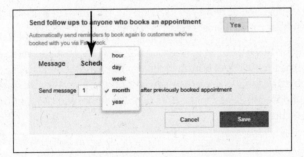

Developing chatbots

As you can see from the previous examples, chatbots help you serve your customers in a way that you never could by phone and email. Think about how you might use them to step up your engagement. In case you want to build one yourself, Facebook provides online documentation at (https://developers.facebook.com/docs/messenger-platform) that will help your company create its own chatbot. If you want to go outside your company for assistance, you can find several third-party vendors who specialize in creating Facebook chatbots. These vendors include:

>> **Botisfy** (http://botsify.com): Botsify provides an app that requires no coding. It offers tiered pricing with a free tier for those with fewer than 100 users.

>> **ChatFuel** (`http://chatfuel.com`): ChatFuel's app also requires no coding and does not charge for its app. If you want advanced features, you can pay a fee.

>> **Conversable** (`http://conversable.com`): This app is scaled for the enterprise and used by companies (such as Sony and Whole Foods) that need more robust features. It can be set up to work across multiple social media platforms.

Advertising with Messenger

We're well past the time when online marketers debate about the value of mobile Facebook Ads. TechCrunch reports that 85 percent of Facebook's ad revenue now comes from mobile ads. The key is to present ads on mobile that load fast and look good.

You have several types of Messenger ads to consider:

>> **News Feed Messenger ads:** These ads are shown in your audience's Timeline and contain one or more call to action (CTA) buttons. If a user clicks an ad, a Messenger conversation starts.

To set up this type of ad, go to `https://www.facebook.com/advertising`. Click the Create an Ad button in the top-right corner and choose one of two ad objectives that give you Messenger options. In the Consideration column, you choose Messages; in the Conversion column, you choose Conversions (see Figure 16-12).

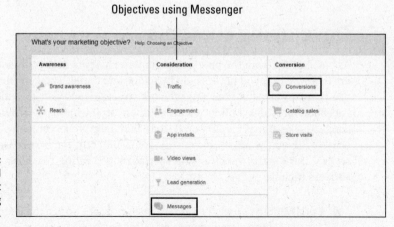

FIGURE 16-12:
News Feed Ad
objectives that
involve using
Messenger.

>> **Sponsored messages:** You can set up sponsored messages to communicate with users who have previously held conversations with your business. Again, go to `https://www.facebook.com/advertising` and click the Create an Ad button. The objective to choose for this is Messages. Then choose the Click to Messenger button and, from the drop-down menu, choose Sponsored Message (see Figure 16-13). Then input your message where prompted.

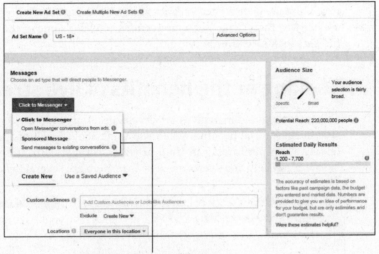

FIGURE 16-13: Choosing to create a Sponsored Message with Messenger.

Creating a sponsored message

>> **Messenger home placement:** This type of ad is related to placement and can be set for any ad objective. It allows you to set up an ad objective (in this example, we chose Traffic) and have it show up in Messenger as one of your choices, as shown in Figure 16-14.

TIP

For step-by-step details on how to set up ads in Facebook, see Chapter 11.

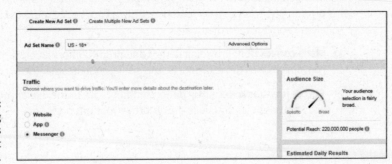

FIGURE 16-14: Choosing Messenger as an ad placement for an ad.

Getting Started with Facebook Live

Another great way to engage fans and find new customers is to broadcast with Facebook Live. Imagine the great opportunity to speak directly to fans and prospects in real time. You can directly answer their questions and find out what they think. It's your very own focus group of real people who are interested in learning more about you and your business.

If you already have a Facebook account, a business Page, or a public profile, you are halfway there! The following sections consider some of the significant benefits Facebook Live affords you.

Looking at the benefits of live streaming

Live streaming and its replays on viewers desktop or mobile can reward you with several substantial benefits. When you think about live broadcasts, you may feel uneasy about performing in front of your customers. But focusing on how your business can help you overcome your fear. Here are several benefits to consider:

- » **Easy content creation:** Live streaming helps you develop video content both easily and inexpensively. You can then replay it on your Page and repurpose it for your website or other channels and platforms.

- » **Increased brand awareness:** Gain attention for your business by promoting your broadcast and educating your customers, which in turn can help create advocates who spread your message.

- » **Increased Loyalty:** Develop better relationships with fans, resulting in more loyal customers.

- » **Deeper conversations:** Tell your company story your way and see whether it resonates with viewers. You'll get both positive and negative comments that will help you hone your message. Telling your story also increases the likelihood that you'll show up in your users' News Feed — a worthy goal!

- » **More engagement:** Providing information and interactions helps build community. You can broadcast directly to a Facebook Group and strengthen interaction between members.

- » **More conversion:** Providing demos and product information can affect conversions, sell more products, and grow your customer list.

- » **Better feedback:** Receiving direct comments about the use of your products and services helps you build and improve your offerings.

Understanding the guidelines

Before you start broadcasting, you should understand what settings you can control in Facebook Live so that you can make better decisions about your broadcast. We cover the setup details in the next section, but first, here are some settings that you control:

>> **Who sees it:** If you're broadcasting from your profile, you can choose who sees your broadcast. You can opt to exclude specific people, show it to only a select group, or show it to everyone. (See the next section for details about broadcasting from a Page.) If you're broadcasting from a Page, you can restrict your audience by age, gender, and location.

>> **Whether it is public or private:** You can determine whether you want to do a private or public live stream just as you can with any other Facebook post.

>> **Whether you can delete it:** You can delete any broadcast after you have completed it if you choose to do so. You can also delete it at any time in the future.

>> **Who can comment:** You control who can comment, and you can delete comments during or after your broadcast.

>> **Where it can be viewed:** If it's public, it can be seen on the desktop, iOS, and Android devices.

TIP

For format guidelines and more about live streaming, go to `https://www.facebook.com/help/1534561009906955?helpref=faq_content`.

Setting up Facebook Live

Talking directly to your fans and prospects will help you maximize your attempt to build a stronger customer base. Lots of interesting things are happening during your workday, and new products and services are being developed and introduced. Pick something you feel passionate about and stream it live to your audience. To get started, you need to set up Facebook Live. This section describes the setup from your computer.

Go to `https://www.facebook.com/live/create`. On the page that appears, you're prompted to give Facebook access to your camera and microphone. (Facebook requires this only the first time you set it up.) If you don't use a Chrome or Firefox browser, you see a message that says, "Please try broadcasting on the latest desktop version of Chrome or Firefox to go live with your camera." Next, a screen called Go Live With Your Gear shows you settings for your broadcast, as shown in Figure 16-15.

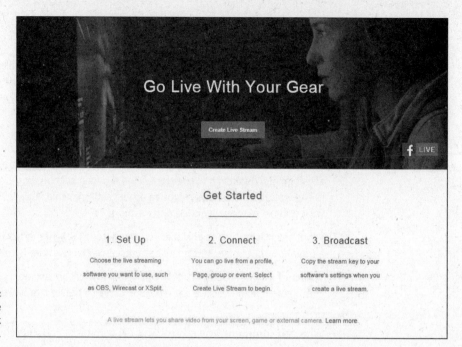

Go Live With Your Gear

Create Live Stream

f LIVE

Get Started

1. Set Up	2. Connect	3. Broadcast
Choose the live streaming software you want to use, such as OBS, Wirecast or XSplit.	You can go live from a profile, Page, group or event. Select Create Live Stream to begin.	Copy the stream key to your software's settings when you create a live stream.

A live stream lets you share video from your screen, game or external camera. Learn more.

FIGURE 16-15:
Accessing the
Facebook
Live screen.

TIP

You can also set up a Facebook Live broadcast on your mobile or desktop from your Page in the section at the top that says Write Something. Click the *live video* icon and follow instructions. You may want to choose this option as you become more familiar with broadcasting.

REMEMBER

These settings may look different depending on the entity you are broadcasting from — profile, Page, or public profile.

When broadcasting from your profile, follow the three items listed on the screen under Getting Started (refer to Figure 16-15) and explained in the following sections.

Set up

Follow these steps to select the live streaming software you intend to use:

1. **Click one of the three choices, OBS, Wirecast, or XSplit (or your own choice).**

2. **Follow the instructions to download and install the software and then return to the broadcast screen.**

3. **Click the Create Live Stream button (refer back to Figure 16-15).**

   A screen pops up, as shown in Figure 16-16.

Use the drop-down menu to choose when you broadcast

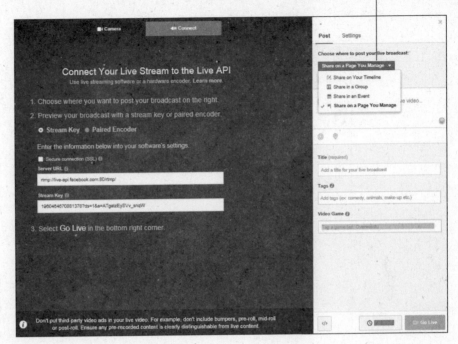

FIGURE 16-16:
Settings for
Facebook Live
stream from
your Page.

Connect

Facebook asks you to choose where to post your live broadcast. From the drop-down menu on the right, the choices are as follows:

>> **On your Timeline:** You can choose to broadcast directly from your News Feed.

>> **In a Group:** If you have an ongoing group, you can create a broadcast directly for them.

>> **In an Event:** Broadcasting live from an event is a great way to generate excitement. It also lets you interview participants and show engagement.

>> **On a Page You Manage:** If you have more than one Page, you can choose the one you want here, as shown in Figure 16-17:

- **Public:** This includes anyone on desktop or mobile who tunes in.

- **Friends:** You can choose those listed as Friends on Facebook to show your broadcast to.

- **Friends except. . . :** You can eliminate some friends from the broadcast.

From your group Timeline or Event

Choose who can see it

- **Specific friends:** You can select individual friends who will see the broadcast.

- **Only Me:** You can use the Only me setting to practice your broadcast. It's a good idea to give yourself a practice run to smooth out all the wrinkles.

- **Custom:** This setting allows you to mix together several of the preceding options.

- **Acquaintances:** The acquaintance list is one that you set up separately that allows you to see less from these people but doesn't unfriend them. Choose this to include them.

Next you are asked to add a description, title, and the choice of several icons, as shown in Figure 16-18. The fields are as follows:

>> **Say something about this live video:** In this field, enter a description of your broadcast that tells viewers what benefit they will get from watching the broadcast. You can edit it after the broadcast if you want.

Icons

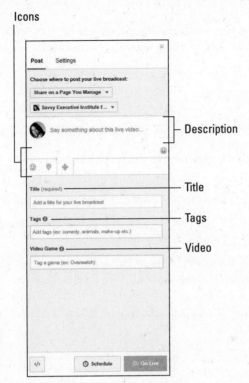

— Description

— Title

— Tags

— Video

FIGURE 16-18:
Adding a description, title, and icons for your broadcast.

Beneath the description, you see icons to insert an emoji, add a tag, insert your mood, and let people know your location. Don't overlook tagging as a way to help people find your broadcast.

>> **Title:** You are required to create a title for your broadcast. Make sure to include keywords that your audience cares about.

>> **Video Game:** In this field, you can tag the name of a video game, if applicable.

Broadcast

Copy and paste the Stream Key and URL into the settings of the streaming software that you chose previously, in the "Set up" section. After copying, you see a preview of your screen with your choices.

REMEMBER

You can use that Stream Key for the next seven days. You'll need a new one if you choose not to go live within five hours of previewing your screen.

TIP

Make sure that you have a strong signal (Wi-Fi or 4G) before you broadcast because if your signal isn't strong enough, Facebook will disable the Go Live button.

Schedule

If you want to schedule an upcoming date instead of going live right now:

1. **Click the Schedule button next to the Go Live button.**

   A schedule screen appears (see Figure 16-19) with important instructions and tips. Make sure you read them. They include two important caveats:

   - Make sure to verify your live feed 20 minutes before the broadcast to ensure that everything is ready to go.

   - The broadcast starts at the time you scheduled it. If you are not there 10 minutes before the start, your broadcast will be canceled.

FIGURE 16-19:
Scheduling options for your Facebook Live broadcast.

2. **Choose the Scheduled Start Time by selecting a date on the drop-down calendar and setting a time in the Time field.**

3. **If you have a Custom Image that you want to use for the broadcast, click Upload Image and choose an image.**

   After you have chosen your image, you see a preview of your broadcast on the right side of the screen. Make sure everything is correct.

4. **Click the Schedule button when you are finished.**

   Your broadcast announcement post will be published when the Schedule button is clicked.

You can choose to boost your broadcast announcement post as an ad if you want to ensure a larger audience. You can also boost your content after a broadcast. Experiment with your most important broadcasts.

5. **Click the Go Live button when you are ready.**

   When you have completed all your tasks, you can click the Go Live button. As noted above, if you have scheduled the broadcast for a later date and time, your broadcast will go live at that time and you need to be there 10 minutes before the broadcast starts.

Creating Broadcasts That Connect with Customers

Now that you're ready to create your broadcast, you need to pick topics that are timely and popular with your audience. You should have an ongoing list of topics (and keywords) that come from an analysis of all your channels and social platforms.

You can broadcast for up to four hours at a time. This gives you the leeway to create virtually any kind of live stream broadcast you want. Although you're not likely to use the full four hours, you should mix things up with a variety of formats and running times.

Here are some issues to consider before you broadcast:

>> **Format:** Your choices are limitless. For example, you can do a product demo, an interview, a workshop that educates people about a topic, a heart to heart with your group, or a behind-the-scenes broadcast. Try experimenting to see what resonates with your audience.

>> **Desktop recording:** If you're recording on the desktop, you need to consider your lighting and microphone. If your broadcast is dark or can't be heard, you are wasting your time.

>> **Content:** Visuals are an important component. If you aren't doing a demo, you should consider using slides or other graphics to make the broadcast more interesting. Think about the broadcast from the viewers' perspective and try to see what they see. Look at your setting. Are you sitting against a blank wall?

>> **Promotion:** Promoting your business is a key component of fostering engagement. If possible, schedule an announcement ahead of time (and consider boosting it), as discussed in the "Schedule" section. (For more about boosting, see Chapter 11). You want to reach new viewers and generate some excitement. Also during your broadcast, try to get repeat viewers by asking viewers to click the Live Subscribe button during your broadcast to be alerted to your live videos.

>> **Mobile recording:** When using your mobile phone to record, be careful how you move your phone. Avoid fast movements so that you don't make your viewers dizzy by wobbling the image back and forth. Go slower than you think you should when panning the site.

>> **During the broadcast:** You want to get discussions going with your viewers. Remember that Facebook is looking for meaningful interaction. Ask questions and respond to comments. Keep your broadcast lively and positive.

TIP

Having someone monitor the comments and help you respond to the inflow of information can be helpful.

A great example of a Facebook Live broadcast was done by Amy Porterfield in January 2018 called "How to Make BETTER Decisions in Your Business (to see BIGGER Profits)." She sent out an announcement before the broadcast to get viewers interested, and during and since that broadcast, she has garnered thousands of views.

The following figures show the broadcast as it looked live from a mobile phone and after the broadcast was completed and appeared in her News Feed.

The broadcast on a mobile phone shows you the Live button in the upper left along with the number of viewers (see Figure 16-20). The comments and reactions are shown in the center, and the Comments field is at the bottom.

After the broadcast, viewers will see the topic and several ways to share and comment. The broadcast also appears in Amy Porterfield's News Feed, as shown in Figure 16-21. Under the topic and to the right is a Follow button, which helps to get more subscribers. You can also see the Share button, which viewers can click. This is a great way to get more engagement, so don't forget to mention using that button.

TIP

To learn about looking at your Insights data for your videos, see Chapter 10.

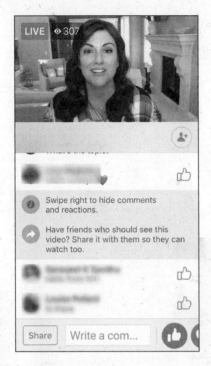

FIGURE 16-20:
A Facebook Live broadcast viewed on a mobile phone.

FIGURE 16-21:
After the live stream, you see the replay on her Page.

5

The Part of Tens

Beware of these ten common Facebook marketing mistakes.

Mind your manners with ten business etiquette tips.

Check out ten factors for long-term Facebook success.

Chapter **17**

Ten Common Facebook Marketing Mistakes (and How to Avoid Them)

Just because you've created a Facebook Page for your business doesn't mean that you won't make mistakes. Mistakes aren't necessarily bad if you can learn from them, but it's always good to avoid mistakes in the first place! Many common mistakes have to do with not understanding how people use Facebook. You shouldn't use a Facebook profile to market your business, for example; profiles are for people. Other mistakes involve unwittingly making a bad impression, such as being too pushy.

In this chapter, we discuss ten of the most common mistakes that you should avoid on Facebook.

Think Like a Traditional Marketer

You'd think that social media would have changed the one-size-fits-all marketing approach that's been so pervasive since the Industrial Revolution, but it hasn't. Facebook — and most other social media, for that matter — is still viewed as a free email list to target and market to.

To amp things up on Facebook, you have to flip this mindset 180 degrees and instead think about creating a space for your supporters to share what matters to them.

Start asking these questions:

>> What's their agenda?

>> What are they already talking about on Facebook that's in sync with your cause?

>> How can you capture that on your Facebook Page?

Use a Profile to Market Your Business

We don't recommend using a Facebook profile to market your business on Facebook, and here are at least three reasons why:

>> **Facebook profiles don't have any analytics tools.** Those tools show you how fans engage with your content. Without these analytics in your information toolbox, you have no way of knowing what strategies are working on Facebook.

>> **Sending a friend request is very different from asking someone to like your Page.** If you're sending friend requests as a profile, you're essentially asking the user whether you can see her photos, friends list, address, phone number, and perhaps relationship status. This request crosses the unspoken social boundaries that most people have between their personal life and the brands they do business with. It's perfectly acceptable for you to like a pizza shop, for example, but creepy if a pizza shop likes you. Pages allow Facebook users to connect with businesses they like without compromising their privacy.

>> **Using a Facebook profile to market your business could end up violating Facebook's terms of service.** After you spend a lot of resources building up a large amount of friends, Facebook might simply delete your profile.

Use a Group to Market Your Business

Another very common mistake that businesses make on Facebook is to use a group to market their businesses. The problem with this approach is that groups are intended solely for Facebook users to connect with one another about common interests and goals — not about a single brand. All group members have an equal say about what's discussed, as well as what's appropriate (or not). Groups that have a single person controlling topics generally aren't successful. Also, Facebook didn't create groups to be used for the purposes of marketing: That's what Facebook Pages are for!

Post with Shortened URLs

Many third-party tools designed to manage multiple platforms are available. Many of these tools, such as Hootsuite and TweetDeck, use URL shorteners to make long URLs fit within the character constraints of sites such as Twitter. Although these tools offer the capability to post links on Facebook, they don't offer the flexibility of posting a long URL when no such character constraints exist, as on Facebook.

Marketing Cloud (`www.facebook.com/marketingcloud`), a Salesforce company, conducted a study that revealed that full-length URLs get three times as many clicks as shortened URLs. In other words, using shortened URLs on Facebook actually has a negative effect on your ability to create awareness about your business!

Instead of using shortened URLs, post content directly on Facebook or use a third-party tool like Post Planner (`www.postplanner.com`), which is made specifically for Facebook marketers to schedule and post various types of content to a Facebook Page.

Wing It

Another common mistake that Facebook marketers make is treating their Facebook Pages with the same relaxed approach that they use for their profiles. People who have Facebook profiles rarely (and should never) have a primary business agenda. For the most part, using Facebook profiles is a completely different social activity that's relaxed and fun. Pages are very different.

Sure, having a relaxed demeanor on your Facebook Page is important, but so is having a well-thought-out strategy that includes understanding your fan base, presenting a unique message, and measuring results. In other words, don't just wing it.

Post at Bad Times

Facebook Page marketers generally work 9-to-5 jobs like most other people, and as part of their jobs, they update their Facebook Page with useful content that (ideally) has been well planned. What they fail to realize, however, is that most of their Facebook fans also have 9-to-5 jobs and don't have time or aren't permitted to use Facebook during the day. Posting during the workday generally isn't as effective as posting in the early morning or early evening, or at any other time when users are on Facebook. The reason is that the News Feed flies by very quickly, so posting an update during the times when users are present increases the likelihood that you'll be at the top of their News Feed right when they're checking it.

Buffer for Business (`https://buffer.com/business`) and Post Planner (`www.postplanner.com`) are excellent applications for scheduling posts at optimum times.

Be Pushy

Selling too much probably is the most common mistake made by Facebook marketers. Suppose that a Facebook marketer sets up a Page and starts posting content that's all about her business or products. The problem is that Facebook users don't care about her products and services, but they do care about things related to those products or services. Hikers, for example, want to discuss great places to go hiking or to share photos from a recent adventure. A sporting-goods store that promotes the latest hiking gear through a discount keeps its fans interested only as long as the Facebook Page discount lasts.

Sell Too Little

Selling too little is probably less common than selling too much, but it's still a potential mistake. Suppose that your friends at the sporting-goods store stop selling too much and start focusing on what their fans are interested in. Their fans start engaging, which is great, but sales don't increase as a result, because the Page isn't posting any promotions or any calls to action. Facebook users love to converse about the things they care about, but they also love a good deal!

Post Lengthy Updates

Posting lengthy paragraphs as a status update is like giving your Facebook fans homework. (And when was the last time you celebrated getting homework?) On the other hand, short updates such as questions and short polls get a higher reaction simply because the barrier to participation is very low.

It may be very tempting to cram as much information as possible about your new product or service into a status update, but in the long run, this practice has a negative effect on the News Feed Algorithm. Read more about the News Feed Algorithm in Chapter 7.

Ignore Comments

Facebook fans are people like you (and us). If they make the effort to leave a comment or reply within a thread on your Facebook Page, they want to know that you're listening. Pages that consistently ignore posts by fans aren't as successful as Pages that participate in comment threads. Fans are less likely to return if they don't feel heard.

The other reason to reply to posts from fans is that Facebook sends each fan a notification, bringing him back to your Page. So in addition to showing fans that they're heard, you get them to continue posting on your Page.

Chapter **18**

Ten Business Tips for Facebook

A s Facebook grows, so does the number of embarrassing faux pas committed by individuals and companies alike. There are occasional slips of the tongue, odd photos, and everyone's favorites: embarrassing tags in photos or videos.

You can and must protect your brand's reputation on Facebook, as well as maintain the utmost respect for the Facebook community. The downside is steep: You can lose your Page, your profile, or both. After you're banned from Facebook, it's hard to get back in, and by that time, the audience that you worked so hard to build is gone. Therefore, it's a good idea to abide by the tips and warnings we outline in this chapter.

Understand That Business Is Personal

Yes, you own a business and use a Facebook Page to promote it. But because people ultimately do business with people, Facebook users may eventually want to get to know you as a person.

Some businesses — such as real estate agencies and law firms — already emphasize the personality of the business owner. People who do businesses with these professionals get to know them very personally. On the other hand, some businesses, such as family restaurants and hardware stores, don't need to focus on the personalities of their owners.

It's important that you understand the level of personal intimacy your prospects and customers expect from you, or at least understand your role in the customer relationship. This understanding helps you appreciate the degree to which people will seek out your Facebook profile to find out more about you and your beliefs and values, which in turn will influence their decision to do business with you.

Don't Drink and Facebook

Your ability to communicate can be impaired by drinking. Naturally, drinking and emailing or social networking just don't go together. You're better off not logging in. It takes only one bad or off-color post to get you reported to Facebook. Members tend to be vigilant about things that they find offensive, so just say no to drinking and Facebooking.

A restaurant in Boston found out about this guideline after it replied to a fan with curse words and insults. Not only did the restaurant's actions turn off scores of potential customers, but also several business blogs wrote about the incident as an example of how *not* to treat your Facebook fan base. Ouch!

Keep Things Clean and Civilized

Sometimes written communication can seem flat and impersonal, so choose your words carefully and be sure to reread your responses before you post them, especially if the situation is getting heated. Better yet, if you think the conversation is getting too heated, feel free to take it off Facebook and address the person via email or Messenger.

Sending threatening, harassing, or sexually explicit messages to Facebook users is a no-no, as it is in the real world. Also, unsolicited messages selling a product or service aren't tolerated. You should refrain from any of these activities, or you may risk receiving a warning from Facebook or possibly having your account disabled.

Remember, reply with gratitude and generosity — even if you're dealing with someone who isn't so polite. Take your mother's advice, and treat everyone with graciousness and good manners. Under some circumstances, it may be difficult to restrain yourself, but taking the high road always makes you look like the winner in the end!

Be Careful Friending Strangers

You can overdo Facebook many ways. First, don't randomly add people to your personal profile in the hopes of convincing them to become fans of your Page. Befriending random people is considered poor form and may make you look like a stalker, which of course reflects badly on your business. The social boundaries between people and businesses on Facebook generally reflect what happens in the real world. If you're the manager of a clothing store, and you've naturally developed friendships with certain customers over the years, then sending a Facebook friend request is simply a natural extension of your relationship. However, if you were to send friend requests to everyone on your store's mailing list, you'll eventually turn potential customers off. This is precisely why Facebook has a 5,000 friend maximum for profiles.

Dress Up Your Page with Applications

Independent developers have written an endless sea of apps for Facebook. One or more of those apps could make a great fit for your business, so find an app or two (but no more) that you can use to make your Page more engaging. The nice thing is that apps are easy to install and don't require any knowledge to build or modify. Each tab has a unique URL, so consider creating individual tabs for each application. You can even send out an email to your customers, asking them to engage with your new application (such as a survey application). But be careful not to overdo it. (We discuss applications in more detail in Chapter 6.)

Respect the News Feed

Your News Feed is one of the most important places on your Page. It's where your fans can leave messages and start a discussion on a topic. All messages on your News Feed are visible to all Facebook users in the Posts by Others stream. Think of this area as a place of public conversation, so make sure that you're professional and courteous to anyone who posts. Make an effort to reply to all posts with gratitude and generosity.

Don't Be Afraid to Ignore People

Many people feel compelled to respond to every message in their email inboxes. Similarly, on Facebook, people feel the need to respond to every comment or post. Sometimes, fans can overuse the various communication features in Facebook. New fans sometimes binge on the information you present. We suggest that you always welcome new fans and respond to comments and posts on your News Feed within 12 hours, but know when to let the conversation rest. If the same fan leaves several comments on a single post, replying once should be enough. If a fan is irate, that's another thing; ignoring the fan can often work against you. See the following section for more info.

Deal with Your Irate Users

Irate users pose one of the biggest challenges that this medium has to offer. You have several ways to deal with an irate fan:

>> **Honestly consider his point, and try to find something (anything) to agree with.** Finding and establishing common ground is a great way to get the conversation back on track.

>> **Correct factual inaccuracies in a very tactful and pleasant way.** The fan may not have all the data, which could be causing her to be irate.

>> **If you don't know the solution to a particular situation, don't bluff your way out of it.** Be honest, commit to finding out more, and give the fan a date when you'll get back to him.

>> **Don't forget that you can always take your conversation offline.**

Don't Forget Birthday Greetings

Through the power of Facebook, you never have to forget any of your friends' birthdays. Then why not make it a point each day to see whether fans of your Page are having a birthday? Just visit their profiles and leave a birthday greeting on their Timelines, or send a Facebook email to their inboxes. (You can see fans' birthdays only if they've made settings that enable sharing that information.) If that isn't enough, you may want to offer people something unique that only you can provide for their birthday. Fans might be open to getting a birthday greeting from a local restaurant with an offer to come in that week for a free dessert or drink, for example.

The power of this platform is there, and surprisingly few companies are taking advantage of this personalized birthday-greeting opportunity.

Maintain Your Privacy

For some business owners, privacy is of paramount concern. If you're a local business owner — say, a jewelry-store owner — you may not want to list personal information such as an address or phone number on the Info tab of your personal profile. Make sure that your profile settings are set to Private (which is no longer the default) rather than Public, which makes your personal information, including your home address, available to Internet search engines for all prying eyes to see. Also be careful what groups you join. If someone you know in business sees controversial political, sexual, or religious activist groups on your profile, she might stop shopping at your store. Often, the less revealed, the better.

Chapter **19**

Ten (Okay, Eight) Factors for Long-Term Facebook Marketing Success

E very marketer wants her Facebook campaign to succeed, but not everyone can be so lucky. What are the best approaches to ensure success? This chapter lists the most time-tested ways to make sure that your campaign makes the most of Facebook.

Know the Language, Eat the Food

One of the best ways to ensure long-term marketing success on Facebook is to use it personally. Sure, you can read books and the latest research on why people use Facebook and why it continues to have amazing growth even after exceeding 2 billion monthly users worldwide, but no book can take the place of the Facebook experience.

By signing up and using Facebook to connect with high-school friends, share photographs with family members, discover new music, and comment within threads about various topics, you begin to understand how to connect with your customers. It's like the adage about the apple: We can try to describe to you what it tastes like, but until you take a bite yourself, you'll never really understand.

Understand Why People Share

Obviously, one of the most important things you want your Facebook fans to do is share content that you post on your Facebook Page. Understanding the psychology of sharing enables you to optimize your content for specific sharing personas. (Find out more about personas in Chapter 2.)

Some people share to promote their careers, keeping everything they share professional and safe for work. These folks are generally well educated, use LinkedIn, and keep their Facebook profile privacy settings very closed. Other people share because they want to look cool in front of their friends. They share new music, breaking tech news, and the latest Threadless T-shirt they bought, and they most likely have very open privacy settings.

TIP

A good person to follow to understand more about what motivates people to share is Jeff Bullas (`https://www.facebook.com/jeffreybullas/`).

Be Useful and Helpful

One of the most powerful social laws that functions across cultures and languages is the law of reciprocity. Helping others is at the very core of our evolution as a species. If I help you shovel your driveway after a major snowstorm, you're much more willing to help me out in the future. Reciprocity is scaled to a massive level on Facebook.

When you make consistent efforts to promote like-minded businesses on your Facebook Page, they promote yours in return. You can also be helpful by joining relevant Facebook Groups and keeping an eye out for questions you can answer.

Listen to Your Fans

One of the biggest reasons that people use social media in the first place is to be heard. The brands that do really well listen to their Facebook Page connections.

One example is ShortStack (www.facebook.com/shortstacklab). When customers post technical questions, they always get a quick and helpful answer. Make sure that the moderation settings on your Facebook Page are configured so that Page connections can post updates on your Page (see Chapter 5). Also make sure that you can be notified quickly when someone comments (which you can configure by clicking the Settings button on your Page and then clicking the Notifications link). It's not as much work as it seems, and the positive effect on your brand in the long run will more than pay for the effort.

REMEMBER

Your Facebook Page is essentially a platform through which you can have conversations with your customers and prospects. You can ask them for feedback on products and services, which enables you to give them more of what they really want. Even if you can't give them what they want, you can at least show them you care by replying (such as by saying, "We're sorry we don't offer that, but here's what we do have"). The fact that they've been heard leaves them with a positive feeling about your business, even if you don't have exactly what they want.

Consistently Participate

One of the biggest reasons that you're using Facebook for your business is to better connect with your customers and prospects. You want to make them aware of your business, get them interested in buying from you, and motivate them to take action. Every single step that they take along this path requires trust. Nothing obliterates trust more than being inconsistent. After you begin to use your Facebook Page as a platform for conversation, fans naturally expect a certain consistency. If you're not consistent, you'll hurt your chances for success on Facebook. If, during the first month on Facebook, you post three times daily and respond to questions quickly but disappear in the following months, fans begin to question not only your commitment on Facebook but also your ability to provide good products and services.

Appreciate and Recognize Your Fans

If you want to stand apart from the crowd on Facebook, make a concerted effort to recognize and appreciate your Facebook fans. Being recognized and appreciated is a basic desire of all people; it makes them feel valued and inspires them to appreciate others in return. The positive feeling that starts with you makes them more likely to share your business with their friends and even give you money!

One way you can express appreciation is to state simply, "We have the best Facebook fans on the planet!" (Notice how many comments you get after that update!)

Measure and Monitor

Chances are that you're a business owner, and if you've been in business long enough, you know the value of measuring return on investment. What you're measuring on Facebook is the response from your efforts. What topics get people excited? Which fan-acquisition strategies are working best? When fans visit your website, how many of them end up as customers?

If you can't answer these questions, you'll never know whether you're using Facebook effectively. In today's economy, you can't afford to wing it. Think about measuring your Facebook efforts as a compass that tells you how far you are from your destination, when you arrive, and how to change direction if necessary.

Be Fearless and Creative

Right now, millions of businesses are competing for attention on Facebook. Many of them are pleading for the attention of your current Facebook fans. They're using video, photos, conversation strategies, and highly interactive custom tabs to achieve this goal. The good news is that you can be just as innovative and have the same capability, or even better capability, to attract and retain fans.

To stay creative, read books like this one, attend webinars on Facebook marketing, and watch what other brands are doing. Still, all this knowledge won't mean a thing if you don't take action. Your competition isn't waiting for the perfect idea, and you shouldn't be, either. View everything that you do on Facebook as a draft — a never-ending beta. That way, you get a real education about what actually works on Facebook and more business in the process.

Index

advertising
  on Facebook. *See* Ads
  traditional. *See* traditional marketing
advertising campaigns. *See* campaigns
advocacy stage, marketing funnel, 20, 21
affinity, ladder of engagement, 22
age
  Ad targeting, 26, 218
  Facebook terms and conditions, 82
  setting access restrictions, 86–87
  target audience, 23, 26
AgoraPulse (website), 164, 198
All Posts Published report, 155
amateur images, 209
Analyst, as admin access, 80
analytics. *See* monitor and measure
angry comments, 160–161
apologies, 160
Apple iTunes Page, 273
Apple Mail, 142
appreciation, fan, 47–51, 121
approvals, 229, 255
apps (applications). *See also* tabs
  add apps to Page, 79, 341
  cautions on use, 97
  cost of branded, 56–57
  create custom tabs with HTML, 105–107
  delete from Page, 79
  e-commerce apps, 100–101
  Facebook Apps, 94–97
  fan engagement with mobile apps, 91–92
  on Groups, 66
  as Page component, 16
  for promotion, 94–97
  search for, 97–98
  third-party, 99–100, 101–102
artist as Page type, 69
assets, reuse existing marketing, 142–145
@ sign, 141
audience
  create compelling content for, 116–117
  knowing, for content marketing, 118

in marketing plan, 37, 39–41
size of, ladder of engagement, 22
targeting. *See* target audience
audience engagement
  appreciating fans, 49–51
  customer-centric experience, 48–49
  growing fan-base, 49–51
avatar (image), 8, 129
awareness
  build brand, 8, 12, 41
  increase, network with friends, 138–141
  as marketing funnel stage, 20, 21
  of Offer, 248

B

Ban User, 87
band as Page type, 69
behavioral aspects
  of fans/customers, 40, 285
  marketing funnel, 20–21
  personas, 24–25
  psychographic, 40
behaviors
  Ad tool, 28
  target audience, 28
benchmarks as key metric, 53
best customer, define, for target audience, 22–23
Best Friends Animal Sanctuary Page, 95, 96
Best Friends Animal Society group, 253
bidding, 221–222
Biggerplate (website), 66
big-picture goals, value proposition, 38
Billing and Payments link, 241
Bing, 136
birthday greetings, 342–343
Bitly (website), 54
blogs, 144, 276
Boosted Posts, 231–235
Botisfy (website), 317
brand
  branding strategies, 41–43
  building awareness, 8, 12, 41

About the Author

Stephanie Diamond is a thought leader and management marketing professional with 20+ years of experience building profits in more than 75 different industries. She has worked with solopreneurs, small business owners, and multibillion-dollar corporations.

She worked for eight years as a Marketing Director at AOL. When she joined, AOL had fewer than 1 million subscribers. When she left in 2002, it had 36 million. She had a front-row seat to learn how and why people buy online. While at AOL, she developed, from scratch, a highly successful line of multimedia products that brought in an annual $40 million dollars in incremental revenue.

In 2002, she founded Digital Media Works, Inc. (ContentMarketingToolbox.com), an online marketing company that helps business owners discover the hidden profits in their business. She is passionate about guiding online companies to successfully generate more revenue and use social media to its full advantage.

As a strategic thinker, Stephanie uses all the current visual thinking techniques and brain research to help companies get to the essence of their brand. She continues this work today with her proprietary system to help online business owners discover how social media can generate profits.

Stephanie has written more than 15+ business books including *Social Media Marketing For Dummies, Content Marketing Strategies For Dummies, Dragon Naturally Speaking For Dummies*, and *Web Marketing for Small Businesses*. You can find her at http://contentmarketingtoolbox.com.

Stephanie's Dedication

To my husband, Barry, who makes all things possible.

Stephanie's Acknowledgments

I would like to thank Amy Fandrei, now an Executive Editor at Wiley, Susan Christophersen, Project and Copy Editor, and Michelle Krasniak, Technical Editor, for their always excellent support and encouragement. I'd also like to thank my agent, Matt Wagner, for his continued efforts on my behalf. Also thanks to John Haydon and Melanie Nelson for their help in making this book better.

Publisher's Acknowledgments

Executive Editor: Amy Fandrei

Project and Copy Editor: Susan Christophersen

Technical Editor: Michelle Krasniak

Editorial Assistant: Matthew Lowe

Proofreader: Debbye Butler

Production Editor: Magesh Elangovan

Cover Image: © SonerCdem/Getty Images